AMAZING
JOURNEY OF THE
CHESTER EAGLES
BOYS CLUB

Four mid-teenagers in a what?
Went how far then survived a tornado?
Don't believe it?

Discover the fascinating truth.

Stanley E. Kornafel,
Author and first person.

WORKBOOK PRESS LLC
187 E Warm Springs Rd,
Suite B285, Las Vegas, NV 89119, USA

Website:https: //workbookpress.com/
Hotline: 1-888-818-4856
Email: admin@workbookpress.com

Ordering Information:
Quantity sales. Special discounts are available on quantity purchases by corporations, associations, and others. For details, contact the publisher at the address above.

Library of Congress Control Number:
ISBN-13: 978-1-960752-99-4 (Paperback Version)
978-1-960752-51-2 (Digital Version)

REV. DATE: 04/26/2023

AMAZING JOURNEY OF THE CHESTER EAGLES BOYS CLUB

Stanley E. Kornafel…Author

INTRODUCTION

This is a true telling of an original dramatically powerful tale of life!

Who would act on a say-so idea? Unique, the huge exploit incorporates many events some large and some small but all true.

For those who love to read for passing time it fascinates from one instance to another, from desire to anxiety, love to hate and from sad to joy. Then for those who like the fantasy of dreaming, some occurrences portray situations that generate wishing while others even relate to similar situations some readers may have encountered.

For those looking for fact based true matters of family is raised questions of values of responsibility, care and love also applying to friends, their friendship and loyalty. Then the same trueness applies to the times of action where the abundance of segments provides telling of physical strains, mental struggles times of surviving life-threatening death situations.

Highly important, is the story being fact based involving of human character that people can relate to. Nothing was left out where, even the verbiage from the small remarks, expressions and slang to the conversations has been recorded enabling feelings of the emotions that were applied or realized. Even professors of psychology and human behavior will find the events within the story useful as having so much controversial matter relative to ego, determination and religion.

Although the grammar is correct it is most important to remember the young ages along with their period of time in life. Misspelled and cut up words and phrases have been intentionally included because such is necessary incorporating the time period along with the essential language as spoken.
The writer has provided the actual feelings during the moment or situations as the five could recall. Moments of anger, joy or sadness, as pronounced are part of the

mental attitudes and as such are expressed of the emotional feelings at the time.

Not from imagination or Hollywood and not written by a second person or transcribed by a third party but, written by the person who actually participated. The original story rises to a full and true portrayal of life relative to persons of all ages and creeds.

Stanley E. Kornafel…Author

CONTENTS:

SECTIONS

CHAPTERS

AUTHOR'S STATEMENT

How could so much happen to so few, in so small a time?

A fascinating true story of ideas, family and friends' controversy along with joys while maturing of young people showed everyone's frailty. Here, "amazing" applies because as an ember of fire the idea kindled a desire where thinking turned into an unpredictable cause of heartfelt meaning!

Not looking to be fancy, but teens simply looking to celebrate where every thought was turned away as not possible. Constantly heard was either you can't do it, not possible or can't be done. During a time when money along with necessities was hard to get, the four coped against all odds. Impeded by having no money and no car such was magnified being under the stress of a constrained time period. Yet their miscalculations may suggest a unique portrayal of just how problematic young people can be.

No travel training along with being without experience dealing with hardships of life the guys set out on a journey. Times of failure and success were had through common sense impeded by periods of immaturity, and stubbornness. Plans and strategy turned upside down abounded. Mental struggles, physical adversities, challenging hard luck and good times occurred even beyond the norm for adults. Yet, for the young teens it resulted in more excitement, anxiety, thrills, and even life threatening situations than most people encounter in a lifetime.

Assumed may be, that surviving their near death situations were simply by luck. But was it faith alone, or luck, or was it the combination? Beyond the team's control, someone or something brought us out and whether intervention or, indirect means by the creator too much surviving makes it impossible to be by luck.

The original five characters' names herein have been retained being true, while people and places visited due to the loss of time were forgotten. Time having passed combined with a lack of a diary, years to complete and loss of memory resulted in the erasing of much detail. However, brought out are all the significant essentials of places and descriptions as as was able to be recalled.

This is the biographical/ autobiographical account taken from recollections of the five and finished in written form by the author. Holding to truth, facts were used along with remembrances where male and female of young and old readers alike may find sections easily relating to their own history.

Not since Geronimo's times has several young boys done so much, with so very little, doing a great deal, in such a short period of time. And it is thanks to the four school comrades who had the character to follow through, remaining a loyal team of trust and comradely.

Based on fact of personal experience, the true story of the Amazing Journey of the Chester Eagles Boys Club is supported by existing resources along with documents and materials while written solely by the person that was there being one of the five.

And all by boys simply wanting to celebrate their graduation, Wow!

Enjoy the, Amazing Journey of the Chester Eagles Boys Club. …. Hi Yo, Nashie! Away!!

THE STORY

SECTION I:

A DREAM,

OBSTICALS,

DETERMINATION.

CHAPTER ONE

BUSTLING CITY, DECISIONS AND PROBLEMS.

Nineteen Hundred and Fifty-Eight A.D., where movie theaters, record players, parks, comptometers, and fireworks occupied parts of the day. The thriving city of Chester, Pennsylvania located in the county of Delaware, was a historical place. Peaking with a population of around fifty- six thousand people, "What Chester made, made Chester", was the sign in an area visible for all to see, especially those riding on a train. A diverse cultural place of all races, colors and creeds the community enjoyed various education means as well as a diversity of religious places and trade applications. The country's first true government center where people practiced their religious freedom while enjoying growth from major industries with the Chester Times newspaper. Prices of items were: bacon a dollar a pound; gasoline twenty to forty cents a gallon; bicycles at thirty five dollars; a shotgun at one hundred and fifty dollars; a pair of man's pants 11 dollars; milk twenty-five cents a quart; post cards three cents; draught beer 20 cents a glass, with Ballantine Ale being thirty five cents.

Headlines were the words "in God" added to the pledge of allegiance; the four minute mile was broken; a person was recorded as having been struck by a meteor with high-fidelity, color televisions, instant foods and drive in theaters for entertainment. Well known songs were; Strangers in Paradise; The High and The Mighty; Don't be Cruel and Three Coins in the Fountain. Many families were still recovering from Second World War hardships or suffering from setbacks or losses from loved ones. Yet, some while forgetting things of the past were trying to move into some reasonable living style. As for the weather, it was winter and cold. Whichever part of the city a person traveled they had no fear and Stan feeling as such always respected the inside of persons not paying much of what others had to say.

Saint James Catholic High School was a finer type of educational facility, not only in the city but even enjoyed a super reputation among businesses as well as colleges along the east coast. From St. Michael's Grade School, except for Larry, the boys went on to St. James Catholic High School where graduating classes were always of a small number. Bordering around five hundred yet, it was that opposition from the much larger schools in any contest knew that they had an adequate competitor, especially, when the opposition felt the bitter sting of defeat.

Just a bunch of good ole boys that could play pool, bowl, shoot darts and shuffleboard plus drink beer with the best of them. Often even challenged were adults in their own inside sporting activities. Though small time mischief or fights there was never any vandalism, stealing, nor any kind of criminal behavior as all came from factory or labor type hard working families bolstered by the Catholic education. Thomas and William were graduating along with David and Stanley who was the author, where having palled around from grade school they had grown a loose closeness. Bill (William) and Stanley also knew each other from years of friendship scouting where open conversations between them flowed easily.

Dave who lived on Madison Street, close to Tenth Street was the Casanova type who liked to drive cars fast while Stan the author, also seventeen from Potter Street at Rose street unnecessarily lost his mother at age eleven. While suppressing his hurt he thought about a trade or high school instead of the administrative because he was good with his hands. Then being a piano player he wanted to start a band but couldn't find any person having a similar interest leaving him void of direction with no idea of the future. From Spruce Street also just off Rose around the corner from Stan was Bill who had lost his middle aged father several years prior. Dave and Tom's family remained the only two families that were whole. Tom at eighteen lived on north Seventh Street where his parents were more advanced in years along with his mother ailing. Although each one had part time jobs, everything revolved around knowing graduation was drawing near. So it was, that winter had peaked with spurts of spring. The season was about to change yet no body thought of making graduation plans when Able mentioned something but the words never stuck.

It was a February, Saturday that he caught Stan by surprise. Without even a telephone call he came around in the morning finding Stan relaxing while sipping on some hot coffee. Both had finished their newspaper deliveries where Stan was trying to relax when Bill unloaded the bombshell. Blurting he suggested of, joining the Air Force on the buddy plan. In a relaxed stupor, Stan broke out in laughter mentioning the military was not on his list where the matter was forgotten. Tom, along with the others of seventeen age knew that being underage they had to be careful. However, once inside of places all properly conducted their selves. Easily blending in with other customers rarely were they questioned on ages plus it was never the volume as each simply enjoyed the taste of good tap beer.

Socializing after dinner at one of the local bars the boys overheard a few men talking about their traveling. Overhearing the men's talk drew the boys' attention where the idea of going somewhere stuck, and boy oh boy, did the matter ever stick. Only days later while on Dave's porch playing Gin Rummy, it started in the coolness of the open porch. Definitely not the usual in such weather, but there was a challenge of fun playing cards in fifty degree temps while sipping hot coffee with warm donuts. Tom, all excited, the street-smart youngster, mentioned how he thought of doing something big as a special for graduation. Quickly responding to his idea the others noted how he was dreaming since having no money where the thought ended there.

Several days later in a parking lot, Dave mentioned about going to Canada while Able mentioned his suggestion of Ocean city Maryland. Laughing in response Stan mentioned how such was done in the past and not big. Subsequent conversations became like a comedy opera of absolute chaos. But, the flame of doing never went out. After school, days later, Bill of mild personality stopped at Stan's house again pressing the military matter. While Bill's dad had passed away leaving him with no one to grow with, Stan's father had his own life interests where the two had something in common. Some days later the two signed up. Following testing and physical examinations the two were scheduled on the tenth of July to report at the airport for going to Lackland Air Force Base in Texas for basic training. Meanwhile none of the boys showed any interest in Washington, D.C., New York or Florida because they were accessible any time. And though Japan and Germany was impossible being too far and costly the spirit of celebrating only grew. As some contagious illness, it drove the minds where Bill suggested of panning for gold, or do some gaming while Tom mentioned mountain climbing. At first, Stan supported the ideas, but later suggested going where none of them had traveled before where all could accomplish each of their ideas while remaining together at the same location. It was as if madness had taken over where the word trip began to be repeated when during a sports discussion Stan blurted out that the four could climb mountains in Colorado while also being able to go fishing and pan for gold.

The next day, it was if a bomb went off. Bill who enjoyed gambling suggested not to stop there when a little further all could go to Vegas and do all those other things".Just when making fun of each other, being fully aware they didn't have the funds, Dave suggested to keep on going to see the sexy women in Hollywood. The heat of doing something big had uniquely increased though feeling it was impossible. But the boys couldn't stop giving the matter consideration as each was hooked as fish in a pond. Even single ideas along with complex thoughts were considered.

Then one night at the Arcadia Bar in Eddystone Dave showed he was on edge. He had something to say but was afraid because of being told to stuff it days before. Finally in the middle of darts, quietly, the boy in a serious tone stated that he wanted to have a real meeting where if truly interested in doing something it's time to act.

SEGMENT – 1. Dave's seriousness with Tom's coaxing caused the four to meet that Saturday mid afternoon at the Pee Wee Diner. Decision making time had arrived where it became a debate of either we dozz or not dozz, dos, or not dos, goes, or not goes. With all the talk of not able to do it was that if a decision of not going was agreed, there would be no more discussion about the matter. Heavy statements brought everyone down to earth where doses of the hard stuff flowed. Neither one wanted to go anywhere without the others yet each had there own doing and places in mind. Then when it seemed getting into some unison, Able reminded the three of the distance blurting out that it was about two thousand seven hundred and eighty miles, which was by way of the birds.

Round and round the four went until Stan suggested for them to compare Colorado to Canada showing it only being matters of miles. But, after Dave noted about the no money matter the team sunk back in the seats tongue tied. Last it was Bill flapping his arms while asserting how we ain't birds and the mileage mentioned was only that of one way, but again Stan countered how it's still only a matter of miles. All energized Dave zestfully slamming his hand on the table pleaded how we aints got wings but we all gots our limbs where if weez waza to really works at it we cans dozz it all.

With everyone laughing, Stan mentioned how not twenty one it could cause problems. A bout of heavy laughter ensued that almost brought the ceiling down. So fired up the four had become where such controversy meant more rounds of hard stuff. Coffee, ice cream, donuts and those delicious toasted sticky buns abounded when at that moment every negative seemed to be turned away. It was only days later during another meeting where other customers stared at the four as if they expected some sort of a performance. Nothing remained other than to go to California as all divisions had been thrown out. As the four were agreeing for making a go of it, the waitress interrupted asking whether the four was going to spend the night in the booth?

A couple of days later at Deshong Park while passing around a quart of beer along with fresh pretzels, various modes of transportation were ruled out. Neither wanted being hooked up with other people while confined to only a certain location where the only choice remaining was a car to travel by. Wow, here the four was making decisions yet not even having the means where Tom noted how they should have started on the matter months ago where quickly Dave added how the matter was brought up months ago but the only interest shown was in having a good time.

Subsequent discussions over money covered ideas as robbing a bank or holding up a train, but at least they had the sense to know if caught it meant no celebration. In the meantime Tom and Stan mentioned hat they didn't want to start something then, in the middle, any of the guys would change their minds that caused a heated debate. Slowly each came to understand the values of committing where it was needed to form some sort of a group where anyone could find dependability with the others.

An exciting time it was since Tom, Dave and Stan had made up a really great intramural bowling team. The struggles in the bowling league allowed close comradely. Having advanced from sixth to first place such competitive struggling enabled the three to grow, as they bested the league in an awesome season and playoff. The long program eliminated the means of simple luck where Stan carried an average of one hundred sixty-eight bolstered with Dave's consistent game ending rallies. Such a combination allowed having two of the league's highest scores of the season while winning the tournament.

Of course, getting to the bowling alley and winning was one thing, but getting to the Pacific Ocean, was another larger matter. During the following meeting, the four gave their word to stay the course until total success or failure was realized where each gave their word while shaking hands. To the team it was a valuable thing being of the heart as back then among the four it had values a person could rely on.

A few days later each put up an equal share of one dollar as Dave and Bill secured the foundation during the first big event when the two opened a joint savings account at the Delaware County National Bank. From then on, the team had official material as well as mental joining where it became established with a kitty that they could work from. Seizing the moment a rule was made that no money would be withdrawn from the kitty except where preplanned or only in emergency situations. At the time, while a dollar being a big amount of money, it represented one hundred percent of good faith binding intentions.

One evening while enjoying a few brews, hot dogs and sauerkraut at the Baldwin Hotel and Bar the four carried away with the comradely moved it to a higher level. Forming a pact each gave their word in an allegiance there would be no dropping out for any reason, except only if something terrible happened. As the glasses were tipped making an official toast to each other they shook hands along with a few cheers. The small event even brought cheers from others that were playing at the pool table.

So let us now return to those thrilling days of 1958, when with the power of the mind, clouds of thinking and much determination the boys set their course of celebration. The four were going to take a well-planned, enjoyable car trip to the west coast and that was that. Aha! Well at least it was the general intention. Parents of the four refused to believe the idea they were told being taken as trivial hoopla but since none of parents or relatives had extra cars or extra money such was an understood. Often Stan mentioned for the guys to look at their situation comparing with Columbus or Washington at Trenton.

If the parents' refusal to get involved wasn't enough sadly, the classmates dispelled the matter as frivolous folly. Some even mentioned how such was stupid, even suggesting to stop dreaming. School days soon became a bore. Meanwhile the type of vehicle needed had to be considered while the trip was thought to take four weeks but such was only guessing. As reality set in the impossible thoughts began returning but the comradely willing spirit pushed each to push each other as each assured each other to cope. Figures for costs of motel rooms, meals, food, beverages, fuel and road tolls as well as needed car repairs surfaced. Costs bubbled beyond all thinking, as the project needed money.

Having no coach or experienced person able to develop a workable project plan and budget it magnified the lack of the team's experience. With the limited part time jobs the four already had, each knew the money made was insufficient. Furthermore it was that all attempts of talking to the parents for fund falling on deaf ears the project became like attempting to purchase the empire state building. Bill's mother was completely against the idea since not only struggling being on her own plus she had never learned how to drive which presented him a huge obstacle being absolutely needed around the house.

Where Tom's mother who had been sickly, needing money for medication prevented any unnecessary spending. Stan's father squashed all ideas of receiving any helpful effort plus he also suppressed any thoughts of getting any support from other relatives as to him the idea was totally so stupid it wasn't even to be discussed.

However, Stan's aunts Rose and Sophie were surprised when told of the idea as also was his uncle Henry where over time noting his persistence the two aunts and uncle offered whatever they could do to help. The very big obstacle was Dave's mother who abruptly put the lid on all thoughts of the matter stating how she didn't want to hear anything more about it as to her the whole idea belonged in the comics.

From then on it was understood that any of the parents joining together to help would not happen. Every day started to turn up new things presenting more challenges. At first the matter was exciting, but getting it started with the obstacles of family along with school friends anti social attitudes caused emotional drudged feelings.

However the team was able to rely on the help from their-own comradely experience from when on the bowling team.

CHAPTER TWO

ENTERPRISING ACTIVITIES, NASHIE AND SHOPPING

Needing to find work, upon Tom and Bill's suggestion advertising was done by putting an ad in the daily newspaper. Though costing money, the priority was the need for work where subsequent to discussion a handy man ad was used where each put in an equal share of three dollars to the kitty to get the ad running. A day later looking all mature, Bill and Dave with a shoe box of change made the deposit in the bank account.

What was it that pushed the four? Certainly it wasn't money or politics. Only Bill and Stan's phone numbers were given at the Chester Times where the ad taker' suggestions met no resistance. Mentioned was one type of work as she suggested plus general handyman whatever type or size. Meanwhile the boys became trash pickers where discarded soda bottles provided pennies for the returns. Then when the newspapers, brass, copper and other metal objects, provided a bunch they were taken to the salvage man. One time Tom commented being unable to recall classes that taught on how to pick trash but, the fact was that those items provided funds where every little bit helped to feed the kitty.

Jubilation time it was, for the ad brought in calls which involved work of a short time period while others called for a long time duration while other work was simply too large or beyond our knowledge to be considered. From cleaning cars, trucks, store warehouses, basements and yards it was to cleaning out garages, cutting lawns, and painting. Calls even came in for scrubbing porches from top to bottom even to helping with grocery shopping. Once the boys took care of one person's needs it was to squeeze in the next customer where any history of normal eight-hour days for socializing or watching television vanished. Every opportunity was used even as time permitted whether before or after a job, the trash picking team scoured the neighborhoods where the job took place. Pennies or half dollars made no difference as whatever could be done to make a dollar, then save it was done.

Moving mid February, the weather started to break for the better when a woman wanted her basement walls white washed. Taking turns calling people it was Dave's turn, where responding he understood it was about the basement walls where the woman quickly grabbed the boy's offer. All excited by the prospect of work, to him the woman's request was taken as accepted. All fired up about the job as had relied on Dave's description the three believed to be handled with ease, after all it was only about washing the walls. What an education outside of the classroom the scenario became when following the introduction it was total embarrassment. Understanding the four could not perform the service the woman knowing our young ages provided a tongue-lashing. Then as she finished the four apologized while attempting to leave. Surprisingly the kind woman questioned for what purpose it was to be done where once told of the cause, she responded in a different tone. Quickly seeing the eagerness, the woman offered other work in the form of trimming the lawns and ridding the area of crab grass. Later seeing how neither of the four took any breaks later the woman wanted the cleaning of her car done, inside and out. Then several days later, work was even received from some of her friends.

Another event occurred where it was a simple job of cutting and trimming a man's lawn. Located in a well to do neighborhood while knowing the job would be easy each brought something to cut or trim. While Numb had brought his parents motorized lawn mower, in a rush to get the job done everyone did their best to push. To everyone's surprise it wasn't when less than half way through the job where the mower without being turned off simply shut down. Tom's unit being motorized needed fuel of which no one thought of bringing. Realizing the error, Dave and Stan went to their homes returning with each of their parent's push type mowers. Afterward, being satisfied about the work, the customer gladly paid the price plus provided other short jobs that were done days later then, even contacted a couple of his relatives. It was like a fever that had taken over. Whether large or small, an hour or a day, as long as there was money to be made the guys were willing. Being able to be performed, along with if the price was accepted by the caller the work was done.

Of course, there were times of not having the skills where the work was turned down. The kitty though growing, time wise it was not fast enough. It was that one day after school where Stan suggested his wild scheme solution. But after he broadcasted his idea to the other three, they simply asked if he flipped his lid? Do what? Sell chances on what? No, absolutely not was the response with a no selling attitude. What other kind of ridiculous brainstorm did he have, they asked? Although Stan was suggestively speaking, he new that he was really reaching.

Meanwhile the boys felt that they needed some sort of fancy title. Daily a variety of suggestions were made such as the Traveling Four, the Four Celebrators and the Chester Graduates Association. Also the Chester Eagles Group was mentioned but the four were afraid of legal confrontations from other groups. Already was the Eagles Club in Chester plus there was the Philadelphia Eagles football team. Really bugged the four couldn't agree any names mentioned yet, refusing to quit, Stan kept pushing his idea for selling chances until one day Bill joined his idea. Coming to grips with the urgent need to grow the pot then with the other two listening and realizing the lack of money they finally agreed to give it try. Then it became a true necessity to devise some kind of a name. A real challenge it was until Dave replaced the word of "group" with "boys club". Amazing what a couple of words can do. Yippee! From then on the four no longer was just a group of boys but rather addressed themselves as the team of the Chester Eagles Boys Club and good timing it was as Dave occasionally worked for a printer who agreed to print the tickets. Samples of size and color were easy to agree on but no one had given any thought as to what prizes to offer.

Once a couple of items were mentioned a non-stop continuous flow of ideas erupted. From a free car wash to washing walls of a small room or a basement floor cleaned was suggested. Even a mixer, toaster and radio were noted, but though of merit there were simply too many items to consider and while Bill suggested a large table radio Tom mentioned a small travel size radio where agreed to, was a table size, yet small enough to travel.

Now it was that up to that time none of the four had ever sold anything plus some of the parents without giving credit to effort indicated the ticket selling as a good idea but stressed there would be no need as not going anyway, and if selling was done there would be no ripping anybody off. Dave was surprised to learn that his brother had talked with their father thinking the trip idea might have some merit. But with mother's objection to the idea, discussions fell short. Since the team didn't have any organization or adult backing, the four truly lacked any confidence. Such atmosphere caused thinking to find a business, person or organization to do the selling. But all efforts to get one in that direction also failed.

At an evening meeting, Stan all frustrated asserted how either the guys should sell the tickets their selves or just let them sit to produce nothing. Quickly, Dave added how he didn't want to be stuck owing the printer needing to be paid. Wow! What a mess, where followed was a quiet that filled the air, as no one had the answer. Quietly Tom all serious verbally pressed starting somewhere where each could learn by doing but in jest Dave responded of what the team needed was more schoolwork. It wasn't what they wanted to hear but the statements got the boys thinking where introductions into the sales field became imminent. A big feat it was that first day, almost as bad as taking a test. Having finished their dinner all piled into Dave dad's Buick where it was like going to a dentist. Amazingly quiet it was with no one talking even arriving at the west end of the city. A stop at the Penn Hotel and Bar was made where discussions usually took place but it was another strange time. Always having something to say it was at the moment not a word was spoken. Bill broke the ice as he sarcastically advised of the tiny sum in the pot where Tom quickly followed asking what they expected since nobody sold any tickets. It only took a few moments to get their selves together where a basic plan of what to say was devised.

So, it was where everyone took a house by their selves then after a few callings the four would meet to compare notes. A raving success it turned out to be where having covered an entire block the total sales added up to two sales each of one ticket. While feeling a sense of embarrassment there was also good feelings since it was realized that no one had complained about the price of the tickets. From then was added about the guys needing a clubhouse. Over time other thoughts were generated as the four began to teach themselves. Along with cutting down on dinnertime all socializing was stopped allowing more time for selling when slowly the boys came to realize they needed help, especially once people had inquired about the prize. Forced into discussing a prize they didn't have, the team quickly moved to resolve the problem. With hope, Bill's mother willing to help knew about sales along with the stores that made it easy to find one. Having the prize along with the good pitch gave the team some needed confidence. With the jobs along with the extra work combined with the sold chances and trash money, the kitty steadily increased.

Reflections often caused discussion in hindsight of what should have done at the beginning but then at the start who could have known what to do. In school it was the same as home as always being told what to do but with the celebration project there was no one to give advice where everything was a struggle. In authority belting out for him to hold up while the man invited the two inside. Always valuing the diversity of the races it was easy for Stan to feel at home. While Stan noticed the various trophies, Dave continued speaking about was a drab type day when standing on a house porch the two were greeted by a large African American male. Answering the doorbell, nothing was expected since showing his age. Quickly while Stan made his pitch, the man demonstrated his consideration of the chances. Surprising the two, the man interrupted asking if going to college while offering to provide some sale pointers. Initially each erroneously assumed the man was simply trying to be nice but noting their respect, they responded with a yes sir plus, Dave all smiles, blurted out, "the team needs all the help they can get".

As the man showed his professionalism explaining his years of salesmanship along with not so fair means the two amateurs realized that the intelligent man was not the norm but worldly knowledgeable. With the two salesmen it was all ears, as the man took charge. Providing lots of ideas along with comparing to his younger years there was much laughter as the two were happy to receive the learning. Then after showing gratitude for having sold a few tickets the two departed. Jubilant Stan was having felt that he had made a good friend.

During a subsequent meeting the information shared bolstered thinking to even looking the part. From then on the four started wearing what the man had suggested. Shirts and ties, along with dress coats rather than the casual or work clothes became the norm. With attire changed to a professional dress code, attitudes also changed where pushing every day to the limit improvement was noticed. When something worked, it was shared where often purchased was a book rather than just a few tickets. Such result not only bolstered the confidence but greatly helped the kitty. Time moving into the end of February breaking of the weather helped with the outside work along with the selling of the tickets. Also visiting bars or watching television became nil where getting to bed early for sleep was the rule. Such good behavior though beyond the norm for the four became unnoticed yet often drove the parents batty.

Early March Dave's father and older son came to understand that the younger son was showing too much determination. Evidently his attitude along with the madness of his actions had become more than the parents could handle. Especially was his mother where his constant rushing around while hardly at home often put them in an awkward position. Although they pretended to ignore what was going it only caused more strife. Dave always tried to make things as amiable with his mother as possible but stress never seemed to go away where was a pot brewing on the home front but it wasn't tea.

During a day in the small town of Eddystone , Tom and Dave were greeted by what at first seemed as a happy elderly couple. Peeking through their storm door the couple showed as if they were almost scared. Then to the boys' dismay the couple for no seemingly reason showed attitude as they refused to believe anything the boys told them. With alarming emotions the two even demonstrated being threatened to even calling the police. Left with nothing to do, the two quickly apologized for disturbing them while quickly walking out.

Afterwards the matter was discussed on how such situations could be avoided but regardless if intentions there was no answer. Such was just accepted as just one of those times and not just was the weather warmng, but so were the boys and the pot. Realizing their good fortune with a hyped up attitude there was no stopping except often to thank almighty God, for providing good health.

Gaining of confidence generated more determination where a serious looking for a car began. Such action prompted the boys to again speak to their parents but each was greeted with the usual deaf ears as all remained against the idea. What remained was only finding consolation in each other. Having respected his mother's intelligence along with good communications, one day Bill inquired what he was supposed to do when the guys would have enough money to buy a car. Surprised he was with her response of how it might be ok, if everything on the home front was taken care of. Not wanting to cause problems, yet with his mind set on going it was about what to do. With Bill, was the same with Dave where all the other two could do was listen while offering opinions. Dave tried dropping hints about the guys starting to look for a car but, his father was so adamant that one time he simply shook his head pretending not to hear what was being said. Then another time, exploding in anger his mother asserted why should her son care if his friends are looking for a car? As a deafening silence filled the room she ended her feelings asserting her authority almost in rage. Boldly she hollered, why would they even be looking for a car, when she was not going to let her son go any way. His mother finished stating how it would be the same even if they took a train, as you're not going, period, and that's that.

But his parent's refusal to budge didn't stop Dave when evenings later, the boy tried again. Awe come on now mom, he pleaded, please try to understand. Then getting an icy look from her, he tried his father. Don't you see, Dad, please help he asked. Didn't you want to make such a trip when you were my age the boy pleaded? His father couldn't respond but his wife with jaw set and her teeth tight muttered how they decided he wasn't going and no need of talk. I don't see what there is to discuss his mother ended walking out of the room. After that, all heartbroken Dave didn't bring the matter up hoping that time would help. Soon the boy fell into a kind of limbo as his house was on pins and needles when he was around. A psychological defense, it was for him that postulated if he didn't say any more about the project. Yet somehow, maybe by the laws of Karma, religion or whatever everything would turn out okay he hoped. But the silence didn't allow any solution.

Meanwhile, each of the boys had been reading their respective newspapers along with other mailings regarding articles showing automobiles that were for sale. Calling it was found either the vehicles were of the sporty type, convertible, two-door, too old, or simply had too much mileage. Then when a car seemed a likely prospect the asking price was so high it prohibited the team from even looking at it. Although each was aware that the price of a car would drastically reduce the kitty so would the insurance. Cost of coverage was found to be almost that of the cost of a car as an entire policy outright for a minimum term was necessary. Then being underage adding penalties the matter was put on hold.approaching end of March, yet only four vehicles had been looked at where on a Saturday after the jobs were done they started the sales part. Early time of day it happened when driving by a small car lot located off Welsh Street. Scaring the day lights out of everyone Bill yelled, yo Stan stop the car! Instantly, thinking something bad happened, the driver slammed on the brakes causing everyone some mild inconvenience. When asked what was wrong, smiling Bill pointed to the cars in the lot suggesting to take a close look at it. Sitting in wonderment, each questioned what it was to look at. When Bill asked whether it was a hippo, the three offered it being a rhinoceros, whale and a large turtle. Stan upset at the situation hollered at Bill of him being an idiot, as if the car was on fire, just to look at a what, a turtle, he yelled? Yet, after the words, the turtle seemed to draw the four as a magnet. Shortly, the salesman, came out wearing all smiles like a shark about to bite asking if he could be of some help. Quickly Dave boldly replied a jesting yes sir as it was noticed that all the doors were attached. Noting of the humor, the man asked if the feature was noticed of the ultra modern drive train of rubber bands under the hood where everyone had a good laugh. Although ten years old, the vehicle looked to be a very capable means of transportation but, then at seventeen what could the young boys know of auto mechanics? Never having had the responsibility of owning and caring for one, every move and every word was a step in learning. Aware of the boys fishing, politely the man suggested of the group having no idea of what they were looking for and to take a ride. Although the driver seat portion was worn, the rest of the interior was in very good condition plus the areas between the front and back seat allowed for good storage space. Perhaps the price to a lot of people may not have been much but being the early time of the boys' life along with lacking finances, to them five hundred and fifty dollars was a large amount.

Where possible the man stepped on the gas then, as it burst forward he noted the good pick up. After covering several streets it was back to the lot where the four questioned wether the car would be able to fully serve the need of a long trip. As the man asserted it to be dependable he walked back to his trailer. Returning several minutes later he inquired if any agreement had been reached where smiling, Tom replied how the price was too high. Uttering their thinking the four departed leaving the man scratching his head

Meanwhile, Bill offering a solution, asked his mom whether she would feel better if he obtained people close by to provide some help. The positive response of his mother urged him to speak to their friend Al. Al's parents living in the corner house gladly offered to help taking her shopping. Also, Al agreed to cut the lawn along with helping in small chores and since Bill's mother had been a Cub Scout den mother along with Al having been a boy scout both families were known in the neighborhood. The family living across the street, hearing of Al's helping also agreed to lend a hand. Lastly it was Bill found the older man at the other end of the street and although he didn't drive he knew the boy's mother having also worked with children where he offered to help around the house. Soon hearing of the help available, Bill's mother felt better but still preferred that he didn't go or at least go with adult supervision. However, five people in the car was not possible.

About then the time arrived where Dave informed his dad that the boys were looking at a specific car when hearing of such, his mother exploded. All she could think about was the assumed danger he would be facing. From the simple phrase, the family got entangled in arguments. As the father showed interest because Dave had asked him to take a look at the car the father attempted to reason with his wife. Noting of precautions being taken even about safety matter, the mother full of adverse feelings remained with a deaf ear. Trying another viewpoint the father demanded that Dave assure his parents there would be no skimping on safety and no reckless driving. Cooperating as best he could, Dave assured them how each guy was responsible being very careful. Although his father understood the mother simply by not listening failed to understand her son and husbands reasoning.

Meanwhile in a conference comparing to other cars along with the short amount of limited time, it was decided to buy the car. When the team returned to the lot the salesman applied pressure, where Tom and Dave indicated concern about the negatives. Simultaneously Bill and Stan walked around the vehicle, pointing to the dents along with its slight tilt. Finding him-self in the middle of a controversy the man asked the question of which one was really looking to buy the car. So intrigued from the answers he started making suggestions as to where to go and places to visit. Then smiling the man asserted how the car would be safe to make the trip while reducing the price to $450.00. Unexpectedly, Dave's dad arrived where he performed his inspection of the vehicle. Then after taking a test drive the father whispered to his son how he only found it a good one with only minor things. While the salesman understood the boy's father helping he was confused about the parent's negative position. After the two men talked, the price was dropped to $400.00 but an impasse was reached. Quietly, the man stated his being tired of the bickering where he went back into his office. Shortly as the four were starting to leave the man came out stating he could adjust the price to three hundred and sixty dollars but not a dollar less. While shaking their heads, the team upon leaving stated they would think about it.

Later stopping back after hearing the conditions along with the financial strain the salesman went back inside his trailer. Shortly back with the four he asserted his wanting to help where Dave responded of the price being too high for the budget. Throwing his hands in the air, the man replied, how the car could be had for Three hundred and Twenty-Five dollars adding it either take it or leave it. In response, the four sounding depressed, Bill hollered how if he had come down to Three Hundred he may have made the sale. Right away, the four turned to leave. Immediately stepping backwards with his hands to his face the man blurted how the team was really something. Then he hollered, you could have it for three hundred even but, no more talk as there's not another dime to be had. As the five walked toward each other shaking hands a verbal agreement had been made. Inside the trailer as the man requested payment Stan signed the necessary papers. Then   while Bill explained of the money still in the bank, the man accepted ten dollars down payment being assured he would have the balance in a few days. As if being relieved from some burden, the man advised of holding the car for only two days.

Subsequently, Bill explained to his mom of having purchased the car where noting dissatisfaction she mentioned of being afraid because of the distance. Showing concern, the boy comforted her noting of Dave's father having given it a good inspection adding about the distance being only more miles than Florida. Then upon hearing of Bill and his mom having a good understanding helped perk the group. However, Dave's mother was absolutely livid when, the next day she found out from her husband. Softly, he mentioned that considering the price and condition he couldn't help but agree with his young son where her temper soared. Unexpectedly the house had become ablaze with anger as feelings of her young son's leaving on some trip that she didn't approve of scared her in a mind of worry.

Assumption of being dangerous taunted her as she pressed her husband for having allowed her son to buy the car especially knowing how she felt about the matter. Whether his mother's failing to grasp the importance of her husband having checked the car out was a hindering of understand was never mentioned but it may have helped. As if crying out in distress the woman pressed on knowing how it was dangerous out there.

How could her husband allow him to do such, she repeatedly asked. Almost in a rant she hollered, not even 18 the boy isn't even of age to drink let alone wonder around the country with juveniles.

Meanwhile, Dave's insides were torn as he hated the controversy with his mom, especially with his father and older brother being in the middle. In tears the woman pleaded. In tears the woman pleaded how she only wanted what was best for her son. Being in his early age it was not the time for him to buy a car simply to frolic around the country she stammered. Then in distress his mother having taken it personally, yelled how she couldn't believe he was doing this to her! Angrily, she blurted of being strictly against the whole stupid idea asserting, just who the hell did he think he was. Immediate anguish had emotionally overtaken the boy as he had no intention of hurting his mom where fully upset the boy noted how his dad had checked the car over to make sure it was a safe vehicle. Sullen he looked toward his father and brother, Dave with a bleeding heart seeking help, but it was only a moment of silence. Only received were expressions of sadness with shaking heads. Unexpectedly the situation had exploded well beyond what he had ever known. As his mother's expressions hurtfully hit home, he of heartfelt feelings, Dave attempted to explain his position with the other boys being a member of the team. But such effort only dug a deeper hole.

Quietly the father mentioned of his son getting older where the time had come to cut some of the line allowing his son to grow up. Subsequent to a moment of silence, as advised, Dave left to go on to school while his father attempted to calm things. But he too had to go to work while his wife was unable to accept her husband's fatherly intentions. Although he understood his wife's reasoning, she was so engulfed in her motherly love that a mental wall had been created. To her he was still her baby.

At school with Dave unsociable the other three tried to console him. But not part of his family, words from the other companions lacked any affect. Then later as his dad was able to discuss into details, slowly the parents comprehended their son's reasoning. Needing to be a team player, then along with the other two men offering their opinions Dave's mother mentioned how she came to understand. Noting her not appreciating how serious the boys were in tears she retreated to another room. Then with apologies and love expressed the following day along with noticing her son's hurting she finally forgave him for what he was doing. Time helped where slowly it healed the boy's misery as well as that which his mother was suffering. At dinner a couple of days later, the boy's mom pressed for her son to promise to contact her often where overcoming the last hurdle the boy promised that at least every other day or when possible Dave would call his mom.

Sunday after church services, Dave's father insisted on mending the atmosphere. Over breakfast talk carried on until interrupted when Stan called but he was cut short as Dave stated that he couldn't talk but would explain later. Understanding each family's attitude improving, a good feeling of relief abounded as if a huge dark cloud had lifted from their space. Days later, noting about insurance Stan's father agreed to add to his auto policy. So with the insurance matter resolved the four went to the bank withdrawing the amount needed for the car.

A 1948 Nash, Ambassador, the four-door sedan was a fantastic piece of machinery. Resembling something like a large turtle yet built like a horse reacting to the reins, the Nash responded well allowing it to easily get underway. With the four inside, space was lacking but the large trunk provided space for holding much beside the jack and tools. Along with the small front and rear vent windows there was the pop up vent located at the base of the windshield that combined provided good air circulation. Another real benefit was the extra gear called overdrive where driving on the open road it allowed for saving gas costs as later realized of getting up to thirty-eight miles to the gallon. Yet, only a six cylinder with all the weight it had to be babied along.

Realizing a long awaited team accomplishment, a huge lift in morale took place. There were no more excuses, as the Chester Eagles Boys Club was in full gear. While people made fun, asking how far the car was expected to go, others suggestively uttered of not going in that thing or not making it out of the state. Soon the four found their selves ignoring them, noting their not offering their cars or help to pay for a better car. Also noted was that the car was purchased with their own earned money and not somebody else's dough or vehicle. First things first it was when the car was driven to a local Sun Oil Service station for gas. Knowing how the cost of the vehicle had seriously dropped the kitty's total subsequent discussions erupted on where to visit. Complications required every place to be planned on along with what routes. Also allowed were consideration for other places that would pop up but constrained by the distance and limited time, sacrificing the norms became essential.

Notions of attending baseball, basketball or football games along with bowling, swimming, hunting and trap shooting were stopped. Then also established was a majority rule to decide all matters and, if not historical, new or different, no visiting plus if no majority the place was dropped. As the four prepared the car Tom suggested the vehicle having a name. Initially such thought brought funny responses. but after Dave started with the Bulldog or Eagle the others offered suggestions. All smiles, Tom suggested Nashieola where Stan went inside only to return with a beer and when Bill saw the bottle he suggested each one all take a healthy sip using it as a toast. When it got back to him, Dave made a scene of tapping the bottle against the side as if christening. Shortly, while spilling some on the car Bill yelled out its name of Nashie. Surely it was not a large commercial vessel, but the significance was high where full of emotion each was clapping with cheers while jumping around.

As the days passed, the four seemed to transform themselves into some sort of robots. Dinners at the table became rear treats as paper plates and soda bottles took over. Food such as the basic sandwiches of peanut butter and jelly or the lunchmeat, cheese, lettuce, tomato and onion types became a common place. Saving money had turned into a real nightmare but nobody ever complained as whatever was made from jobs, work, trash picking and chances all ended in the bank. Such success energized momentum affecting the comradely where the project brought the four into a new level of high friendship.

One day while finishing the borough of Parkside, Stan and Tom had already finished their block but Bill and Dave had one house remaining. Decided was to make the sale together where once on the porch, Dave rang the doorbell. Seconds later as Bill rang the bell again the door flew open as if the person was trying to tear it down. While the older man looked the two boys over all anxious, Bill started in. Quickly after interrupting he invited the two inside where he suggested for them to continue. Started in where his partner left off Dave ignored the man's gruff tone. As the scene unfolded into a hornet's nest, interrupting rudely the man asked why Bill was not the one doing the talking. Suddenly, the atmosphere turned unpleasant with Dave attempting to restart while the woman aggressively yelled for the man to shut up and don't interrupt the boys. Suddenly, an argument developed between the two it became apparent the two had been in an argumentative state even before the boys rang the doorbell.

Attempting to quiet them down Dave spoke in a lowered voice. but all the man did was give the boys a glance while pursing his argument with his wife. Shortly the man threw out questions in a disturbed manner regarding their age along with why not in a uniform. So, with all efforts failing the two realized they were wasting their time where simultaneously both moved towards the door giving the excuse of parents being outside. Angrily, the man yelled out, how if your parents are out there, go, get the hell out of here!

After finishing for the night, a stop was made at a diner where over coffee and treats the four discussed the situation ending where one would put on an act of being sick. As Tom mentioned of hoping it was not a bad sign of things to come though affected by the situation the four settled down. Graduation was on the horizon with the four not the same that had started. Pushing the regular jobs along with the odd work while also selling of the chances took their toll. Yet with all that, discussions started on the matter of time as class testing preparation time would slowly approach compromising available time.

Realizing the long distance to California developing the budget for maximum saving was furthered. Knowing there was not being enough money to go around mentioned was no spending on anything except when necessary. Later it was made a rule of absolutely necessary where things almost got ridiculous in spending. Helped, were the longer days of sunlight enabling more selling plus taking on more side jobs. Meanwhile, Stan's helpful Aunt Rose provided a huge four-foot wall map of the United States. Just in time it provided a good means for estimating distance and travel time.

Then there was the question of who would be driving, how long, as well as how the driving would be shared. Rules were made that no driver behind the wheel would be drinking any alcohol plus no drinking before the driver's shift. Aware that neither one had ever experienced such a long trip they came to respect each one's lack of knowledge. As each felt the pressure from not having any supervision other than their selves doing the planning it became a real monster. It had become clear how the simple pact made at the beginning had grown into heavy responsibility. Don't forget the pact, became the phrase of the day when after initially using it as a jovial slang, the remark seemed to carry the team's weight.Intense hustle became the word applied to everything where even usual thoughts of putting off till the next day was stopped. Also unnecessary conversation with perspective buyers was shortened to a minimum for saving time.

On one of the days, it was off to the library but it offered little as maps that could have been used were not permitted to be taken out. A short drive to Dave's house where picked up was the telephone directory. Travel agencies became the direction. Although the first one stopped at, though small in size had several racks of various kinds of brochures. But along with thin books it was found to only contain matters relating to air travel, trains and bus lines. As it was the four were of a mind that a travel agency was of all travel forms where neither was aware that agencies specialized in different means. After not getting what was hoped for from a second and third place, the team headed for the one in Brookhaven.

Operated by an older man and woman there was also a young couple offering their services. Following a short, the four provided the kind of maps needed for the trip, along with their first hand experience that became a big help. When noted of visiting Hollywood the two couples really opened up with their knowledge on attractions and resorts. Families go, women go, even men go shopping, but what would young teenage boys know about shopping other than carrying the bags? Then too, what did they know about preparing for a large trip of which they had no knowledge of?   W h e n Bill mentioned not to forget the beer Dave asked whether he was a broken record while Tom questioned what would be done if stopped by the police. On a rainy day not productive of outside work or chances, a stop at the bank was made for some funds. Too early for supermarket food, other stores were visited which had a variety where metal cups were purchased being on sale.

Finally the team stopped at Pep Boys on Ninth Street. Even with the dismal weather the auto store was really busy with customers. Looking around Stan started thinking of the four having a lack of funds.

While thinking how the car used oil, considering it an ongoing expense the boy was moved into action. Suggestively he asked the other three to ask the clerks questions regarding trailer items, camping supplies and prices of tires. Then seeing the sales personnel preoccupied along with all of the counter attendants busy, while starting to sweat, Stan took the risk. With his heart racing, he grabbed two five-gallon cans of thirty-weight oil and headed for the door. Earnestly his thinking was only to help the trip's budget. Shortly at the car while trying to catch his breath, not being a thief such action caused him to reconsider knowing it was wrong plus also contrary to his way of thinking. With actual thoughts of borrowing, he knew he would pay for them after the three returned. Then while moving the metal cans around to find a good spot, the boy prayed asking his Lord for understanding of the team's financial situation.

Seeing the rectangular cans standing upright didn't take up much room Stan went back inside when at the right moment he helped himself to another five-gallon container, but of fifty-weight oil. Back inside the car, he waited for the others. Although Dave bought a couple of tail light bulbs, the two only got prices on headlights and tires yet neither of them realized what had been done. As the group talked about prices, the questioning started on Stan. All anxious he pulled the car away where following a moment of quiet he responded by giving them a choice of where either he had borrowed, or that the Pep Boys made a contribution to the gangs cause. Shortly noting their concern with insinuations, Stan became irritated. He noted how they should have been thankful since it meant less money out of the kitty being spent on the car. Finally the boy suggested that if they wanted, he would return the items but, having realized that they insulted him, they started agreeing with him. Suddenly Stan pulled the car over to a stop leaving the three sitting in a stunned position. As he got out of the car he lit a cigarette while contemplating the situation.

Then moments later, Stan started driving back while asserting the three could pay for the oil when needed out of their own pockets but not from the kitty. As the other two responded, in an angry tone, Bill banged his hand on the roof. Mad, he hollered for them to just shut up and think of what they were doing to their partner. That kind of personal situation between the four had never happened before where every word carried its own weight. Showing his anger, Dave shouted, asking whether the children were going to come to their senses when right away, Tom asked Stan to say something, Sternly responding being so upset Stan replied that since they started the mess they should clean it up. Displaying some temper, Tom blurted out how the team had better get themselves together cause if such was the way things were going to be on the road, it was time to bring things to a halt. Instant silence took over, as everyone was stunned by what had developed. The statements had hit home where full of emotion each felt the sting of the words. Then as the three made known their appreciation of Stan's efforts, it was almost as if the boys were riding in a funeral. Finally the team patched their selves up while going to another diner.

Another learning experience was had, but had the hard way. Such was simply because the boys said things without giving thought. A crystal ball reader or fortune-teller would have been nice to consult with, but the boys didn't have either plus didn't believe in such things.

So, it was always about the present day where the team was taking each day at a time. Meanwhile the four had regrouped with even more respect for each other as the team pulled closer together.

CHAPTER THREE

ADVERSITY, A DISSOLVING TIME AND THE RACK

Wanted was to be prepared for any type of situation that may arise but there wasn't enough room for everybody with everything that everyone wanted to take. As Bill blurted out if taken was everything everybody wants, weez needs a truckz where Dave responded that what weez has, is what weez gots, and what weez gots is what weez uses. To help save needed space it was agreed washing powder would be taken along to allow washing clothes when staying at a motel. It was unbelievable how thick headedeveryone was where looking to bring way too much stuff had to be overcome.

It was as any other day when out selling the tickets that it happened when

Tom hollered for the driver to stop the car. Then he pointed to one of the yards sounding all excited. "I got it, I can see it working guys, that's it"! While the three looked not able to understand they asked him if he was having some sort of hallucination. Slowly upon seeing the upside down canoe it brought a solution. Tom suggested how a container for the top of the car is what is needed, but the car's roof being like an eggshell in shape presented a mental stumbling block. From then it was another new challenge searching for a container that could be used. With the need to keep spending down it was to buy only certain parts then use big pieces that could be found in the picked up trash. Once the four saw how various items were constructed it was decided to build their own however, with the car having a semi-bowed type of top the team was stumped how to secure the item knowing that speeds would be over fifty miles an hour.

Considered simple to be done was the weight along with building a frame to attach to the base, then a top to cover the holding container but, nothing could be found. Newspapers and magazines were searched where if they had the shape the four felt they could fix it. A solution had to be found since after the purchase of the car, there wasn't enough funding remaining to purchase such a large item. Visiting various types of stores they searched for anything that would work yet, nothing was found. Surprise it was, when days later, Bill unexpectedly paid Stan a visit after school. While banging away on the door he was hollering, hurry up when as Stan opened the door he couldn't imagine what his friend needed. In an alarmed stated he thought that maybe his friend's mother was in trouble. Rather, Stan was greeted with a smile on Bill's face that was lit up like a light bulb. Friends and school buddies yes, but it was dinnertime where Stan thought such timing was ridiculous. Puzzled, seeing Bill carrying a child's bedspring Stan asked whether he was drunk, or lost his marbles. Then as the boy laid the item on the porch floor upside down Stan comprehended how it made sense.

Bill's mom without even seeing the car had solved the rack problem. Rushing to set the thing on top of the car it was upon seeing, as if it had been custom made. Not only a perfect fit from front to back but also from side to side. No dancing or hugging but the euphoria that that was created between the two could have been cut with scissors. Of course tying it down with permanency was another matter. Also needed was to find a solid covering to enclose it. But at least the problem of a base frame had been solved. Often the question arose of why neither had thought of such an idea where it was a female not even involved that solved the problem. About that time it was amusing where the boys felt regarding the chances that it seemed as if people were actually waiting for them, almost rolling out the red carpet. Wow! All of a sudden everything was going so right where even the home fronts seemed to have improved where happy days became the words of the days.

It was an afternoon in Brookhaven when Dave and Bill were finishing up at a large single house. After ringing the doorbell an attractive middle-aged woman opened the door where surprised the two were. Seeing the fully developed woman in a revealing wet bathing suit interrupting Dave's slow pitch she invited both into the house where the shapely beautiful woman created a terrible distraction. If that wasn't enough, just having gotten their breath three other women came into the room dressed accordingly. A heated swimming pool in the rear explained the situation and though such a difference in ages yet the gentlemanly actions allowed the completing of the sale where all four women bought some chances.

Twas the day of big advice when all through the school not a teacher was edgy not even the class. April had arrived, yet none of the four was able to find any information regarding the school's schedule as notifications only asserted of getting serious about preparing. Several attempts were made trying to figure out how to tie the massive spring thing to the car. While tom suggested drilling holes in the roof to bolt it down, Dave mentioned using rope or chain with the door handles and the bumpers in the back until understood those inside would not be able to get out. Days later Tom provided L shape straps with funny hooks from his father who had done some traveling while using a trailer. Proving a secure means of leverage the straps allowed stabile support for the unit on the car sides yet not long enough for the front and rear. With the four metal legs facing the sky it allowed the adding of four sides using the legs as posts. Dave brought a bunch of bolts along with Able having brought some electrical single strand covered wire and brackets from a hardware store which enabled attaching the frame to the bumpers. It wasn't pretty and though it did the job there was still the need for finding a covering. Sheets, blankets and painters cloths were determined unable to stand up to the wind or rain. What to use for the top of the rack became the on going question.

Quickly word was spread for the need but nothing found. Days went by with nothing found in the trash collection, along with no one having anything to offer. Unexpectedly one evening Stan received a telephone call from his uncle Henry suggesting he may have found something. Hank as his friends called him was a Second World War veteran who played semi pro baseball. Accessing one of his old buddies he was able to provide a covering which came from a small truck it. Not only waterproof but the heavy gauge fabric was strong enough to withstand any kind of wind. Then with the tiny metal grommets it allowed for applying tie downs without tearing the material.

Meanwhile as Dave suggested buying a couple of tires since the two on the rear showed wear starting with the trunk the team made sure everything was accounted for having to do with things requiring car repairs. Everyone was in high spirits since the last obstacle had been overcome operating well as any fine-oiled amateur team, the four found their selves in a state of disorganized organization. Yet at least they were learning to do.

Now it was around that time where the school testing schedule had been distributed noting that one of the tests would be on one day at a certain time while another test would be on another day at a different time, where there could be two tests on the same day but at different times.

SEGMENT - 3   Who could have known, but a day it was when Tom showed up at school displaying a sloppy appearance while in a miserable state. Highly irregular it was as just not like the boy. With everybody else was in good spirits who would have known that life was about to pose big time problems? Everyone was healthy where nobody gave any thought that sickness would come into the picture but, unfortunately the team forgot about the relatives. Then during lunch period Tom broke the bad news where, horror filled the room. As the other three boys listened the boy announced that he was pulling out of the project. At first the three thought he might be jesting, but his beaten looks brushed all hope aside. Each was aware that his father had suffered a stroke but that was months back where recuperation had been doing fine.

Overwhelmed, Stan hollered out, "oh God, why now"? Immediately in a pleading tone Dave yelled, "yes God, and why now Tom? Slowly bending his head Tom advised how his father's health had taken a sudden turn for the worse as the doctor had told him that his father's health had deteriorated to the point of being critical. Tom was without other relatives near by, the only healthy person living in the house and the only dependable person where the situation demanded him to be there every day. Suddenly it was the boy found himself doing all of the chores, even assisting the parents with their personal matters. By any normal or even stretched means such critically disabling home situation on any young boy at age 18 was more than any one could handle.

Especially taking into consideration his feelings having gotten attached to the project and car, because things on the home front had drastically changed, so also did his life style. All broken while shaking his head, Dave prayed, "oh God, of all the times why now, it just ain't fair". Having been inside their friends' house the three remembered of his very sickly his mother where the sad combination left his parents in a scenario totally out of their control. Stunned, all the three could do was show comradely offering their full assistance but the boy's face showed how all was in vain. Cutting short the discussion Tom stated how sorry he was but he was forced to say goodbye to the project. As the boy left for class Bill very mad while upset belted out a few choice cuss words simultaneously banging his fist on the table. Deeper the four sank into a depressed state as the four realized the tragedy. Dumbfounded comprehending what had struck the team, the four sat motionless, unable to talk.

During the following days, driven into a deep low of emotions, the three felt completely lost where all talk ended in doom and gloom. Since Tom's matter was too personal the three became totally frustrated with feelings of uselessness. Control of the project seemed lost where all activity came to a halt. Even abandoning the project was considered. Time passed where thinking became strained as all the three could do was pray for the other boy's father to regain his strength. And pray they did every chance they had, at church, at home and in school. What a heart wrenching time it was where the three, supposedly the closest of friends didn't even know what to say to each other. Mentally shutdown and heart broken, the three attempted to bury themselves in their school work yet forced to face the music seeing their friend but, only between classes. Often Tom showed him being curious how things were going which only created more miserable time at school. It was as if a heating pot was waiting for some boiling. Where needed was for someone to say the wrong thing at the right time.

We should all keep the lid on, each suggested, since if either got physically hurt it would do the team under, where, would the mess end? Although the three still did their regular part time jobs the odd work and selling of chances floundered becoming as just putting in time. With the matter festering it was into moods of discord stretching everyone's nerves to the breaking point. Leaving an unexpected wall of meanness created, soon all that remained was to cancel the trip.

What to do, carrying heavy anxiety feelings there still remained some urge to find a way, With the three so upset they seemed glad to get it over with where they decided to call off the whole idea. Questions of what to do arose with the odd jobs, tickets, radio and stuff inside the car as well as the car plus the money in the bank and Tom's share. Finding a time that allowed everyone to get together was tough but, finally there was a night. With Tom a meeting was held but so distraught unable to start each could only listen where the boy at least broke the quiet. Although Bill attempted to start he choked over all the negatives where Dave thought to continue but also failed as couldn't say it all. Seeing both all choked up from being so close friends, Stan got right to the point asserting how it had been decided to stop the fiasco closing down the trip. Right away as Dave offered Tom his equal share, Bill added that whatever was sold from the tickets, car, contents and kitty would be divided equally among the four. Almost in tears, Stan uttered how such would finish the entire matter, bringing the fiasco to an end.

Instantly, the phrase hit the ears as winter's arrival with chills running up the spines when with heads shaking in dismay, Dave mentioned how it was all they could handle. Quietly standing up, Tom being a sport responded how he would only accept a portion of the pot to cover any monies he had personally put out. Yet, without giving thought to his feelings the three squabbled. As the three attempted to force some extra money on their friend, such only agitated him where although it was friends' good intentions, the three had actually insulted him. With a stern face Tom stood while asserting himself stating how after all the team had been through he would be really disappointed if those actions were all there was. Are you now a bunch of cowards, ready to throw in the towel and quit without making a full effort, the boy quizzed? If you finished the trip making it a success he hollered, at least there would be the memory of all the difficulty, efforts and times but, if you three quit now it would be a big let down to the friendship declaring him a total waste time.

All of a sudden it wasn't just a bunch of school buddies after a game or a simple set back, this was life smacking the three in the face. While ending the meet, Tom displaying a sad face added how he had no choice due his home situation, but the three had no excuse, angrily adding that if they quit, the three would be breaking the pact. With the four having given their word never to quit, for them to give up would have been a big insult to him where the pact would end up having no meaning of value. Nodding their heads realizing their wrong assumptions of self as well as misplaced values each agreed to think the situation over where the meeting ended.

Over the next couple of evenings the three telephoned each other but lacked any form of direction as was just talk and talk but without meaning. Feeling down in the dumps one early morning Dave, way before breakfast called the other two stating he needed help hoping there could be a meeting to decide on what to do. Outside school that morning the three stood on the corner noting their feeling helpless yet, each blurted out of feeling compelled to complete the trip. With much affection the three placed their arms on each of the other two's shoulders asserting it was no longer a celebration but turned into a cause. Bill uttered how the circumstance gave heavy meaning, but what to do? Displaying their resiliency, another meeting was held after classes but where to start was the question? Slowly suggestions were put from shortening the trip's time to eliminating some of the visits but shortly the three were void of answers. Finally it was decided that the original plans would not be changed and since missing a driver it was to find one. Each knew the school schedule was about to change so all efforts had to be a rush.

As April rolled on with a bang completing of the odd work and trash collecting became the target along with the selling of the tickets but the duo system could not work. Without Tom it left a third boy operating by himself along with causing bad memories as the boy had been too big a part for to long to forget him. Regrouping to restart struggling to overcome the misfortune, was not easy where often it was heard where one would mention how they were still the Chester Eagles Boys Club. Then another would respond that they were definitely going to make the journey. Although arguing was put to stop the evading of the classmates' insulting sayings along with pacifying the parents and relatives, almost closed the door of the mind. Soon though, things became easier since they at least could only confide in each other. Also there were the occasions where it was mentioned in conversations that those other people were not going anyway or not their money or not their car. Slowly it became as if there were two different worlds. First was to find someone at school where written notices were taped on the bulletin boards along with the doors. Even if another person agreed to go Tom had priority, if his situation allowed it.

A rule was made that if anyone would go, the person would have to give some money to the kitty plus share in the gas, driving, motel room and road expenses. Many boys showed interest but disliked the restricted short amount of time. Others reasoned that for them it just a matter of going along as a rider. It soon became apparent that most were only thinking about what they wanted of enjoying the fun, but without any of the work. The fact that none started with the beginning of the idea became a high priority and after days of seeing good words going nowhere, a newspaper ad looking for a rider was started but it too produced no results.

About to give up on the ad, a surprise it was when one morning unexpectedly a classmate from a different section approached Dave inquiring about the flyers. Although the talk was short the boy wanted to continue, so in between classes the two spent minutes talking. Then demonstrating serious interest, the three met Larry after school.Dragged into a consuming discussion Larry mentioned he had planned on going to college in California but skepticism abounded. Questioning of why the other driver dropped out raised concern of foul play when as the three responded it seemed to dampen his interest leaving the three not giving the boy any credibility as just full of talk. During a subsequent meeting the boy mentioned needing to get his parent's permission, adding how with a girl going along he doubted that his parents would agree. At the time the three had ignored Larry's utterance of there being a girl along thinking that he meant his guardian angel or was to meet someone.

Time was slipping by where the testing atmosphere was daily as instructors offered suggestions as to the materials. Although none ever gave specifics of where to look or concentrate they did provide clues. Yet there was no clue coming from Larry where not receiving any word the three was only able to assume that the boy wasn't going.   Surprised the three were when days later after school the four met where not at all seeming enthused Larry only had more questions. Yet, as Bill started to close the meeting the boy stated how he was looking forward to joining in on the trip. Without even being asked he agreed to all the requirements put by the three but, with a big condition. Boldly the boy demanded to be taken to his destination. What had taken so long for his decision was his parent's objection. They did not care for there being no adult along with the boys being under age. Also there was the assumption of having a girl along.

A day later when Larry saw the car for the first time, doubt could be seen written all over his face. Giving a heavy smirk, while he shook his head from side to side the boy blurted out, "are you guys kidding me"? Sarcastically in a raised tone he uttered how the thing may be a nice heap, but they were all crazy thinking they would go that far a distance in that thing. All upset over the remarks, Stan reacted asserting, "listen bub, if you don't like the so called thing, you could just leave", where Dave blurted out how the team would even smile as they helped him leave.

As if to change the subject the boy asked where Naszee the little girl was but, not understanding how the guy wanted to see a little girl, the trio assumed more wrong thinking. The guy wanted to meet Nazzhia before they fully agreed where just who the female was. While Dave advised him of the correct spelling Bill added for him not to forget it. The boys' seriousness about the vehicle caused Numb to change his tone where he noted how he wasn't aware of their affection for the car. Instantly being adamant, Bill advised that they had gone through a lousy mess to get where they were. Following a brief silence, Stan added for him to remember that they had scrimped, sweated, scrounged and saved pennies to buy Nashie, where each all worked up added, "yeah, and remember, your only a passenger taking advantage". Following more words of sarcasm by all, the three asserted of being happy to educate him.

All smiles displayed, Larry walked forward where he gave the car a pat while also offering his apology to the car. Then showing his serious side the boy mentioned how if being allowed in, he would help anyway he could. Then before departing he added his intended bus fare for making a kitty contribution which solidified the agreement.

With the month soon turning the corner, and test periods soon to start the senior class would then be reduced to only three full days a week. Therefore the rest of the week being half or partial days allowed a schedule which enabled more completing of jobs, picking trash and selling tickets. Times changed where whatever a problem was, if it would take too much time, it was passed by or let go. Time meant dollars and any dollar to the three was a lot of moola. Soon Larry, after hearing some of the stories had become so fully enthused about the whole idea he wanted to be an actual part of the club. Although a regenerated foursome was again off and running, him not being from the start with the transportation means already purchased, he wasn't allowed to be a part of the original but an associate member. Meanwhile some students in the school realized that the boys' trip was true where some even tried to muscle their way. Through use of their parents or offering to pay their way as well as meeting all the boys conditions was offered but, they were too late as the three had already committed to an established agreement with Larry.

Time was where the kitty had grown substantially. Then with more testing days it was known being only a matter of time before it was prom time. It was also time to start on final car preparations One evening the four stopped for a brew where the three asserted it was a time to close the door on all past matters so as to make a fresh start. Each of the three had been holding things inside where it was necessary to rid the garbage. All relatives' and friends negatives would be handled only as past events. Not understanding, Larry stated, "you guys telling me that things were that bad"? Attempting to get his words out, Stan strained, replied how it wasn't that bad, but worse

Along with the car holding non-food necessities other items were kept in inside Stan's basement. Intended was to have everything possibly ready in one place. Knowing it to be a trip for a month, at first each brought large pieces of luggage accompanied by smaller bags fully packed to the brim of clothes anticipated for all needed situations. Big problem it was where one person's baggage had to be multiplied by four. So prepared it was that they had enough stuff for a year. Instead of what was needed, each was thinking of what they could use Though they already had the spare tire, jack, small hand tools, a tire gauge, flashlight, extra batteries, a pump plus the oil, extra bulbs and rags, everybody scrounged whatever extra stuff they could get.

While each's folks provided a small satchel of soap, wash rags and towels, Bill's mother provided one of her old but large handbags filled with various safety items such as a flashlight, band aids, cotton, iodine, hydrogen peroxide, gauze, tape, body strapping and sun tan lotion. Along with providing tiny head pillows Dave's folks gave a medium size heavy blanket plus a small rubber blanket for ground cover. Meanwhile Stan supplied a couple of umbrellas, with Bill's parent's furnishing a small ice chest, which fit nicely in the back on the floor. The scouting sleeping bags from Stan and Bill ended on the top.

Quickly the alarm sounded when realized there was way too much stuff. Stan suggested how a trailer should be rented or trade in the car for a truck where amid chaos a plan was developed limiting everything to the minimum. One change of casual clothes plus one sport coat, dress shirt, slacks and one pair of dress shoes became the rule. Bill and Stan provided laundry detergent, which helped reduce the need for extra underwear and outside garments. Meanwhile there was still the ongoing selling of the chances. Completing the blocks around Melrose Avenue was easy as most had houses on one side. Flying high, the boys were not only showing better attitudes but selling more everywhere they went. But unexpectedly the team's easy times ended as calamity started. Larry needing a break, found one day to have some free time where he joined the four for a few hours of comradely.

It was while completing the small borough of Sun Village of about seven thousand people with small row type houses that scared the two. Bill and Stan were on one side with Dave and Larry; taking care of the other side. Dave had finished where he joined up with Stan who had one house remaining. While a woman answered the door, Dave commented how it should be an easy sale. Then as she listened the woman asked whether the two were from around the neighborhood while asking them inside. As the two boys stood inside wearing smiles the woman explained to her husband what the boys were selling. With him showing little interest while sitting on the sofa reading a newspaper, the two felt they were being treated as if not even there. Slowly after giving his wife a glance while he inquired about the chances, he asked where the two worked.

Questions seemed to abound in normal curiosity, until he stood up while asking where the two lived. Immediately the man requested to see the prize but no one had ever asked to see the radio, so why the big deal the two were thinking. While attempted to explain the man changed his tone demanding that he see the radio. As the man approached the two, it caused them to back up becoming alarmed. Thinking was the man pulling a knife where the two adjusted for a brawl. In a smooth motion the man had reached into his pocket only pulling out his badge with identification. Who would have guessed, but the boys had hit a jackpot. Of all people it was the Police chief of the borough.

Having run out of words all the two could do was listen. Sternly stating his authority, while demanding to see identification he grabbed a pen. Then while copying down the names, addresses and telephone numbers he questioned Stan if was related to Henry who lived on Terrill Street. While the two were thinking all was ok, the man asserted how the two were in violation of the laws on drawings. Growling he asserted, there will be no more selling of the tickets to anyone, anywhere at any time, and your done where he confiscated the extra blank tickets the two had on their person. Stammering he asked if the boys understood then added he would see the prize. While displaying an angry face he stated how if his order was not followed, all four would be jailed on running a scam plus would attach theft charges for stealing people's money. Upon leaving, the man required a repeat of his instructions then added not to forget, in three days to be back with the prize. Happy to exit, the two answered, yes sir with a solid thank you.

Once outside the other three fully aware of the time spent, the three anticipated how the other two must have sold at least a couple of books. But as the five walked away Dave sarcastically mentioned how he was not interested in any more hassles like what they had just experienced. With Dave and Stan still rattled the other three could only prod them to say something where Stan responded for them to stuff it. Well on the way to a local diner the two dropped the bomb of what happened where Larry blurted out how there would be no more sales time for him and for the guys to stop or they would all be in trouble. Upset, Dave responded about having put too much effort into the matter to even think of such things as quitting. But Bill feeling all down mentioned that for him the trip had come to an end.

Suddenly one remark led to upsetting words that caused a rift where Dave quickly put a halt to the discussion mentioning the pact. While taking a big breath he asserted how such would be going back on his word. Then while staring at the others he reminded them how it was only himself and Stan who had the meeting with the policeman. Perhaps it was Stan's situation or the police chief's episode or the older couple's confrontation or even the combination but, whichever it was the combination had made a substantial impact. With everyone feeling jittery it was no longer business as usual. Like dragging an anchor the zip was gone yet the enthusiasm remained where a complicated team emerged.From then, except for class times, with Thomas out of the team's activities he was rarely seen.

Only a couple of days later, having the prize in hand Dave and Stan returned to visit the police chief. Once inside the chief mentioned how he was impressed finding it to be new along with one of quality plus being in the wrapper. Then following a pause, the man reminded the two of being advised of who won along with their telephone number and address information. As the two made for the door, the chief hollered out for them to hold it and stop where you are. Right away, Stan in angry tone asked him, ok so what's the matter now, where smiling, the chief offered a few dollars while expressing his friendly gesture to help for the trip. Lastly he added for the boys to remember, that there would be no more selling until a permit was gotten, then with a few handshakes along with thank yous the two walked out.

During the following nights the boys thought contrary wise as had their jobs and ways to do. Showing his concern, Larry blurted out how the guys should stop the selling or might be in trouble yet, surprising the other three he stayed showing being a part of the team. The four steadily pushed in new areas until there were no more tickets to sell. And what a lift it was as the pressure stopped like a big vacuum had sucked out the three's brains.
No more people to complain about plus no planning was needed for any area to sell in. Such completion of the selling project allowed contacting more potential customers that allowed completing more of the odd work and trash picking.

Finally, it was to determine the winner where the four simply dropped all of the stubs into the back of Bill's jacket then folded the arms making a satchel. While giving the bundle a shake each was expressing their hopes that the winner would at least be someone they knew. Once a few tickets were drawn, in memory of Tom the three stubs were tossed to obtain the winner but as it happened, none of the three tickets was of any name that either of the five knew. Tis a shame because being an unknown there was no reason to keep one of the stubs and ticket. What made the team feel better was during delivery to the winner who made compliments on the radio being good quality. With a bunch of smiles the four left the house where once off the porch they started singing the old song, De Camp town races sing that song, do da, do da as we won the race all do da day.

Such a tune was easy for Stan as he used to play the song on his piano. Having awarded the prize, the four stopped at a diner over ice cream, cake and coffee celebrating the ticket sales success. Happy it was that the sales had come to a close but sad because each knew much fun they had enjoyed. While, Bill's mother had cancelled the ad of looking for a rider, Bill called the police chief notifying him of the winner's name, address and telephone number. Tom however, was a continuing shamble being bogged down by his parent's matters along with the chores. Sadness for him was felt by the other four especially rarely seeing his face it reflected the stress.

Anxious the four was to get started on the road quickly and though the day of the trip had no real connection with the historical meaning of the sixth there was a connection, as the team had cause. A rush hit the four aware that the last two weeks of May were not far away. As with all things about trips being new the whole situation presented feelings of uncertainty. One of the days the three went to Stan's house where the sleeping bags and small pieces of luggage along with items not often needed on top then secured the rack tightening the bolts along with the straps plus doing a tuck and tie where needed. In jest, Stan seeing a large bubble mentioned that a dirigible should have been rented to save gas that drew a barrage of innuendos.

Afterward, the last of unwanted things to the junk man were taken. As much planning the four did, they could have planned one of the Second World War invasions. With preconceived ideas of places to visit while reviewing the brochures, flyers and advertisements decisions were made. Easy it was to be, straight west over the turnpike, then hook on to route forty until connecting with route sixty-six. Heavy black lines were drawn along with light lines for alternatives if time permitted. After leaving Larry in California, being uncertain of the time element it was decided to leave the return part up to the three.

Unfortunately, there was no thinking of souvenirs plus no one ever suggested to keep a diary and collect items for memory. Result was not only were the ticket stubs and remaining sections discarded but so were the maps and other materials assumed not needed. Anticipated was that driving to California would take about fifteen days from when the trip was started. At least the plans along with the rules of the road had been established.

SEGMENT - 4.   Time getting short, Bill and Stan withdrew some funds for last of the shopping. A gas station located at the far end of Sun Village was the first to be visited. Along with the tank being filled, the tires' air pressure was adjusted. While the station attendant filled the tank, with curiosity he questioned where the four were going. Thinking to be funny,

Larry asked the man, why he felt the team was going somewhere. When replying the man mentioned how he didn't think the stuff on top was for rowing a boat where smiling, Larry advised how he didn't look hard enough since the vehicle is a boat. After a short pause he continued how he was unable to see it since the man was looking at it upside down. Quickly all five ended up caught in a quagmire of vocal humorous fun.

Heading for a diner they stopped at the nearby Sears auto store to check on tire prices. Both front tires had very good tread while the rear tires were showing heavy tread wear. Larry decided to stay with the car suggesting that the three could handle the matter. Only after several minutes had passed with the other two occupied with attendants when Stan walked out with a tire in each hand. When Larry saw him with the two tires he inquired of the sale price where Stan could only put on the big stall. As soon as the other two climbed aboard, Stan drove away. Dave and Bill inquired as to which one had paid for the tires.

Following a pause, Larry suggested to ask Stan where relentlessly they pressed Stan on how much he paid for the tires but received no answer. Unable to hold back, Stan coping with the pressure mentioned how he was aware the kitty was of small funds needing to save every dollar. Then smiling Stan added how he sort-of borrowed the tires from Sears on a long-term pay back plan. As Stan let out a blast of hot breath, he asserted that he was not going to argue the matter like the oil stuff and for them to stuff it.

A moment of silence took place until the other three pressed on how he managed to carry such big items out without anyone in the store even noticing. Feeling his temperature rise Stan only responded asking who was noticing what. Right away Larry insisted on knowing about the so-called long-term plan that put Stan on the defensive. Mad from the others' vocal abuse, Stan made a quick u-turn heading the car back around. Seeing the action Burb yelled for him to hold up asking where the driver was going? Fed up, Stan sternly responded how the guys didn't appreciate the effort only interested in criticizing. Boldly he finished asserting he was returning the freaking tires. Angrily he added, but if one of the old tires should give out they could pay for any new one out of their own darn pockets.

Quickly the three insisted how they weren't really serious, but Stan, emotionally upset replied how he just didn't give a darn and for them to shove it. All upset, Larry blurted out to pull over because he had a cramp. Then at once, the boy jumped out where looking through the open window he yelled of having enough of the arguing. Noting his anger the boy hollered back inside for the guys to get some reality. Moments passed when with Larry back inside, the four sat motionless until Dave quietly suggested to go for some coffee. Frustrated, Stan asserted, how along with the Pep Boys incident and other things he just had enough. Madly he uttered how they could just forget about him being on the trip.

When he added how he had it with their useless insinuations, a stillness crept over the car when suddenly it had become so quiet it was almost as if the four were riding in a funeral. All upset, Bill showing signs of struggling, quietly urged Stan not to go back to the store as the guys needed a chance to think and regroup. Remorsefully Larry quickly asked to turn around and head for the diner so they could reduce the friction. The team was trying but their egos along with the lack of communication hindered their intentions.

Upon reaching the diner, the three rearranged things from the trunk where it ended with putting one of the tires in the trunk. Easily it was to see the people in the diner sitting next to the widows having a good time smiling as being amused. Noticed was that some had even nodded their heads as if they had some vague idea of what was going on. Seeing the faces that were watching, Stan with temper, waved to them showing his frowns. Once inside it was almost as if the four under stress didn't even know each other.   Over coffee, Danish and sticky buns Stan mentioned his having doubts of the four being in the same car for three thousand miles, whether they would even survive.

Continuing angrily Bill belted out that perhaps others at school had it correct asserting of the group not even getting outside of the state. Sullen, Dave brought the group to reality suggesting how the episode might be a lesson since the kitty is all there is even to get the three back home. Immediately everyone sat back in disappointment over what was transpiring. Listen guys, Dave blurted out we ain't gots the money to spend, as we will still need to return. After getting there and if we doesn't pull together we ain'ts got enough to spit at. As tensions reduced, the three noted how they forgot about what the cost of the two tires would have been and then as the air cleared, the three thanked Stan for his effort.

Quietly as the four engaged in a calm discussion pursuing matters on the need to help the kitty with minds working together again it was off to the beer distributor. Purchased was two cases of different beers that easily fit in the rear with one on each side of the hump. While the ground cover mat along with the blankets laid across the cases along with the oilcans covered any view, the ice chest able to be moved allowed good space for the feet. Some re-arranging as needed allowed space to spread out where sleeping became only a small problem.

Next was a stop at the liquor store where having learned a little bit more about each other to minimize any chance of being carded Dave and Stan went inside. Bought were half gallons of Old Crow and Jack Daniels along with a fifth of Rock and Rye. Concluding the shopping was a supermarket visit. Thinking of the weeks' time it total the boys purchased six large bottles of soda along with large bags of chips, pretzels, peanuts and boxes of cakes. Then inside the car, Stan yelled how they were all idiots removing need space, so no more stuff!

Right away each realized how they had thought of themselves, rather than buying as a team. Shortly a discussion took place having learned something by the fiascos of the day where from then on it was agreed that everything would only be done through majority agreement. Money, money and the lack of it kept everyone on edge. With the car, food and beverages taken care of the days remaining were spent on the part time jobs. Completing the remaining odd jobs. Studying and taking the exams with the growing anticipation of departing everyone was stressed out.

"D" day had finally arrived. It was the sixth of June and unfortunately the three had to say goodbye to Tom. Heart rendering as all met at the diner to do some socializing. All emotional, the boy mentioned how he appreciated the comradeship that still existed where at one point the atmosphere was so close that it could almost be felt.   During the beverages and cakes able noted how graduation only comes once in a lifetime, so why not have a little celebration before going? Larry was aware that his parents had a party waiting at home while Dave's mom had also made preparations. Yet suggestions indicated that each wanted to do something together where Bill mentioned it was good but only if everything was ok on his home front. Although he agreed with the ideas, Larry noted that he had other considerations.

So, it was early that evening where Dave picked up Tom, then Bill at Stan's house, but Larry left word with Stan, that he along with three other pals were going to Atlantic City. Across the Delaware River by way of the Chester-Bridgeport ferry the two separate parties headed to their respective cities. As it turned out, the happy eight fell in with other happy celebrants.

The shore places were jammed with the young crowds where adults had vacated, leaving the loud music and crazy acting teenage high school graduates and college students to enjoying the joyous atmosphere. Giving consideration to the safety of the customers, most places had secured the hard liquor serving only beer. Also card checking was reduced which allowed more time for serving everyone. Simply too much toasting was ongoing where it was non-stop from the time the foursome arrived. As the dark of the night grew, none of the four could hold any form of straight talking. Dance yes, talk yes, have fun yes, but think straight, no.

Even when trying not to drink so much, other girls or boys found their way to coax the four to join in where some drank others passed around their own small bottle of whiskey. If questioned as to where going or why, one of the three would only mention that it was all Stan's fault as senses became so affected that everyone forgot about the next morning's appointment.

On the way back home sometime after three, the team stopped at the diner on route forty-seven. The stop did little for the time element of the tomorrow. By then the tomorrow had already turned into the today where all the best laid plans as well as good intentions flopped. Around five in the morning, after Tom was dropped off, it was the other two off at Stan's house. But, before driving off Dave made the suggestion that everyone should sleep then start late. All Stan could manage was that it was all wonddderffful.

Laughing, Dave stated, that with his stuff in the car he would carry all else to Stan's then both go from there. All smiles, Dave belted out for the two not to forget they were going the next day. Yet, so under the weather was Stan that while removing his shoes and falling asleep hitting the mattress he had forgot to take off his clothes.

When morning arrived, as Stan awoke at ten thirty being hung over, he thought the clock had run amuck. A short while later Dave telephoned mentioning how he was in no condition to go anywhere. So, after a short conversation it was agreed to start on Sunday Stan called Larry leaving word with his parents while Bill telephoned Dave who was told by his mother of their son being sick with the twenty-four hour bug. With no one of good mind the big start was put off.

Common sense having gone out the window it wasn't till after church on Sunday morning that the new target was set. Monday morning, eight a.m. where the months had passed by as the final week and weekend closed yet, after all of the effort the team had spent they still failed to depart. With the sun shining and targeted time of day three days behind schedule the team had finally begun to make their move. In a manner where the four dragged their selves around no one would have guessed that they were actually supposed to be in a celebration mood.

Aha! But the hours and days would help change everything. The idea turned into action actually resulted in a time of a journey all its own.

SECTION II

CONFIDENCE,

NASHIE

& PILGRIMS.

CHAPTER FOUR

SOCIALLY VICTIMIZED, ATMOSPHERIC PRESSURE AND DOUBTS.

Already it was the first day of the second part of the journey where the guys together again as a team was finally to get on the road heading west. Monday, it was the ninth day of June. Although the morning started with the usual routine of wash, dress and grab something to eat, there it was, where normalcy ended. In his eagerness Stan found himself rushing. Plenty of time for a full meal but he was caught up in a frenzy. While his self sufficient farming grandfather Nickolas and other grandfather Joseph had died years before, his loving, intelligent mother had passed away under formidable circumstances when he was eleven leaving him with much bitterness.

Stan's grandmother had taken up residence providing needing help to raise the two boys. Petrunella's last name was spelled Gurska but people always spoke it as Gurski. Having a maiden name of Skcabickie the lady of small stature, petite in size, grandmother Petrunella was of much character. Being of good spirit along with a strong will the woman showed much heart where along with speaking five languages, she wrote in three along with self taught English. While Stan often watched the visitors thinking of the League of Nations in session he was disallowed to learn any language by his father. Breakfast at the table he along with grand mom and his brother Ronald began to enjoy the great breakfast of eggs, Kielbasa, fried potatoes onions and peppers. Then over rye toast, olives, horseradish and coffee there was much talk about the trip. Although the boy wished to take his brother along the boy at fourteen was too young plus couldn't drive. Involved with their presence Stan lost all thought of his team especially since Bill hadn't telephoned.

Abruptly, conversation was interrupted by Bill when after banging on the back door he walked in. Displaying all smiles, the all excited friend while motioning with his hands hollered, as if going to a fire for Stan to hurry up and get going! After his sandwiches and other fixings, ice cubes and pieces of solid ice were put into the chest it was loading of everything else from the basement. Added was what Bill's mom provided which was a roll of Scott Paper, paper towels and facial tissues along with peanut butter and jelly to cold cuts with the works sandwiches. Quietly the four enjoyed a few cups of coffee when unexpectedly the telephone rang. Hesitation abounded with immediate apprehension as the two had thoughts of one of the others being too ill to go. But, relief it was as Dave had called yelling news that Larry had already been with him waiting to go. In a change of plans, Larry's parents insisted on helping, where they drove their son to Dave's house.

Time to go it was all good byes at Stan's place with much hugging then arriving at Dave's house it was found of Larry and Dave with all of their personal stuff and food sitting on the porch steps. While getting out of the car the other two greeted them with their verbal jestings of what took so long. Wasting no time, within minutes the car was loaded, ready to go when teams had to be decided along with who was to have the privilege of being the first driver. Using coins it was the two first names with the heads enabled the starting team. Then since Stan had provided the chances idea the three chose him to be the first one driving.

All loaded and ready to go Larry asked if anyone had brought a bottle/can opener. Bill responded asking how it is that cans and bottles we has, but no opener, gee wiz what else? Right away, Dave replied asking, how it was that being boy scouts and high school gwaduatees yous guys doesn't know that an opener is needed? Quickly he ran inside returning with his parent's hand model can and bottle opener. Once the boy was back inside the car Larry asked if anyone remembered to bring water. Jovial, Stan hollered asking if everyone remembered to bring their heads? Clowning around Stan yelled how whatever weez is doing it's enough, as weez is going!

What a morning! Wait Larry hollered where smiling he asked that with all of the rolls, jellies and different spreads did anyone think of forks and knives? Shaking his head, hearing no one admitting to bringing the utensils, Dave was absolutely livid. Angrily getting out of the car he yelled that the group was a bunch of stupid idiots. As soon as the boy was back inside Stan again turned the engine over ready to go. But while Stan was looking to go another hindrance. Larry started clapping while suggesting the need to say a prayer giving thanks for the good weather, plus everybody being healthy and able to go. Another pause then, after the prayer, Stan blurted out how if there is any more requests by anyone, to have the person being given a message that the team had departed for the west!

SEGMENT - 5.   Pulling away from the curb was an electrifying moment. Tenseness was so thick, that if turned into material matter it would have filled the car. Moments of absolute silence took place. Then as if New Years Eve, expressions of yeas, yippee, and hoorays were loud and many as finally the travel part of the journey began. All excited, "Oh man, finally its rolling wheels", Dave hollered where, "Hey, we're actually doing it guys"!, Bill yelled. "You better believe it, and thank God", Larry hollered! Perhaps it was not so much expressions of happy but a way of relief from all of the strain, as for sure each had buckets full inside. Suddenly in an excited voice, Larry showed his enthusiasm as he hollered out the window, "Hi Yooo Nashie, wagon ho, let's go team"!

Emotions erupted as the three began beating on the outside of the doors. In good sink, it almost sounded like a drum group. Then while slowly moving along with Larry the copilot while padding the dash in a rhythmic sound he suggested the three should really take the time to consider what they had accomplished. Starting to relax, various thoughts were noted on how the guys were leaving their family's homes for a longer period of time than had ever been done before. Attempting to be funny, Stan suggested in making a quick stop at Di Constanza's sandwich shop for a hoagie, when Bill aware of Stan's type of humor responded stating to also stop at Stacky's and pick up a few steak sandwiches. Shortly adding his note, Dave suggested making a stop at Anna's for a couple of Italian sandwiches then also the Polish butchers shop for a few good Kielbasa ones. Sarcastically Larry ended the rhetoric stating how the guys could go, but first drop him off at home. As everyone laughed, Stan asserted of not being too far from there, so if he wanted he could be dropped off. "Never mind smarty pants", Larry replied, "just keep on driving".

With all the windows down there was a lot of fresh air flowing that helped everyone to settle down. No, it wasn't a wooden covered wagon with the canvas top or a classy convertible with its top down, nor was it a little red wagon. And the crew was not a part of a wagon train yet, in certain respects the guys felt they were riding in a wooden wagon. Unexpectedly, not even out of the city, Larry exclaimed, "quick, pull the car over"! Awkwardly when Stan asked why, the boy replied how it could be anywhere, but just pull the darn car over. Quick it was when the big boy jumped out with a big body stretch while letting out a couple of big grunts.

Following a few loud yells that sounded like a small bear the boy jumped back into the car as if it was something everybody did. Immediately Dave belted out asking, what the heck that was all about where showing a big grin Larry replied where it was either out there or in here. "Gee guys, there's a gentleman among us", Stan uttered. While Stan responded the rhetoric flowed heavy. All excited by finally being on the way, Bill blurted out for the guys to think there is only two thousand and eight hundred miles to go of this crap. Displaying a raised voice Bill in a sarcastic tone asserted how nice it was with all being stuffed in the metal box and all together. Then he hollered of wow–wee are we going to have some fun.

Soon quiet came about when Stan pulled on to route three fifty two heading for the turnpike. Excitedly Bill hung his head out the window singing when right away the others joined in singing the lyrics of the school cheer of hoorah for Saint James, hoorah for Saint James someone in the crowd is hollering hoorah for Saint James. Then with all in hype, they changed the words singing how only a few thousand miles to go. It could be puzzling for people to understand, but the truth is that everyone had already thought of how difficult the trip would be. Proceeding, it was on route 352, then route 3 until route 100 was reached.

While looking for a tree or a place to use as lavatories a diner was spotted. As Stan pulled in Dave suggested of the guys being a bunch of children asking if they were going to stop every short miles just to wet the trees. With quick jesting responses the other three challenged him to feel free to find out what kind of children they were.

Boys' fun, then with straight faces the four moved inside as if what had just transpired was part of a heavy work-day. As seats were taken at the counter on time the Greek waitress came by with the waters. Unable to resist the temptation of a tease, Dave uttered in a soft tone, "and how about Nashie, wasn't she terrific"? Such a timely phrase caused the waitress to show curiosity where the other three seeing such joyfully joined in with their remarks.

While the waitress took the orders, inquiring about Nashie the waitress must have assumed her being a celebrity that opened a door of fun. The more she listened her entire focus went from serving to inquiring when at one time passing by she set the coffee pot down while leaning over to hear better. Later, as Stan decided to enjoy additional dessert the three expressed how they didn't wish to stay. But once they saw the dessert trays it was a quick change of minds along with the continuing of the waitress episode. When leaving the crew advised the woman how it was the name of the car where instantly showing surprise, all busted out in laughter. Hearing her whimsical reply along with seeing her smiles the four departed with the four having separated in good spirits. Good people respecting others ethnicity along with good food enjoyed life to the maximum when it was onward to the turnpike.

A beautiful June day for a drive happily the four noted there being no shopping, selling chances, odd work, part time jobs or trash picking. Also they were riding in what they had worked so hard for. Appropriate words were spoken with emotional feelings of gratitude for each one's doing what they did. In their cheerful state the four watched as the scenery went passed. As the car approached the turnpike entrance Stan suddenly swerved the car stopping by the guardrail. Turning to face the crew with a solemn grin he blurted out, "all right you guys, this is it"!All excited as thinking something bad had happened the three responded, "what the hell is going on here and yeah, what the heck's the problem"?

Displaying a big grin Stan replied, "look guys, if anyone is not going, say so now because, once Nashie is driven through that entranceway there will be no turning back, for any reason"! Instant replies abounded such as "are you kidding, get this darn car back on the road and are you insane, move the vehicle forward". At the entrance tollbooth, the man inquired if there was any problem along with where the crew was headed. As Stan took the ticket Dave yelled out the window how they were conducting a highly secret atmospheric survey taking them to California. So there the crew was at the threshold of land space of which the foursome had never ventured into. Going forward with spirits soaring, the team was looking forward to traversing new territory of new people leaving their humorous attitude to grow.

Moments later Dave stated, "what the heck you think we're doing here selling Girl Scout cookies, get your darn foot on the metal pedal and move this wagon"! With a big smile Stan yelled, "man oh man, are you guys are something, you betcha"! The crew was not in any kind of wooden wagon or any type of crude vessel about to battle rough seas. Rather they had it easy being in a mechanical vehicle on wheels protected on all sides by steel armor and a metal roof. With a planned route, maps for direction and provisions for days, what should they possibly fear? No bands were playing nor were there any firecracker displays or a news reporter with people around to give them a send off. Yet the foursome was as confident like eagles soaring.

Proceeding from the tollbooth, Nashie was headed west with an atmosphere of excitement. Banging was done on the sides of the car with continuous yelling bouts of hoorays, yippees and yos. Simultaneously the four added their own rendition of singing, California here we come, though far from where we started from. Well on their way repeatedly sang was words from de camp town races sing dat song, at last, at last de turnpike here we is.

Some time down the road Stan feeling worn out pulled over where Larry took over the driving. Shortly, Dave commented how the whole thing was building to be one heck of an interesting trip. Turnpike speed limits were posted off and on at 60 miles per hour depending on the area, weather and road conditions. The toll rate for cars was about 1-1/2 cents per mile. Of course the car needed to be babied to get to sixty, however being aware of its age it was always maintained a couple less than the sixty. Considering the weight the car was carrying the crew appreciated it was doing very well. With the four guys each over a hundred and fifty-five pounds along with the spare, two new tires, three five gallon cans of oil, full ice chest, bottles of soda and two beer cases, food and blankets there was the pounds of tools. Also, there was the rack's weight along with its contents of luggage and sleeping bags. Perhaps it wasn't on a wing but for sure it was on wheels with help of occasional prayers. Such was the weight that the body of the car was fully resting not on the shock absorbers but directly on the frame. This meant that when a bump was hit, those in the back seat felt the brunt of it, that is, there was no bounce to the ounce. Not comparable to sitting in an outhouse during a tremor. But gee, how many people remember those days of outhouses and honey wagons? From time to time the guys talked about their graduation ceremonies, the prom, school matters, and sports activities. Also reflected were the various situations and negative moves they coped with plus the errors they had made and not to be forgotten were the often prayers of thanks for their health.

Excited by the moment, breaking out the Old Crow, Dave suggested of making a toast. As the others greeted his suggestion with cheers the driver took his eyes off the road. Quickly in response, avoiding a mishap, the driver hollered, look out while he swerved. As the car came to an immediate stop, happily Bill suggested they should all take a short snort. As if an alarm clock went off, Dave and Stan received a piece of minds from the other two as they noted of the wrong idea of showing something ok, when it wasn't. A heated debate ensued regarding the rule of the driving team and drinking. As the bottle was passed around it was where the first toast was to Tom. Wow, did that stuff warm up the inners. For the driving team it was only a short sip. But it was the significance of the matter where only a few minutes of debate were needed when matters on care along with responsibility were hashed out. Result was a rule of no more reckless handling of the car, no slamming on the brakes, no jerking the steering wheel and no swerving around or speeding. With Nashie well underway sandwiches were passed around as the four watched the panoramic view of God's creation go buy. Except that the car was moving, the episode was almost that of being at one of the drive-in theaters.

Temperatures helped the minds as had warmed to the mid eighties. Along the way there were various farmlands where various expressions regarding the area popped up. Fascinated, Larry raised the thought of saving some money for a few years to go into a partnership. Instant joyful response by all was heard where thinking was to buy a farm. Shortly and unexpectedly, it was as if the team had ran into a garbage heap. Put upon by a change of wind direction it was as if a plop of concentrated fresh cow manure had been deposited in the car. Urging the driver not to slow down for anything Bill attempted to make sounds imitating a siren.

Although the windows were rolled up along with the vents closed nothing worked. It was too late where the strong boys almost showed tears while having little to say. As if someone threw a can of laughing gas into the car, intensely laughing, Burb suggested the others to breathe heavily. Take in fully and feel the affect of Mother Nature's finer odors he hollered. Dave trying to catch his breath suggested how it wasn't nature but rather a disguised FBI form of laughing gas. Shortly, while Bill recanted his suggestion on buying a farm the other two expressed their thoughts of never mind.

A restaurant area was nearing only a short distance passed the exit for Lancaster. Being around dinner no time was wasted as the team pulled into the area. Following a good wash, a booth was settled in for some good food. But, Bill and Dave upon reviewing the literature mentioned taking a detour to Gettysburg. With time to get there and back along with time spent at the place considered, it sank the four into a controversy. Quickly the debate ballooned covering visiting other towns where Larry asked whether a debate would occur over every place that one or two of the team wanted to go. Result of the matter ended with recalling the rule of requiring full majority on detours.

Once all was back in the car, it was Larry behind the wheel with Stan his assistant but from the heavy day the two admitted they were too tired. With a quick glance it was noted a good distance before any rest areas. So, with the sun down leaving nothing to see it was decided to stay. Being aware of the restrooms and food, availability the crew watched how other cars, trucks and buses parked where Nashie was placed in the midst but a spot not drawing attention. After enjoying a brew over the events of the day, discussed was what was intended for the next day.

Tuesday morning, the Tenth of June where sleep problems it was for those in the front. As it was they had no means of stretching out. However those in the back had the covered padded floor where though somewhat cramped it was easier than those in the front. As the four took advantage of the facilities and restaurant for breakfast it became apparent that the four was attempting to communicate as a team. What to do about Pittsburgh was put off until really close. Following a thorough check of Nashie, the driving team of Dave with Bill the copilot started the driving.

While approaching Harrisburg the driver pulled into a roadside stop for taking in the view of great scenery. Then with food along with beverages enjoyed it was too nice of a day to waste sitting in the car. While having good weather, food and beer along with the travel maps it was discussed which roads would be taken regarding Pittsburgh. Although maps on Ohio and West Virginia were originally penciled in from the start a big problem arose. The team's inability from not knowing the road conditions and lay of the land became a burden where thinking was to ask people around the area again the matter had to wait. Driving a long stretch of the highway it led to the Blue Mountain tunnel where just in time as a short distance before the tunnel there was another restaurant.

Taking in an early dinner, after the car was parked, Dave and Bill went inside to grab a table. As the other two remained outside to check the car over everything under the hood showed up ok. Shortly it was discovered one of the straps securing the rack had worked its way loose. "Just in the nick of time", Larry exclaimed.   Then once inside they alerted the other two where considered was how if the cover flew off everything would have rolled onto the highway that could have caused an accident. From then on, every morning or night resulting from long driving the car would be inspected in detail. Plus done by pairs to ensure everything was double-checked.

Stomachs full, along with feeling great the driving resumed with Dave's team behind the wheel. The highway might have been great for the newer vehicles but, the group's progress had slowed. Traveling across the bridges along with going through the tunnel, some had reduced speed limits which slowed the pace to fifty miles an hour or even below. Some many miles later having gone through the engineering marvels of tunnels and bridges, Bill took over the driving. Getting buggy, he suggested stopping for the night but his copilot feeling his oats didn't want to hear of it.

As it was, once Bill took the wheel it was only soon when he realized how tired he was. Understanding the situation, Stan mentioned that having been a long day, finding a place to sleep seemed like the safe idea. Slowly the four was learning of the new long distance traveling experience.

Welcomed sight it was when Cove Valley appeared on the horizon. The crew couldn't wait to pull in for the night where it was the same as before where four followed the same plan of washing up, eating and sleeping over. Once Nashie, was moved to a secluded spot they conversed about everything from the tunnels to the magnificent beauty of the land. Smiling, Larry blurted out for them to remember that they had a dignitary in the car.

Asserting how he was going to college stimulated some interesting conversation among the four where the three noted of his need to watch what he said. Preparing for Nevada it was playing black jack till the crew sacked out. The temperatures dropped into the low fifties, which made for great sleeping. Things seemed different the next morning but no one was able to say what it was. Yet without realizing it, the four had trained themselves into a method of wash up, eat, check the car and hit the road. Such was it that it became a habit of trust where neither one asked each other what was doing, or what to do. Having enjoyed a good night sleep it was over a good breakfast the four discussed the travel plans as if holding a big business board meeting.

Later checking the car it was found to need some oil where the teams of two moved as if a team from the local car wash. Gee whiz, Larry blurted out asking is weez gonna gets Nashie on the road or what? After waiting for the others to take their turns Larry was forced to swallow his pride as he too was called by nature. Wow, the fun of traveling down the highway with Larry's team doing the driving. Although the car had taken to the road well, on the hill climbing it definitely showed having a burden. Yet each was thankful that it wasn't raining since it was necessary to have the windows down.

With the sun bearing down on the roof along with the high humidity, everybody agreed to keep the car moving since Nashie was not air-conditioned. Just when the crew thought they had seen it all, the crew came to a pull off place, called Breezewood. Wow! Was all the four could exclaim. As each beheld what the eyes were seeing the four got caught up in the spectacular view. Understanding what the constructors had done while comparing with the mountain, left the gang in awe as they enjoyed the cold beer, cookies, pretzels and cigarettes.

Stan's team took over the driving where later upon reaching a place called Somerset the crew pulled in where decided was to use the time of an early dinner to discuss the issue of Pittsburgh. From the start, Wheeling West Virginia was the main target allowing the crew to head into Ohio. Although a state road was an option saving driving time, using the turnpike would have meant going north out of the planned way. Bill, wanted to visit a steel factory, but when noted of a steel factory in Delaware the thought was dropped. Later after the crew had stopped to change teams, traveling along suddenly, Stan belted out for the guys to look at that as he quickly, pulled over! Immediately as Bill inquired, Dave suggested for him to look out the side window where the scenic view was nothing less than breathless.

So extraordinary was the view it became a problem since they had stopped immediately after going thru the Laurel Hill tunnel. The problem was that it was not a designated pull over. Hearing Dave suggest how the history books did not tell the whole story, Bill asserted how it was all God's form of entertainment. Such remarks stimulated exciting subsequent discussions that became fascinating ranging from creation to paintings. Rolling down the highway trying to push for time it was to play it safe. Agreed was to lie over at the New Stanton restaurant area. Just the right place at the right time of night it also turned out to be a good spot to start from the next morning.

Upon waking after sleeping nine hours cramped up, Bill remarked how he felt as if he had already traveled across the country. Then as the other three followed they yelled out their yeah and me-too on the way to breakfast. Once in a line waiting to give their orders, Dave was the first person in line and being the Casanova type he decided to do some socializing. Candidly referring to the young, female Afro American attendant in a joyful tone he remarked, "well look at her, she's beautiful". But forgetting his place, Dave said it loud enough where she also heard it. As she turned facing him he immediately said, "helloooo sweetie, going my way"?

Displaying a face of shock from Dave's attitude the waitress returned a sternly glaring mad look. Surprised yet not expecting anything he was really taken aback when while looking at the other three she passed by Dave. Smoothly the woman moved coming to face Bill while inquiring of his order. Subsequently she did the same with Larry and Stan where after realizing what had transpired, Dave asserted something to the affect of, what are you drunk? As if everything was normal, with Dave still standing waiting she started on the other three orders. Finally, aware that she had kept him waiting long enough, she went back to wait on Dave. No sooner had she asked him what he wanted to order, the boy feeling offended while not thinking responded. In a gruff yet teasing manner he blurted out something like, what's the matter bimbo, not going my way? With the other three stunned from seeing Dave's action they watched and uttered things of politeness. Displaying an unhappily look the waitress gave Dave a stare that registered her feelings where it was obvious the waitress was so mad she wanted to slap him thinking the guy was a real jerk.

Obviously the attractive waitress had felt offended, yet caught up by her position since knowing he was a customer. Meanwhile as the very young woman minded her manners, the other three could only watch. Dave seemed dumbfounded yet, not knowing when to leave well enough alone. As she had started to walk away Dave remarked, "wow, isn't she something". About then, the entire scenario was bent out of shape. What could the three do as thoughts were of leaving but they were also hungry. Disturbed, the other three mentioned to Dave, how he may have thought he was some sort of Errol Flynn but with them there it was he just flopped. Right away Larry all upset blurted out that Dave may try to attach to the ladies, but he never takes time to think of their feelings.

As the waitress returned she served the other three their beverages then to Dave's startled amazement the waitress walked away again. Surprised everyone was when she returned with the manager. While the older big sized man approached, he stated his name while asserting him being the manager. Then with a stern look he stated how it was brought to his attention that one of you boys insulted my waitress, so which one is to blame. Standing with Dave wondering what to do there was a moment of silence then without a smile the man looking at Dave asked him whether there was anything else he wanted to order. Fully aware of what the man intended Dave replied how he didn't mean to insult her but thought she was pretty, thinking to pay a compliment. Seeing the manager not moved, he added that he never meant to say anything harmful as was just trying to be friendly, nor did he wish to stir up any trouble and was sorry if done. Quickly the manager turned asking if the waitress understood and was satisfied. Hearing her affirmative reply he requested her to finish serving them.

Subsequent quiet words exchanged between the three quickly cleared the air. Surely the manager would have wanted the four to leave, but instead he showed his finesse when while smiling at the girl he asked the waitress to finish serving as he walked away. Meanwhile receiving stern looks from the other three along with those from other customers looking on, Dave didn't make a scene.

Looking to finally sit down and eat, after several minutes, Dave mentioned how he understood his socially upsetting the waitress where Stan added how ignoring the three being inconvenienced was stupid. While the group discussed how to hook on to route forty to go through Wheeling West Virginia, Larry and Bill asked several people for their opinions which only a few offered any suggestions. Then upon leaving, Dave asked the waitress aside where in a gentlemanly manner he apologized for his actions. Quietly accepting his apology she nodded while saying, "ok" then added for him to learn how to talk to new women when trying to give a compliment. As the four walked out they displayed a wave of hands where she responded with a smile that would have melted the table.

The next morning it was the last day on the turnpike where that Thursday, twelfth day in June, Stan's team started the driving. When the crew arrived at Youngwood it was after the exit, unexpectedly Stan caused everyone inside the car to be rolled around as if on a roller coaster. Swerving to the left then to the right the driver pulled the car over to stop as he jumped out. All excited Stan hollered how he realized the full magnitude of the construction projects it must have taken to build the road. While he pointed, the three noted how they felt how traveling over the state super highway by itself was worth the experience.

Then back in the car, Larry let out a screeching yell of, hi yooo Nashie, let's go big girl, causing a laugh with Dave commenting how Larry forgot his boots and hat. Stumbling into a place called Monessen it was close to mid-day when the crew stopped at a quaint little eating place for relief from all the coffee. Before leaving, the front seat team switched places where Larry took over the driving. The narrow twisting road provided some times of fun entertainment. After being on the straight highway that lasted for days the twisting road was a treat. Shortly it was noted how the area resembled New Jersey farm country except that there were the hills and curves where Dave mentioned how he could relate to the early travelers in their covered wagons..

A short time later it was to go across a small stream where crossing the little bridge Dave blurted out, "stop the car, hurry up, stop the car"! When the driver stopped, Dave suggested for him to back up, all the way back to the clearing on the other side. Back over the bridge the car was parked near the stream. As Dave stripped to his shorts Bill yelled that it was drizzling where Dave only responded that if the three were afraid of water to stay inside the car! Seeing the possibilities the other three followed him over to the bank while stripping to their shorts. So tempting it was where each wanted to go for a swim, but it wasn't realized since it was too shallow. Yet, the large creek did provide use as a large tank where the four wasted no time in grabbing the soap and towels.

While not the same as taking a shower, it beat the heck out of trying to wash in the restroom sinks. Soon each demonstrated their joyous feelings as the scene was turned into a water splash throwing event accompanied by all sorts of innuendos. Quite refreshing since temperatures had jumped into the mid eighties with high humidity the hilarious episode ended as they recalled similar times in the swimming hole at the rear of Deshong Park. Cars had passed by when one even slowed down while blowing its horn. When voices and whistling was heard from the female occupants the four boys tried to coax them to come in but without success.

Afterward, the four gathered under a tree for a smoke where Bill and Stan reflected on their camping days in the boy scouts. Calling the meeting to an end Larry stated how it was time to get the wagon moving where Stan responded how he sounded like some old wagon trail master. Larry responded how the guys were lucky that there was no whip handy.

Heading towards where the crew could hook on to route forty Larry drove until the town of Washington where a diner late in the afternoon was taken. With each desiring some cooked food there was no hesitation as each headed inside. While the country air stirred the mood, all excited, the waitress was greeted by Larry mumbling, huba, huba. Then with Dave following with his note of, well hello doll, Stan looked at the two he remarked how he wished, not again. Meanwhile the waitress taking the orders acted as if she didn't hear a thing. Often the tall waitress showed her being curious when asking the right questions she opened up the guy's vocal cords like a can opener. Of middle age the smart waitress was also street savvy constantly showing interest to know where finding her interest amusing the four felt compelled to oblige.

Meanwhile the curious people in the eatery had seen the car as it stood out among all the newer cars in the lot. Having gone outside to look the car over, the owner must have been impressed when shortly he showed his appreciation.

Displaying a wide smile the waitress advised that he had allowed seconds on everything without any extra charge. Of course not wanting to turn away good food the team found some extra room as euphoria erupted where if one didn't know otherwise some could have thought the four hadn't eaten in days.

Spotting a telephone booth it was to call home where decided was for Bill to be first, because his mom being by herself. Along with having agreed to take turns also was to ask to reverse the charges. Although his mother was not concerned over the reversing of the charges she really voiced her anger because her son hadn't called before then. While assuring her that all was well, an understanding was reached where the four would not be calling but every few days. Afterward she agreed to explain to the other parents how each of the four would be taking turns in calling where all ended well leaving Bill in a good frame of mind. Meanwhile knowing the team were visitors, with the cook's obliging and a lot of laughs the whole place responded to hearing the story. A resort of goodly natured people it was before leaving, directions were inquired to see if there was an alternate road but were informed of none that anyone was aware of. Resuming the driving with Bill his copilot, Dave drove while reflecting on the good food and friendly waitress. Already getting on into the evening the car was driven through a short heavy thunderstorm but the downpour was considered trivial being a passing cloud. Passing through a small town it was decided not to stop where to save time the crew made use of the sandwiches and sodas. Then with the border only some distance away, moved by superstition, Bill stated how he wanted to wait until daylight to cross when the sun would come up over the horizon. Thinking by the others was, that such was foolish hocus-pocus. Yet it was that such words caused the driver to stop the car understanding it would be big moment.

Bill asked whether to wait or keep on going which caused the crew to consider their position. Comments abounded regarding the historical significant as compared to Lewis and Clark crossing their first border. Shortly having decided while looking around, found was a small unlit area. Being without supervision or adult at such young ages, the entire situation exploded into a big matter of significance. While moods changed, the four consoled each other as if the crew had just survived a tragedy rather than celebrating their success. Finishing the evening was cards, aided by a cool evening breeze where the worn out crew retired for the night.

SEGMENT - 6.   Day five, Friday the Thirteenth of June. Though the sun was up temperatures were in the low sixties with cloud cover where washing was done with water from the bottles along with the melted ice in the chest. Followed was a short run that allowed the stretching of the legs. While Stan and Larry were only interested in getting the car on the road, a few superstitious comments were made noting a day of caution. When Dave suggested a matter of history to walk across the border, Bill responded maybe even pulling the car across. With everyone serious, the tone changed to hysterical upon hearing the suggestion yet, considering they had already traveled across the entire state, the suggestion took hold. Heavy deliberation ended where it was agreed that since Dave was one of the initiators of the trip, he should have the privilege of the first driver's seat to cross.

The crew was insecure and full of doubts where only if seeing would people have believed the excited atmosphere that had developed. To the four and especially the original three it was a most important time period. Along with a short prayer there was the bowing and shaking hands until finally the boy got behind the wheel. As he drove the car across the border out of Pennsylvania into West Virginia the team went wild. Having driven the car to the side of the road, so enthused was Dave, that as he stepped out of the car looking back at Stan full of meaning. With all smiles he asserted, "so, what say you partner, tis you think it may be about that time"? "You betcha you assa, it most assuredly is", Stan replied! Vocally expressing the joy of comradely it could have almost exploded where even changing to a misty drizzle the weather along with a small thunderstorm was unable to hinder the joyous occasion. In a moment of anxiousness as if needing to yell, Dave hollered, "after all guys, we did make the start didn't we, and did get the car on our own, didn't we"?

Tears formed, Bill looking for credibility asserted, "and we did make it out of the state, didn't we? Smiling, he continued all excited with mentions of Tom as the four ended up with expressions of hip, hip hoorays, yippees and yeas. While jumping up and down along with some barn type swing dancing the four failed to realize what impact it was having on their personalities. All the pent up negatives and cynicalness garbage the three had been carrying as received from the start was being put behind them. While the bottle was passed around it was a most meaningful toast since at the time the four were maturing.

Ready for anything the world could throw at them such mental attitude was growing. For the young boys of the Chester Eagles Boys Club from Chester, Pennsylvania it was a big moment in their lives. No fooling, really! Well anyway, that's the way it was with Nashie the one car caravan as Bill grabbed a towel to wipe his head. Only if seeing would people have believed the excited atmosphere that had developed.

Dave again took the wheel while all hyped up where toasting with soda and candy, the four just gabbed away as if they had just had a long escaping voyage. Meanwhile, all excited, Larry expressed thoughts of him being privileged to be among such a great bunch. Headed to Wheeling West Virginia, it was found the roads were not of the same smoothness as the Pennsylvania turnpike. When Larry noted of another toast, emotionally Bill raised the issue of who would accept the responsibility of notifying the family that their son was hospitalized or dead. Also Dave added which one would want to explain to their parents of how the person was drinking before driving causing their son to being in the morgue. Slowly, the debate concluded as the four realized the impasse of each one's weakness along with consequences being understood, where established was their rule on drinking alcohol. What a terrific day as the team had not only crossed the border out of the state but also expanded their self imposed rule on drinking.

Arriving in Wheeling West Virginia a quick stop at a small diner was made. Intended was for the restroom use but it being a root beer place none of the team could refuse. Following the enjoyment of draught root beer and a float with snacks it was back on the road where Bill resumed the driving. Some short miles later the rest of the crew noticed the speed had gone past the set pattern as Bill's foot had gotten heavier on the gas pedal. As the others belted loudly for the driver to slow it down he acknowledged having gotten carried away thinking of the next border. Bill's statement urged Larry to suggest for everyone to be cautious also urging no more stopping, and no more booze for a while. Smartly Stan added how there should be solid driving cause there was just too many miles to go. As the number of miles climbed the crew noticed how the windows were steaming up more oft. Although weather was dismal, the minds were clear. More happy cheer as the club had reached the next border.

Crossing the West Virginia border into Ohio was done with making the most of it. Music on the radio was enjoyed with sodas, chips and pretzels as the team really started wanting to cover a lot of territory. Avoiding as many delays as possible, Nashie was kept on the move along route forty heading west. Meanwhile Stan and Larry grabbed a catnap knowing their turn was next. Slowly it started where the skies clouded with constant drizzle along with an occasional shower. As the driving teams complained it seemed the weather responded with unexpected down pour periods of ongoing rain. Perhaps there may have been something said on the radio but, at their age why pay any attention to the forecast? Driving mile after mile through the wet weather did little to give the crew anything to talk about. With the windows closed it meant limited visibility being denied any looking at scenery where negative comments abounded.

Upon arriving in the town of Cambridge, a welcomed sight there was of a small diner. Bill without mentioning a word parked the car where in a flash, Dave jumped out. At once he scared the three as he started banging his firsts on the car's hood. At first it seemed he was attempting to take out his frustration on the car, but the others understood he made a melody. Simultaneously he started repeating at the top of his lungs how you guys did it, along with and darn it all but we did it. Unison of the tapping on the huge

drum along with the chanting provided a moment of mental relief where right away his antics caught on causing all four to get fired up with cheering.

Waving their arms while shouting yeas, yos, yahoos and yippee, the four let loose. With anxiety fading while water was running down his face, suddenly Bill stopped then showing all seriousness. Repeatedly he asserted how the four really did do it, we did it. By his tone it was noted that Bill had trouble believing what they had done. While jumping up and down the four shook hands over and over while also clapping. No, it wasn't New Years Eve or a birthday, yet for all intense purposes it could have been a combination of the two. And to think it was all emotion where in jest, Larry expressed how he thought the three were going looney. As he walked away in the rain, all smiles he added how the three goofballs could stay out to play.

Wow, inside did they ever get the looks! While gulping on hot coffee the guys briefly explained to the waitress what they were doing. Yet from the customers, received were only smirks. Apparently what may have transpired was from what the customers seated by the windows may have seen of the boys' behavior, thinking the car may have been stolen. By customers inquiring, the waitress found out, then advising the four how one of the customers had called the police. While attractive, she had been sociable as well as good at tending to the service. But though the coffee, hot Danish and donuts were enjoyed the crew due to the unfriendly atmosphere departed not wanting to have any delays.

A bigger town was only an hour away where it was Bill's turn to drive since Dave was not feeling good. As he pulled away talk drifted to the waitress where Larry asserted how it was his beautiful face and brute strength that was a magnet for the waitress. Jesting, Stan mentioned for him, Joe Hollywood to show his strength and carry Nashie to the next diner. Everyone was looking forward to stopping in Columbus however, wanting to keep moving the group decided passing on through to Springfield. Meanwhile with the two in the back catching some sleep for some reason Bill glanced at the fuel gauge. Instant alarm there was as he pointed to the gauge while mentioning to Dave for him to look. While asking what to do, easily noticed how they were riding on fumes since the needle was not moving but sitting on the empty mark. Just in time as just ahead was a gas station. As the driver stopped, the other two woke up where after hearing why the stop was made Larry and Stan took a look at the fuel gauge. Taking advantage of the stop all four hit the trees in the rear of the lot, using the area as a rest room while tempers soared. While the attendant filled up the tank the four used the time to check the car over in detail. Angry expressions over the fuel situation had already started yet, for some reason the talk diminished.

As Nashie was pressed onward it was noticed of the increased number of signs indicating the people had celebrated the sixth of June. Then further seen was signs which showed where the town was getting ready for celebrating of the old civil war days. Again, Larry and Stan went back to sleep as their shift was next plus there was no reason to   remain awake when there was nothing to see but moving windshield wipers. Driving was steady till the town of Zanesville where time for brunch coming across a diner, Bill pulled into the parking area. No sooner had the car stopped when Larry jumped out of the car slamming the door. With anger he yelled about the guys being stupid along with a few other choice words, regarding the fuel episode.

Immediately, Bill attempting to side with Dave made excuses relating to the scenery and road conditions. Angrily, Larry as a cat springing on a mouse, loudly asked what the heck they would have done had the car quit from lack of gas? Adding how on the road without any lights who would have stopped also he added that since there were no telephone booths around what would the guys have done? All upset amid the heated atmosphere, Stan suggested considering alternatives so that it doesn't happen again. Like a parade each visited the men's room where they dried off while cooling down before going to the booth.

After the older waitress arrived starting with the usual about the specials while sporting a quiz type of face while noticing Stan joining the three, with hands on her hips she asked whether the boys had finished playing musical chairs. While not receiving any response but aware sparks were flying among the three, the woman strongly asked if she could get to her business. Once the boys questioned some of the menu items orders were taken along with the beverages served. Again the fuel issue was raised where quiet talk turned into a full-blown debate. Upon being served, Stan had gotten so upset over the antagonizing situation that he sought some quiet from what to him was sheer madness. Not saying a word, he carried his plates and beverage to one of the isolated tables.

Was everyone in the diner giving the eye, as they wondered or just seemed that way? With the heated arguing ongoing the voices were raised along with the tones showing no let up. In the meantime, the cook having heard from the waitress, had looked at the car where his curiosity moved him. While he inquired as to where from, why and where going, about in his fifties, the man mentioned a few of his exploits.

Also the cook mentioned how he had also owned a similar model

Nash. Who would have believed that out in the middle of nowhere, in such a small place of a tiny group of people, that someone would have recognized the car.. Surprised at what Stan had done, walking over to his table Dave attempted to simmer the guy down. Suggested was for Stan to be a little mellow expecting Stan to return to the booth but he was taken back as receiving no reply. Stan felt that the three were not ready for the trip where as silence took hold while eating, Stan indifferent refused to budge. Aware of the adversity, Dave blurted out how Stan was doing wrong. Yet unmovable, Stan looked up at his friend then also over at other two while shrugging his shoulders.

Once more Dave went back asserting how Stan was deserting his team urging him to get back to normal with the guys in the booth. After Dave rejoined the other two, only moments later the three started waving for Stan to come back. But he simply kept on eating as if nothing happened. Having finished the food along with his head cleared, Stan calmed down then went back to rejoin the team. Attempting to sit while receiving their innuendos, Stan unable to communicate let them know that if they didn't change their attitude he would surely move again.

Finding himself in the middle of his friends, standing up displaying an angry face Dave blurted out how if they didn't allow some peaceful discussion there was going to be serious trouble. With tempers simmering, scratching of faces and rubbing of hands stillness came over the group where Larry stated how he understood Stan's position. With opinions offered an agreement was made using the last quarter mark with responsibility laid on whoever was driving. Meanwhile, the cook running back and forth thrilled with what the crew was doing became amused where the attention drew others like flies to honey. As the cook noted his own personal experiences he related to what the four were doing. Not only was the European style food very good, but piled on in good quantity made the team almost feel at home. Very happy when leaving, the team provided the waitress a hefty tip along with smiling compliments to the cook. Tis a shame that the great little diner of big social means, in such a small town had its name slip into history. Back in the car, noted was the town formerly known as the pottery capital of the world.

Then energized from the inside there was no attention paid to the driving where with little interest Bill resumed his place behind the wheel. Pulling away without looking around, unknown to Bill, was that Dave had not been fully settled in. With one foot hanging out of the doorway Dave was holding on to the swinging door. In alarm, Dave quickly yelled for him to hold up, stop the damn car! Startled, Bill while slamming on the brakes blurted out something like, ok buster so, what's up? Struggling to hold on to the door while also grabbing the ashtray, Dave in anger called Bill, a stupid jerk where responding, Bill called him the jerk. Adding how he was supposed to know how and shut the darn door both looked as if they were mad dogs. Seeing the madness, Stan and Larry hollered for them to both shut up as all four became emotionally upset where the attitudes seemed to match the conditions outside. Once the car was underway, Bill while apologizing pushed the accelerator as attempting to drive away his frustration. Through the terrible weather and water puddles down the road the crew drove no knowing what to expect next.

Later, Larry took over the driving duty cussing the weather and miserable road conditions until after a long period of time he noted having enough of the soup where Stan took over the driving. The conditions had become such that no one wanted to even think about driving in the miserable stuff. Late it was but just in time when after the hours of pushing, the team looked for a place to close down where a tiny but muddy road was found. Observed was no buildings or houses in view plus it allowed for an easy start in the morning so, with no streetlights or traffic, the spot was taken. Having advantage of the close trees the crew settled in where each began enjoying a cold beer along with good conversation. Shortly, the spot made known of the site's nuisance when unexpectedly while playing cards under the aid of the flashlights and dome light the boys' amusement time really began.

A bunch of flies along with several mosquitoes had taken up not wanted residence where right away Larry inquired whether anybody remembered to bring a fly swatter. Of course the response was a classic example of young boys thinking. Instead of everyone enjoying a game night, it was a new form of entertainment of close action search and attack. With the flashlights turned into searchlights the hands and sneakers became the guns as many of the flying invaders attacked with a formidable offense. But they didn't stand a chance against the educated defense of the crew as all the intruders were eliminated. By that time there was plenty of peace but also, by then no one felt like playing cards. Then with the rain drops hitting the roof along with everyone quieted down it was sacking out where the quiet area enabled sleeping till dawn.

Saturday, the Fourteenth of June, when the turbulent mental atmosphere had stabilized, but the weather was just as gloomy as the day before. Who knows what evil lurks in the hearts of boys, especially when subjected to such strains of unwanted continuous miserable confinement? Still upset, Dave belted out asking how the heck we all squashed up in this tank was supposed to enjoy the sights when can't even see. Frustrated with the view along with hearing the ongoing radio give the weather reports, Bill suggested going back home.

Stan starting the day not wanting to hear such, responded how there ain't no way of turning back, especially after all the work we all did to earn the trip. Nothing further was said where silence took over since no wanted to talk about the matter. At the young age while not having being trained how to handle such a situation, the boring monotonous traveling was taking its toll on the minds as no one was really able to comprehend how it was affecting them.

Some miles later Dave mentioned of going to Detroit while Larry suggested going to Lexington Kentucky. Surprising everyone, Stan pulled the car to a stop while asserting the agreed rule of not going too far off the planned routes where banging on the door Bill, showing signs of strain suggested to do away with all the rules then after going to both places, drop Larry off at a bus stop. Cooped up while unable to have good visibility and speed reduced due the water each was having a time of it. Dave in total sarcasm added, sure then go see a ballgame and party on the way home which only increase the arguing until heated everyone became fed up. Only a few deep breaths could be heard when exasperated, Bill throwing his arms in the air asserted how he had enough of going against the plans. Then following a moment of quiet, while holding his face Bill stated he wanted to quit the fiasco and go home.

Sadly, Larry noted how he was ready to end it and catch a bus when as if a door had slammed, the crew realized they had been confronted with an issue they created but did not anticipate. Moments passed as the four sat shaking their heads when Larry stated that either way of what was decided, if there were any more delays he would be pulling out having had enough of the bull-crap.

Minutes passed until later the four from discussion, showed appreciation for the plan made at the beginning agreeing to no more outbursts or heavy confrontations. Little did the crew know that over the miles there was to be serious times of testing even beyond what they had already endured.

Slowly, Stan restarted the engine then headed Nashie westward. It seemed as though everything was working against them where the celebration had slowly turned into an unexpected struggle. Miles went by steady which accompanied the four where they steadily sat as if strangers in a new environment. Driving through constant rainy weather over flooded conditions that never seemed to end caused mental meltdowns. Then too, lacking sunshine even the radio didn't help since repeating of clouds, rain, showers, rain and then rain with thunderstorms.

Such situation meant that the wipers never stopped and windows stayed up being water logged. Was it all hopeless the four was thinking as the hearts of best intentions that started out had become depressed. Not even reached was the half waypoint where the boys couldn't get their minds out of the dull drums.

If such deplorable weather continued onto California what would they do? None of the conditions were ever brought up during the planning stage yet the team was in the thick of it. Such a constant mental drag was contrary to thinking of enjoying and in hindsight people could think of many things they could have or should have done, but at their young age of inexperience such was not within thinking.

Perhaps Nashie was the only thing steadfast as she moved forward, but as for the team, it was as if Zombies in a state of limbo.

CHAPTER FIVE

STIFLED GOING, STRAINED MINDS, ANXIETY AND WHAT ELSE.

Attention was quickly grabbed from the three as the driver pulled off to the side of the road. Quietly Stan sat with head in his hands resting on the steering wheel as moments passed. When the three inquired what was wrong, as if a mummy he moved outside while letting the three know how upset he was. Emotionally the boy screamed of what the guys had put him through in Cambridge along with the other two places he was beat. Forced back inside by a cloudburst he sat only to face the looks of the other three who were sitting speechless. Sarcastically, he asserted how they had pushed his tolerance point asking whether such was to be expected every time they passed thru a city. Angrily he added that if that was to be, he was taking the car back home.

Without thinking, Larry in bad timing questioned what the problem was since no one was in any hurry where immediate sparks flew. It was not the thing to say which even rivaled Stan the more causing him to asserted just who the hell he though he was, with all the garbage of no one, just who was he speaking for. Seeing tempers flaring, immediately Bill showed his frustration angrily stating how the guys had come along way acting like a bunch of spoiled brats. Then boldly he added how he too had enough where it was time to find out just where the heck the group was going.

Gruffly Bill added how nice it was for them, so happy not being in any hurry, then banging his fist against the door he exclaimed that others beside them that were going where the two idiots should remember that Stan and his self were confined to a months limited time due the military obligation. Showing strain, Stan asserted that having started the thing, damn it, he can also end it. Stammering he hollered out how he had no intention of traveling to places that would take away from places originally planned on being visited. Following a moment of quiet Bill displayed a face burning red almost breathing fire where he asserted how they should drop Larry off at the bus stop and go on back home cause this ain't worken.

Instantly Larry, in a miserable tone stated how he had enough hearing of the dropping Larry off fiasco but, it was all right with him. Highly emotional he added that he could be dropped off at the nearest bus depot as there ain't no more cause for celebrating where the guy's words hit the mark. Slowly the boys started real thinking of what they were doing to themselves where a sudden quiet took over. Quietly, Dave acknowledged seeing the two's points of view, suggesting for the team to consider all the work done to get where they were. Then taking a big breath he pleaded for the team to get a solution cause he didn't want it all to fall apart.

Amid moments of gloom Dave stated of him being really sorry about the stupid hurting of feelings, yelling how the team should knock it off before they really hurt each other and realize how they let the miserable conditions affect their small minds. Cramped like putting four dogs into a small box the boys simply could not see what they had changed into. Slowly words were exchanged when feeling ashamed of the way they had been carrying on, one by one they attempted to get themselves back into some sort of unity.

Stressed out, the four were walking on eggs essentially unable to communicate since just didn't have the maturity to know how to handle the situation. Ever so slowly the boys crawled out of the ego barrel they had fallen into when all serious, Larry uttered whether it was to be a part of the celebration or a ride to the bus stop? Only a light drizzle was falling where Stan after grabbing a beer, walked down the road. Several minutes passed while the gang called for him to return, but in disgust he simply raised his left arm displaying one of his favorite number fingers.

Needing some understanding Larry asserted as he drove the car to go alongside his friend. While the other two mentioned some jesting insults, one asked if was going to walk home while Dave offered an umbrella noting it was a long walk to the coast. Finally, while Dave stated his apologetics in a drone tone he mentioned they had resolved the differences, where Bill added of needing him involved so they could patch things up. All smiles, Larry mentioned how the gang wanted to continue where then it was Stan was holding up the works. Slowly realizing how the others were trying, Stan climbed in while grabbing a towel then dared them to say something. Amidst the broken atmosphere the four sat quiet where nobody spoke a word.

Larry in the driver's seat pushed Nashie as if he was trying to take his frustration out on the car when strongly, as Bill grabbed the driver's shoulder, Dave banged on a door while both hollered for him to slow it down. Was another milestone in maturing reached? Once on the straight and narrow Dave suggested for no body to say anything about anything but enjoy the weather while talking to the birds. Swallowing their arrogance the four finally began speaking with each other yet, the trip of celebration the boys had in mind during planning had yet to develop.

Heading into the city of Springfield personalities changed as attitudes were affected. Perhaps other persons would have handled the road conditions differently pushing to keep on moving, but the crew was still having their mental problems. They wanted out of the vehicle. Aware of being uptight the crew agreed to stop for some fresh air to allow their minds to settle. Spotting a diner almost simultaneously needing some space all blurted out instructions. Driver, do it, don't even ask, just pull in", they hollered! Something good was coming about where the four showed effort for pulling together making good of what could have been a disaster.

Once inside each treaded softly aware they needed to regroup where thinking caps needed to be worn. Ordering was slow as the Irish waitress reached the booth with the usual hello where attempting his sophisticated nuisance, Dave belted out his "hellooo doll". But, it flowed in a tone that was humorously taunting. Tammy the waitress with piercing eyes made eye contact with Dave as she passed out the menus then walked away. Actually the guys were glad because Dave had no time to make any other remarks about the woman. Soon returning with the beverages the brunette only gave the boys a stern look causing them to stare in wonderment while boldly she remarked that the place was not some red zone in New York City. Displaying a put on smile the cute woman blurted out how it was a place for food and beverages with manners appreciated, so watch your mouth!

In only a few words she had set the group all humbled where right away Dave thinking to make things better thanked the waitress for her courtesy. Meanwhile all smiles, Bill and Larry paid her a compliment where such niceties were returned during the entire meal along with her questions of wanting to know where from, where going and, how come. Here we go again with the third degree, Dave remarked which stimulated some conversation helping to simmer the stress. Curiosity was shown regarding the area known as the Shawnee American Indian nation because it was noted of the famous warrior Tecumseh but when raised with the waitress she offered her opinion leaving the place of less interest. Estimated was the town being slightly larger than Chester yet with many attractions it demanded selection.

Every time the waitress came around she had newer questions where when in the kitchen Tammy must have blabbed with the cook about what she found out. Bill, looking to make conversation mentioned how he was glad the bowling team never acted in such a manner or there would have been a lot of gutter balls, but instead the team was without words, afraid of what they may regret later. Eventually the simple meal turned into an enjoyable social resulting from the waitress who was prompted by the cook's curiosity. By the time the meal ended the boys had settled down to some normal behavior allowing true discussions.

Having a break from the rain the guys gave the car a thorough checking over where the engine needed a good bit of oil. All excited, even showing some smile Dave was heard to say, how with the guys and the car all fed, there should be no more need for stopping, so let's go. Driving around to certain places of historical significance enjoyed was some education but when Larry objected to visiting any burial grounds the others agreed. So, while finishing up Larry took his turn behind the wheel.

Back on the highway Larry drove as if in a demolition derby avoiding the large puddles but such was halted when he ended up getting parked behind a car. After thinking he had solved the problem by passing it he found himself that quick behind another and then another. Seeing his actions, the other three vocally jumped with heavy assertions till he recouped realizing his efforts were useless as the crew pressed on to Indiana. Hills were found to be more like high mounds yet not mountains where up one side then back down the action generated some conversation. Of course, at all the bottoms was where the problems existed because there the deep water gathered. Driving was far from the speed of the turnpike but at least the crew was moving westward.

Not making unnecessary stops the guys were bent on making time where Dave mentioned his thought of visiting the raceway at Dayton. Right away needing to react, Larry responded by agreeing with him but such wasn't to be as the other two objected since they could always go to tracks in their own or other close states. Thinking was to make some time where the crew while hurrying any of the visiting spurts showed a little spark agreeing to drive straight though the night. Obvious to each was how the guys were down on their prior actions trying to regain some togetherness. Somewhere there actually occurred a break in the wet weather when although there was no sunshine, at least it wasn't pouring down, when a creek was spotted. Obliging the others, Larry pulled into a tiny road that accessed the creek where not bashful the boys made use of their washcloths while wading in the water. Along with a refreshing cold beer, chips and pretzels the place afforded some space where relaxing out of the car was highly enjoyed. Since nature was ruling the time, a restarting of the drizzle curtailed any hanging around where already having stopped driving, the crew changed the driving teams.

With Dave back in his favorite driving spot, all was quiet except for the moving windshield wipers. Boom, boom, boom and boom they told their own story as Nashie moved onto the highway. Catching the crew in their slumber mood, unexpectedly out of nowhere, in a flash some sort of a rocket passed by where each hollered asking if they saw what it was? Surely everyone knew it had to have been a car, but it was one that had traveled at a high rate of speed. So fast, it was recklessly excessive when considering the road conditions plus it caused Nashie to rock from the wind while splashing mud all over the place.

So quick had it happened that Dave never even noticed the car's fast approach in the rear view mirror. Responding to Dave's remark Bill prompted asking, gee whiz man you're the one that's driving, didn't you see it? Serious comments quickly sounded, noting how the idiot could have lost traction ramming ole Nashie. Showing his sense of humor Stan reached over the front seat grabbing Dave by the shoulder while pointing in the car's direction hollering, "Dave, quickly follow that car". Asserting his authority, Larry screamed out, "hi yo Nashie, go big girl" as moments of action gripped the crew. Not even over was the matter as red lights could be seen approaching where all riled up Dave uttered how there was no dull moments for the group.

Settled down with Dave driving, the boys kept a close eye out looking for the speeding car that may have slid over to the side somewhere but such was never seen. The Indiana border was approaching on the horizon where the team bushed from the stress of the day closed down. As another day came to a close the boys with a change of attitude celebrated knowing that another territory had been conquered and most important was that the team had remained intact.

Starting out the new day was greeted with more lightning, thunder and showers but being a new week it was also Sunday where Bill reminded about getting to a church. With a change of teams Stan took his turn behind the wheel when also the fifteenth of the month it was the crew rushing around to find a church. Arrived early for the mass service, the four were glad of the place found being a Catholic Church but it was truly different.

Intrigued the crew found the service usual but the structure was educationally highly worth the visit. Very old with its aged rustic atmosphere it was also different in style then added to the atmosphere was the padre. Attending the service was just what the four needed. During the mass it seemed each had found some inner peace that continued even until after the service where occurred a coming to grips with their responsibility to each other.

With everybody screaming of being hungry the team of Larry and Stan headed for the diner of the night before looking forward to a breakfast of some really good food. At the eatery immediately it was agreed not mentioning anything about the weather or road conditions as all negative problems were swept under the table. As Larry and Bill showed they could really put the food away, conversation finally carried a sensible tone. Dissatisfied with the way they had acted the days before each coping with their feelings brought about a change in attitudes.

With all the commotion created along with seeing the toasting of coffee cups, other people in the diner must have assumed some sort of reunion was going on, but when the curious waitress raised questions she was became of value. Happy smiles that were genuine began occurring as the four gobbled up everything the friendly waitress had presented. Even the extra portions disappeared when as the meal ended the four shook each other's hands with expressions of thanks. While Stan moved Nashie along, not having any interest in the city, the team departed the diner as well as the city. Slowly some singing started where shortly the team in better spirits even found it making up words to fit whatever tune was being sung.

Singing farmer in the dell, the boys changed the words to, no arguing we will do, no arguing we will do, on to the Pacific, but no arguing will we do. Whether it was the confinement in the car or the poor weather and road conditions the combination added to the past day's sour episode that had taken its toll. Once or twice would have been more than sufficient but, for some reason the melody got repeated over and over. Interesting it was where sung the four came back to it again and again.

So caught up in the mood Larry wanted to have a toast where noting of being happy that the crew had pulled back together Larry grabbed the bottle of Rock and Rye. Then displaying a huge smile he suggested passing it around for everybody to have a swig but the other three reminded him of the rule on drinking since soon he was to be the next driver. Understanding the situation, the bottle was passed around, except the driving team only took a sip allowing a help to spark the spirits.

As the car rolled along, while the four brought up wondering of what the other graduates as well as what their own families were doing singing was off and on again where absolute chaos took over. Expressions were mixed with incorporating into various tunes of no school days or exams to worry about, no teachers, no quizzes, no tickets to sell , no customers to be afraid of, no part time job, no owners or managers to receive objections from, no trash to pick, no odd jobs to go to and, no negative or sarcastic remarks to listen to. While shaking his head Stan asked if that was all of it elements of the weather along with the poor road conditions could not be put away.

The first thrill of get going at the start was gone where time of day along with the days of the week all seemed to run together. Every day became an arduous time of riding through the soupy roadway of light or heavy rain, downpours, showers, wind or drizzle while looking at the wipers working and or hearing them go boom, boom, boom. Never had the four seen such weather where Larry suggested for the team not to consider being on a trip. But rather more like explorers. Laughing, Dave suggested for the crew to relate to the early settlers heading west traveling in a covered wagon where Bill and Stan responded noting only the fabric had changed where theirs was a metal wagon.

Later, when Bill mentioned, relating to a group of misfit Vikings or even stowaway Christopher Columbus sailors Dave suggested the crew needed more rain to put the car on a raft making like Noah rowing the rest of the way. Verbal comedy had became truly appreciated since it generated some weird form of entertainment.

SEGMENT - 7. With much hype the Ohio-Indiana border was crossed yet not as much as the eastern Ohio border which had the most feeling. To save time, the four changed driving teams with Bill the new driver. As the crew reached the city a notice about a diner had been spotted where Dave responded with his official negative position that he was not interested in having another meal at another diner. Responses made by the other three fell on deaf ears where stubbornly Dave stated how if the guys stopped at a diner he would stay in the car or go elsewhere.

All attempts at reasoning failed as he asserted being sick of all the stupid weather, the simple diner food and rotten smell of the car. Followed was a resounding by the others demonstrating their not caring for his attitude that caused a noting of his outburst being unfair. However when Dave apologized the three noted of their also having similar thoughts being ready for some decent food with atmosphere. Actually comical the entire scenario was since no one had any suggestions. When Bill suggested some restaurant that had cloth napkins and tablecloths the crew stopped at a telephone booth where Dave and Stan picked a few names from the directory. Afterward the four asked several people for their suggestions when surprise it was that a few people actually noted a couple of the names.

Relying on the people's opinions regarding quality and the budget doubt was replaced with anticipation leading Bill to pull into a parking lot.
Gazing at the Greek Restaurant while shaking his head in doubt Dave asked if either one ever had Greek food the three responded with a no. Only a moment it took where the four grabbed their dress shirts feeling they would suffice hollering they would soon find out. Each felt they weren't sloppy yet little did they know the conditions that awaited them inside.

Once inside they passed a waiter while heading straight for the men's room. Stern customers' eyes told the story in the heavy atmosphere of ethnic Greek created by sounds of light classical melodies, along with ethnic music and a dress code. Amidst the hum of conversation the four returned to the entranceway knowing to wait. After the maitre de escorted the four to a side booth a waiter returned with the waters and table condiments. Then while a waitress appeared handing out the menus she surprised the team when asking if it was their intention to stay.   Not comprehending the meaning of the question in reply the four stated not sure while reviewing the menus. Only a glance it was that allowed a comprehension of the prices along with the type of American and Greek foods served when shortly the

Greek manager appeared. While each agreed that the place had the right menu it was about the prices not in anyone's budget that caused the manager to hesitate.

Considering the grubby appearance along with the four not being of the place's ethnic background would have made it difficult for any employees to truly be hospitable. Low lighting, along with the ethnic and American music playing while speaking with a slow accented voice, after introducing himself the man inquired if from the local area. While Larry replied of where from, Stan asked if the man was from Chester. A disturbance was caused when while asking if staying for dinner, dissatisfied looks along with noise from spoons being tapped against glasses were heard. As if in answer to some form of code he turned around facing the many tables while giving some sort of a hand signal.

Was the management going to ask the four to leave because attire called for casual semi-formal dress?
Hospitably, the manager advised that although in a dress shirt, the four was out of place where not giving the man a chance to finish Dave and Larry spoke up apologizing for the lousy appearance. Quickly the manager seeing the boys' effort, smiling he stated the necessity to care for his customers where the minds had to be made up quickly. Neither one was interested in eating at midnight where as Larry advised the manager of the decision to stay, the man inquired of the names along with the ages. Then while advising of loner ties as well as coats he led to a small back room of loner sport coat and ties attire.

Wasting no time amid items of solid dark or neutral colors, suiting up with their coats and ties along with our shirt styles was easy but, tops of semiformal with the trousers, sneakers, jeans and khaki pants with ties and dress coats was anything but picturesque and one for Ripley's believe it not. Noticing the other patrons' looks, Dave whispered how the crew could apply for clown jobs in a circus. As the youngish middle-aged waitress noticed the out of style attire the four were wearing, she smiled but at least didn't laugh hearing of the for needing time. It was all about the budget along with the fact that the personal funds didn't allow any splurging. To help costs it was agreed to water down beverages as well as share any desserts or extras that came with the meals. No ordering anything from the top of the menu was definite as prevented by the cost. From that moment on it was to make the most of the place being a time for some celebration.

For sure the waitress was unable to understood the strain the boys were under as she took the orders but as the woman later questioned of where from along with where going it was easy to recognize her having given some considerations. Meanwhile Stan had actually flipped over the waitress of good looks, dark hair and striking features of which though much older was quite pretty. Cornering Stan with a personal comment thinking he was of Greek nationality the cordial waitress reacted in surprise seeing Stan having taken an immediate liking to her. While stating he was not of Greek descent, he asserted that for her, he would gladly become Greek where the two seemed to hit it off nicely easing of the communication for all five.

Surprised the three were seeing how Stan acted so natural as if the two had actually known each other from years back. Softly Stan mentioned of being on a tight budget to which with all smiles she replied how she understood such being aware of the younger ages. Then walking to the kitchen, she stopped to speak to the manager while at the same time the three jested Stan's on being Greek. Although the crew noticed the manager along with one of the waiters had disappeared unbeknownst at the time was that they had actually gone out to look at the car. Meanwhile also noticed was the waitress often seen speaking with some of the customers.

Shortly thereafter, what ever had been spoken must have had an affect as a big change on the looks of the other customer's faces became apparent. Even customers that noticed the trips to the men's room often gave a smile, yet seeing the comedy outfits did not laugh.

A time it was during the meal where the waitress mentioned with a smile how the manager noticed that no one had ordered any of the high cost items. However neither of the four readily understood what significance her statement had. Then shortly later it was noticed the quantity of food served was well above any normal serving size. Also, unexpected extra side dishes were served which had not been ordered.   The extra items shown on the menu were costly specials and at the time, to the management any type of red carpet gesture may have been taken as a small matter but to the boys it left them sitting in wonderment. With everything provided but not ordered it was an extra expense, when with the waitress watching over his shoulder, Stan pointed at the items noting that such did not accompany the main dish, plus hadn't been ordered. All smiles, the waitress advised how the abundance of food along with the extras provided was complimentary from the manager being his idea of helping with the celebration.

Not expecting such good treatment, the four joyfully responded raising their arms with a clapping of hands while simultaneously saluting the manager. As the woman exclaimed for the guys not to be so loud, while giving the woman a questionable look Stan lowered his holding of his napkin while also lowering his voice. As the motion drew the waitress closer she bent over close beside him where he smiled while attempting to make a pass. Stunned, yet smiling, she put a halt mentioning her being married while displaying her wedding rings. Voicing his feelings Dave uttered his appreciation noting what a great place it was to be in with great food and a great bunch of people, which all had made his day.

Following two courses, the waitress all smiles brought over desserts, which also hadn't been ordered where alertly, before anyone could say anything she quickly stated that the dessert was on the house being the manager's way of showing his appreciation for having stopped at his place. All freshly made, rich and thick loaded with tons of sweet calories desserts were followed by the generous portion of baklava. Indulging in the sweets Bill all excited, asked whether the Greeks danced the Hora or whether the place was where they break the glasses. Laughing in a state of genuine joy it was for at no prior time had the four experienced such attention of superb hospitality. As the meal ended, the manager showed up inquiring if the soups and salads were to each one's liking. Then he questioned if the meat was done to satisfaction and if the fresh vegetables were ok? Not expecting such care, each of the boys showed their best responding with many complements assuming it was time to leave.

Surprising everyone, the man turned with his back to the table while ringing a bell that he had on his person. Loudly, the man hollered for everyone's attention while he motioned for the crew to stand. Then as if announcing some celebrity, joyfully he requested a welcoming for the four having visited their place all the way from Pennsylvania. once while the four was standing came the response of tapping of glasses, pounding of feet on the floor and clapping. Turning back around with a big smile the manager expressed his wish for good health and lucky traveling to the team from the east.

With the meal finished, the waitress looked at Stan in a teasing manner and in a smile that almost melted the table where she asked if there would be anything else. Aware of what Stan was thinking, seeing his red face, the three broke out in a hefty but quiet laughter. Softly Stan told the woman that she was truly a real sweet potato adding, a big thank you. Then surprised everyone was when the waitress handed him the billfold Stan gabbed her hand where smiling they shook hands while exchanging a glance of appreciation. In leaving, the manager with much warm hand shaking stated how he wished the four could come back again where the four responded in kind while waving to the customers. Upon reaching the car, completely overwhelmed by the exceptional hospitality, comments abounded how lucky it was to have stumbled into a place of such great people while Bill added his thinking, asserting how to him it was an excellent education on human relations.

Back on the road as the miles passed each was feeling clammy where Stan blurted how he couldn't take it any longer as was in need of a shower. Since the rest of the team felt the   same there was no squabbling where seeing a place on the outskirts of town Bill pulled in. Hesitant at first, as from the distance the cottages seemed small but, all being tired there was no discussion. Initially the older couple showed they were concerned showing no interest to even discuss renting anything where even after seeing the driver's licenses the man had to see the car. To the team every penny mattered where after some haggling, the man wrote the bill for a single of double occupancy. Assumed of what was rented was a very large motel room. But soon found was four big guys as opposed to two adults with tiny children.

There weren't any extra beds. However, since it was a place to shower along with sleeping outside the car while each was exhausted, no fuss was made. A while later the man brought around extra soaps along with extra towels, plus a few extra blankets followed by the woman who provided glasses with a tub of ice-cubes. Totally unexpected the efforts of both was truly appreciated. At first it was thought the showers would have to be quick due to lacking of hot water, but it was found the guys didn't need much hot as the cold water was already warm. So, taking full advantage of the place, it was while one person showered, washed by others was clothing in the sink. Shortly having gone to the car, Bill brought back a roll of strong string, which his mom thought might come in handy. Strung across the room it allowed the hanging of the washed clothes. Meantime, as the four took turns in the shower, Stan and Bill engaged whoever was not in the shower for playing black jack. Although the two often played Three Card Monte or Black Jack for fun while walking to or from school, once it was known of the trip to be had, it was practicing when as often as possible and for money. However, during the trip simulated chips of pennies and other change enabled some real practice, always planning for the casinos. Surprisingly the second beer along with being stuffed from the large meal took its toll where Larry and Bill grabbed the bed thinking they had gotten hold of a good thing. Such quick action left the other two to sleep on the pull out sofa bed. Actually, had they looked first at the pullout the first two would have found it was of a fairly large size, which had been hardly used. Later in the night as the two complained about the bed being too small and lumpy, so as not to be offended, the other two also gave off moans about the springs popping through, but such was false as the pull out was comfortable. In reality, for the four not being curled up like a donut inside the car, just the space alone being able to spread out was a treat where the team slept well past normal times.

It was Monday the sixteenth of June, where refreshed and cleanly shaved along with wearing clean clothes, the team pondered over the brochures. Starting the morning off with a good attitude the crew found that the city was one of the first to have the name of a federal highway. Known as the National Road along with reading how the KKK had been prominent in the city about the early twenties the boys expected to see many sites. However, realizing a lack of information about the city, lost was all interest in touring. Shortly recalling the extra effort made by the Hispanic couple of good hospitality, positive comments were given the older couple while returning the extra blankets and glassware. Elated, feeling they had caused the older couple to be a little more gleeful then when they had first arrived, it was with the bill being paid the team departed while expressing warm gestures of gratitude.

Stan's team started the driving while the happy travelers found it easy to reflect on the night before at the Greek restaurant where feelings abounded that their celebration finally had some meaning. Not wanting to waste time it was quick to find a place for some grub but, the car and weather, well that was another matter. Just too much water, where ole Nashie could not be pushed. After stopping for breakfast while on the highway Larry riled everyone stating there was nothing like a little rain to help the flowers. Dismal it was since there was no shining of the sun where in every direction there was only light, puffy, dark, low hanging clouds. Yet the four attempted to overcome the radio and disappointing weather singing, let it rain, let it rain, let it rain.

All serious, Bill mentioned his thoughts that someone had permanently tilted a bucket of water attempting to ruin the travel plans. Water would come down in the usual manner of rain then in gushes almost as if thrown from a bucket and although it would slow to a drizzle there were no breaks as the heavy stuf followed on and on. All traveling had turned into coping with rain, driving over the road of water, muddy slush, and potholes. Then with windshield wipers constantly going bam, bam, bam, much disinterest was shown for anything. Yet the four had become determined to make the best of it.

Indianapolis and Terra Haute were next but the average speed of 55 mile per hour planned on was not being realized where a steady loss of time was known but there was nothing they could do. As the miles went by the four minded their manners where all was quiet, except for the stops. Time passed into the afternoon then into the early evening where dinners though not at any particular place was special. Slowly the four found their selves getting back to some normalcy, even able to jest each other about their ugly conduct.

Then it happened where discovered was that the last of the sandwiches were gone plus there were no cakes or cookies. Mysteriously, the food had disappeared as no one had mentioned anything about eating the last of whatever. How could the guys do such a thing to each other was the wording expressed. Beyond the goodies each spoke of the situation as bordering on dependability and trust that needed to be resolved. Without cookies cakes and pies there wasn't anything left to munch on where the matter was beyond trivial. Ticked off at each other the four could not understood the lack of communication and failure of respect.
    Finally, when Dave admitted to having the last of the cakes, the others angrily questioned how he didn't think telling anyone was of any importance. In a serious tone, Bill stated how it was no wonder that men are foolish in the kitchen as they have no idea of food supplies or inventory but this is between the four relying on each other where such was selfish. Unexpectedly Stan pulled over, where Larry surprised everyone asserting how he was tired of sitting with nothing to do. Needing something to get his mind off the situation and the weather he pressed on driving.

Having run the food situation into the ground, tired of it all there was no quarrelling with Larry as he took the wheel. As the hours of the day passed, feeling sluggish from the day's mental problems driving became a problem as nobody felt like driving. Fighting the ongoing onslaught of the weather with the sloppy soup on the ground took its toll. Rain, rain, rain and then along with the steady rain there was the occasional heavy downpours. For the drivers it meant the sheer excitement of constantly looking through the nonstop windshield wipers going back and forth, back and forth. And then

Also added to the abnormal deluge there was the occasional lightening with the unexpected thunder that moved everyone where it seemed like mad dogs in a cage. Even the radio with its noise didn't help the sanity plus, it did nothing for the view and your simply reading about it. Try placing your self in the car at age 17 with three others.

Tensions were every day with each actually asking how much more could they take. It wasn't just about being in the car for twenty-four hours but there was the four stuffed inside along with other stuff leaving nowhere to move. It had been the same since leaving the middle of Ohio that was totally contrary to everyone's expectations of the thrilling trip they had looked forward to.

As the car droned along the rain swept highway, Stan questioned why nobody thought about bringing a sundial? Such a great question, but at the wrong time yet, it did generate some replies. Stan refusing to be glum asserted some humor noting how a good one would have taken the crew around the rain. Responses were flat as the tone indicated the boys' lack of enthusiasm, which was also flat.

Same old stuff hour after hour, even into the late evening where a side road or area could be found. In one area, Stan yelled for the driver to hold up and back up since he spotted a place to pull into. While the others replied how they didn't see anything, right away once Bill had stopped he started backing up. Loudly as if at a fire, Larry screamed out to the driver. "hold up and stop the car"! Immediately Larry yelled out for him not to back up in the rain, especially not in the dark as he could get everybody killed. While Dave blurted out asking what the problem was since no one was coming, hollering yeah, yeah, yeah Bill turned the car around.

A stop at a soda fountain was made for some banana splits, ice cream sodas and milk shakes, where aided by the woman, girls and man's conversation made it enjoyable.

Another customer played a comedy tune on the jukebox stirring up the atmosphere while the manager commented how business was really bad from the weather and when he stated with a huge smile how the four were the best thing that happened to his place it helped curb the driving misery.

Only a short distance, the narrow dirt road was found. Just as he pulled onto the muddy road, a car, went past. Zoom, as if flying, it went passed without any lights and of dark color where the speed of the car caused muddy water to splash on the car covering all the windows Visible for only a moment and a short distance, wow, Dave uttered, did you guys see it! You bet the three replied where discussion led into instant recalling of the minutes before when Bill was backing up. How lucky you guys were, Larry stated, as there may have been a crash. Once parked the rest of the evening was passed by playing cards where over the minutes the matter kept resurfacing. All four were affected by the occurrence wondering if other maniacs might be on the road. Setting the flashlights Bill asked why nobody had ever thought of bringing a couple of lanterns.

The whole country sides being swamped under water, any other time may have caused some conversation but after day and day of it, the situation dashed any good thinking.

Sometimes, going was so slow it was as if the team felt they were in a rowboat. What didn't help the situation was not just the road but that the land was flat. Except for the hills, which were tiny in size it was level plus flat as a pancake where some high water places it was well up to the running board.

Frequently police had established detours or roadblocks preventing any use of the highway where rerouting of traffic may have been easy for those living in the area but for the crew meant only going from slower to slow retarding effort and time. Being unfamiliar with the areas often left the team in a state or ratted nerves where such anxiety was had at times causing expressions of anger. Needless to say the whole unexpected ongoing scenario stretched everyone's patience. Beyond what they had ever experienced minds were tested and stretched even to the limit as none of the boys had been prepared or trained for such abnormal activity and daily trials. It was slow in the boys maturing, as for sure the team was at their wits end. A journey it was in the making but not the kind they had planned for, yet in a way they were getting their money's worth.

People, times later when told of the ordeals but lacking such experience could not relate while others were found unable to comprehend how the boys' mental stability was affected. Of course they were all adults who had never encountered such and, as such could not comprehend. People that waited on customers such as in gas stations, stores and eateries all had sad faces or, less than happy attitudes. It was enough putting up with each other then also having to put up with the dismal people only added to the challenge the young guys didn't need. Also there were the radio stations that didn't help matters repeating the same subject of rain, the flooded areas, or alerting of storms and various detours.

Indianapolis was a place where visiting started in another diner where after grabbing some food a quick tour of the city was made. While the old and historical buildings could have rivaled the cities of Chester or Philadelphia not caused by the difference in the various ethnic groups. With visiting over, it was back to the highway where heading west the small openings of the windows combined with the vents allowed a much welcomed movement of air. While the temperature had dropped into the mid seventies the humidity still denied any relief.

Leaving the area, Bill asked for the driver to stop a minute as he alerted the others to notice the sign for specialty sandwiches. Suggesting about getting a few to go heard was no one being anxious as not hungry plus, in several hours it would be close to dinner. However, strongly pressing Bill raised the other's curiosity as the four did have experience in such matters as coming from Chester where the hoagie originated. Giving the place a try, ordered was one of each of the three different types in the large size with all the trimmings and each cut into four portions. This gave each of the crew a real chance to taste the variety of the sandwiches.

Seeing them being constructed, neither could imagine what could be so special as each only had lettuce, tomatoes, onions, cheeses, sweet and hot peppers along with the meats. No specialty plus the tomatoes were flat as not from Southeast Jersey, which are superior in flavor from any other part of the country. Once back in the car the crew covered everything up as the wheels quickly rolled until later where the odor took control. It happened even with the vent opened and the windows down a fraction allowing air to pass through.

Miles traveled with time passed, it was almost as if an explosion took place when the four found their selves unable to resist as the wrapped food aroma strongly made its appearance. So overwhelmed, all self-control of the four failed as nature called requiring a pit stop where the sandwiches were consumed. As if a team of professional taste testers was at work each voiced opinions of nothing special being found but at least the sandwiches were still enjoyed. Saving time from making another stop the teams changed places where it was Dave's team with him having the driving duties. Miles past along with time when late in the evening the crew looked for a road where they could call it a day where eventually it was onto a road in an empty field. Hands of Black Jack along with a brew and good conversation ended with the crew bedded down for the night aided by the sound from raindrops hitting the roof along with the cool air. All relaxed Dave remarked of, what a day and night where the others merely responded for him to shut up.

Tuesday morning, the Seventeenth arrived with Stan greeting everyone mentioning that since the halfway point hadn't been reached a real push should be made. Boldly he added limits on visiting should be made even on those planned stops. With the team of Larry and Stan to drive the choice of which was to start the day was resolved by the game of Rock, Paper and Scissors. While Larry won, the other three pushed on making better time where from then it was to be most meals would be to go.

Starting off, Larry drove the crew as they enjoyed their on the go breakfast as he played out his enjoyment of being catered to. Being the copilot, Stan was forced to hold his food, somewhat comically waiting on the driver where the situation enabled some humor. Some distance traveled Stan took his turn behind the wheel, where like the others he rode in the center portion of the highway whenever possible. Such helped in maximizing the avoiding of the huge deepwater areas.

Phrases expressed such as, water, water everywhere but not a drop to drink while recalling matters from school and work even to things from television helped in being social but it wasn't a cure all. The best was Larry asking, how with all the years getting educated he was never taught how to change mud into gasoline. Uh oh, something different! Miles down the road the driver mentioned how he felt ole Nashie seemed not to be handling the way she should where a moment of quiet took hold as each listened.

Attempting to feel something Dave murmured how the car seemed to be going crooked. Right away, Larry responded how he sort of felt something but whatever the something or going crooked meant, no one was ready for. Shortly, Bill pulled the car over where the crew jumped out with each looking around amidst the drizzle. All smiles Larry hollered for the driver to look as hees does gots a flat tire where almost in disbelief Bill responded asking how it could be, out there in the middle of nowhere. Adding to the humor Dave hollered how it was all part of Stan's idea of making good time.s Bill looked on, Larry and Stan hollered how it was the driver's duty to make things right. Angrily Bill pressed the issue of being a team effort but, the others only responded it being the driver's duty to fix the flats that occur. Then as they jumped back in the car they hollered for him to jump to it. Mad at the situation, Bill yelled how the guys were traitors being not fair and would get theirs one day. Moments later they looked around seeing Bill having opened the trunk, getting the tools and replacement out. After watching for a time seeing Bill's effort, the three got out where faces told of each one's feelings. Quickly, the four did short work of it, replacing the flat with the spare then when done it was taking advantage of the clear deep water on the other side of the highway. With shoes and sox removed the four washed as if standing in a large tub then it was back behind the wheel. As before Indianapolis there were very small towns, so it was after the city that there were very small towns. Yet it wasn't the towns causing problems but rather the posted detours where if anyone knew what the thaw in the north was like, they would certainly be able to relate. Lots of miles and comments ended with having a few beers and playing cards which ended the day.

SEGMENT 8. Already the Tenth day of the trip it was Wednesday the Eighteenth yet June stayed what was to see, water everywhere, up, down and sideway. Being the day's first driving team, Larry was first to drive and two days behind schedule, the crew pressed taking care of the personals while getting food and drinks to go. Impossible it was to make up lost time but the measure did help greatly in saving time. Meanwhile the temperatures at night had been in the upper fifties allowing good sleeping then went into the upper seventies during the day. Although it wasn't hot or steamy it was always very close.

Amazing how each struggled to keep a happy spirit where often it seemed like the harder the four tried to be happy, the more negative things caused each to be agitated. Trying to generate some laughs, Stan suggested the guys look at the weather as Mother Nature's way of helping to celebrate as rather than throwing rice or confetti she was throwing drops of water. he added. Response by the three was dropping Stan off at the nearest mental hospital.

Terra Haute was the next targeted city. Noting its location comments were made on how the first travelers across the country must have measured the distance to ensure it was in the center. Comparing it was noted of the city from Richmond to Indianapolis to be in proximity the same distance as from Indianapolis to Terra Haute. For a while being something new it stimulated some conversation where every little bit helped coping with the boredom of the situation.

While Larry suggested fitting the car with pontoons and a sail Dave replied also buying some oars. Yet, with all of the nonsense effort, the drudgery was overwhelming where the crew could not help but keep falling back into the same dumpy mood. Each day seemed as if the weather was getting better but it really wasn't as it was only hope. Once trying anything, Stan suggested doing a native Indian rain dance where Bill mentioned of singing about the sun. As if from another planet, Dave started singing the tune of dashing trough the snow where it was at times the guys were actually daffy. A choirboy at Saint Michael's Church, Stan was also a learned piano player. When he started singing the others of high mentality upon hearing altered the words to splashing o'er the waves, in a four door Nash sedan, on to Vegas we go, to play our Black Jack games.

Down the highway a time of depression had its time where Bill again raised the issue of turning around to head back home. But Dave and Stan asserted how it was not what they wanted. Yet, Larry mentioned that it should be considered as he also had enough of the lousy weather. Dave gruffly stated while there was no indication by any of the weather reports that it would be clearing soon he felt it would not last. With tempers driven by frustration, each was so upset they were unable to even discuss the matter. All they could do was to wait till the end of the day for listening to a long range weather forecast.

Depressed emotions abounded in Indiana, as the four had reached an impasse that seemed never ending. So upset they had completely forgot about all the obstacles they had overcome just to have the journey. Of course the immediate problem was that neither had any control. So continuous it was beyond the team's ability to plan as the team had sunk into the dump's bottom. Nobody gave any thought as to how far they had come where immature inability to apply tactics that would have allowed a better frame of thinking had slowly taken its toll.

Reviewing literature entering Terra Haute it was found that at one time period it was called Sin City. Not even asking the others, Larry pulled the car in at a Howard Johnson's Restaurant and while parking he loudly stated how he had enough of the driving conditions, where it is up to the guys. Then as the others climbed out he shouted how it was Stan's turn but didn't care whether he drove or not. Seeing the look on his face along with the tone of his voice, the others knew that Larry had become fed up and though they could relate his disinterest stunned everyone.

Once inside a booth Larry asserted that he had it with the soup, mentally finished and ready for a bus that caused an instant quiet. Everybody for a moment became like robots not knowing how and unable to respond. When the waitress inquired about needing help with the menus Bill mentioned how it was the four needed help then questioned if the city's sins would affect the food. Oh yes the waitress replied, asserting it being hazardous needing the four to be careful when eating! Laughter by the four helped a turn of the atmosphere into a more at ease semi pleasant period. However Larry had become so far down on his self and the situation he was out the picture for any socializing. Realizing the demoralizing affect the situation had on the guy all the others were able to do abide the time

Taking his turn, Stan handled the driving finding the city comparable in size to the city of Chester. But the older neighborhoods and center of town along with the sullen mood left everyone disinterested where it was the visit ended shortly. Heading for the highway a stop at an automobile service place was made where a checking routine was performed with the flat tire being ruined was discarded along with the tire on the other wheel replaced with the new ones. Moving things around taking allowed advantage of the available space where expressions were heard of even being able to breathe! Heading toward Illinois changes in the cloud formations were noticed but the sun was not showing itself yet, the crew started being hopeful. A sad day it was as closer to the river the crew got even higher water greeted them and if that wasn't enough, there were more detours to cope with. Totally frustrated, Dave at one of the detours suddenly jumped out of the car yelling, "this is stupid, absolutely ridiculous where the world is changing into a huge shower stall".

Without any warning of what for or why, the boy stood as if in some sort of trance with water running down his face. As if making some sort of gesture, the guy raised his arms while looking up but, everyone else sat while stunned only watching. Then when loudly the boy yelled out asking God, when He was going to cause the rotten weather to stop Larry responded asking whether such actions did any good. With head bowed Dave, not happy stood speechless!

Illinois, by way of route forty was not straight across but in fact diagonal where not being a wide state the team anticipated it wouldn't take much driving time to traverse the state. More erroneous guessing as contrary to their thinking, the closer the crew got to the Wabash River, the speed was even slower. All assumptions of optimism were stymied where absolutely ridiculous, Bill belted out in a boisterous tone of total frustration this crew is encountering a situation actually worse than what we had already driven through. As if in pain, Bill screamed out asking if the crap will ever let up?

Struggling in the drive going through the area the eyes were opened unable to comprehend what the crew was seeing. Not far before crossing the river along with the high water there was deplorable destruction everywhere. Then forced to take detours only leading to more detours so disgusted with the moment all serious thoughts of turning back had substantially increased, The guys felt as if time was being taken away from them on purpose where recalled was that no one, not even the travel agencies had mentioned such possibilities. Even once across the river it was still the same and yes the guys had been hoping that for some reason crossing the river was to make a difference.

Often restricted to the lowest gear, moving faster may have been the intent or wish, but nothing was doing. Slowly the car wheels turned but even slower was the boy's patience wearing. Further driving away from the river, the more stabilized things were getting yet ever so slowly. Hopes that existed before had become strained to the max.

Arriving in the town of Effingham the crew stopped at a place called, "Steak and Shake" Some new or different items were found. Almost empty, of only a few customers the worn, plain faces along with the proprietor's sad looks made it clear of their feelings. Dog on a stick, was it some sort of cult place, Larry was heard asking? Gazing at the small menu to everyone's surprise, there it was and although only another version of the hot dog, it seemed as a happy type of food.

Unexpectedly without warning, it happened when suddenly there were rays of the sun shining through the window. Instantly the people rushed to the windows as if a celebrity was passing by where a couple even started clapping. Then while the rays peeked through the clouds one voice was heard of a short of thank you to God. During those few moments the mood in the place was truly moving as the atmosphere inside the place changed with happy expressions. Such momentum by the others helped the minds of the team where it was all ears became glued to the radio as each was waiting to hear some kind of improved forecast.

Back on the road another moment occurred where the clouds moved allowing the full strength of the sun to shine. Loud cheers of hoorays, yos and yippee sounded as if the crew was rooting for their sport team. Time and miles went by when the moment arrived where a pit stop by the highway was necessitated. All ears listening the four strained to hear while praying with hope for some type of clearing when the voice box suddenly let out an extra bulletin. Heard was another improved forecast, but Larry, still mentally down, mentioned his doubt angrily suggesting for the guys not to listen, but look at what was seen in the sky.

Although caught by the phrase while looking the three decided to wait for the next couple of forecasts to make any decision. Having taken over the driving as slowly as miles and time passed he mentioned of the road conditions getting better. Speed increased but not continuous as only in road sections yet, eagerly there was newly generated optimism. Zigging one way avoiding the large puddles then another, it was like learning a new way to drive but, gleefully the crew simultaneously be heard yelling, go Nashie, go Nashie.

Driving with a little zeal the guys still had to avoid the many awesome sized puddles but, even the little gradual change greatly helped ease each of the crews' frustrating tensions. Some time it was where the foursome stopped at a small diner simply to get refreshed. Grabbing the beverages and snacks to go, it was quickly back on the road again where taking his turn driving, even Dave demonstrated renewed enthusiasm.

SEGMENT 9.   Finally the crew reached the next place planned on. Granite City was the old entrance way to East St. Louis popular back in the Steamboat era however lacking cause for a serious tour, to avoid wasting time the town was passed through. Down the road while dragging along the crew approached the big Mississippi River.

Desiring a close look they passed up time of crossing where found was an area to park in. The restricted truck loading area did not allow passenger vehicles in the area but, all excited, Dave drove as close as possible ending up at the very edge of the lot.

Such was the good view that it was void of all buildings, cars, trucks and trains where Bill mentioned how the Delaware River was not as wide. As if waking from a long sleep Larry spoke up surprising everyone suggesting how ships are ships and water is water wanting to get back on the road. About then a police car arrived where seeing the team was just visiting he permitted a few minutes. Shortly after waiting, he was forced to escort the crew to the exit. Upon reaching the top of the onramp Dave surprised everyone when he unexpectedly pulled over. Everyone had ants in their pants, wanting to express their feelings but Dave was doing his thing.

Out of the vehicle, he suggested it being Stan's idea of the west coast that he should have the privilege of driving across the river. Not a big matter Stan hollered, yet with all of the hoopla generated by the other three he found himself helpless. As feelings of joy soared among the four while realizing the spot they were at, responding to the guy's kindness Stan got behind the wheel. Appearing as if in shock to everyone the guy simply sat as if daydreaming. Are you sick or hurting, the three questioned not knowing what to expect? Moving in response in slow determination the guy hollered out asking if the three were ready for the big event where only positive phrases of, yes, yes, do it, don't wait and let's do it, rang out.

Stan started off slowly then kept the speed slow so that each could look at both sides but shortly the engaging traffic forced him to move on. While passing over the center of the span seeing land in the distance, Larry suggested how he could relate to Columbus's day when he discovered new land. Hearing Larry's voice suggesting being back with the three along the ongoing crossing event caused an abundance of cheers to each other as emotions exploded. While Nashie carried the four over the center comments flowed from looking at all the boats and ships, as well as seeing how wide the river was. Contrary to the other traffic making the simple or normal drive across, to the crew it was a huge event where feelings were high with emotions even beyond the norm.

Reaching the other side Stan quickly pulled over into the first available spot amidst watering eyes. While mumbling prayers of thanks by the crew ended with a loud, Amen Stan, then out of the car while moving his hat across his chest displayed his being fully caught up in the hoopla. As if before royalty displaying a huge smile he made a formal bow to the crew. Entirely moved by the situation, the other three got out reacting with humorous antidotes indicating somber emotions of respect for each other. Amid shouts of pent up miserable feelings with watery eyes the four grabbed each other's shoulders with much comradely ending with a shaking of hands.

Dave retook the wheel where moments of quiet followed as the four sat realizing what transpired. All excited Dave hollered how this was one weird way of making a celebration. Wow! No booze and no smelling salts but it was almost as if mannequins had come to life where with many shouts of yippee, even Larry showed enthusiasm as he led the gang belting out repeated choruses of, "Hi Yo, Nashie, let's go".

CHAPTER SIX

ARISTOCRATS, ORIGINAL AMERICANS AND A PARADE.

Determination had been rekindled as if the Chester Eagles Boys Club had just begun yet, unknown what was to befall them. Aha! Euphoria was pouring out as good thoughts clouded the air. Darn it, we're finally on our way out of this mess, Bill hollered in a strained voice. Seeing his face with head shaking to the music, the four rallied with yeas and thank God for big favors of His help. Something was happening with the weather while the personalities of the four were changing, as weren't the same as had started from their city. Who wouldn't feel great if allowed to be a celebrity? Even if for only a short while, who wouldn't want the experience?

Saint Louis Missouri, which each knew only of a little from what history taught. Although the city had historical significance, for the team it had huge significance since the big place was designated from the start as the half waypoint. Upon getting close, happily the four cheered with ok, yea, yahoo and yippee, while on the outside of the doors they banged in unison resembling something like a metal drum. Often recollections popped up regarding some of the negatives received from the families and friends but noting where they were, the criticisms faded understanding as not of any importance. Keep on going, no matter what, became the new resolve as the closeness of the heat and humidity along with the limited space that before was big matter became more tolerable.

On and on, the crew drove with the sun baking the mud soaked dark paint. Inside the vehicle it was like a steamy rolling oven and with the crew, hot, sick of being pent up in the car along with coping of the adverse road conditions, each desperately wanted a change. Thoughts of enjoying some type of a comfortable place to get cleaned up expanded into also having a celebration party as fed up with the motels and sleep in car nights, the guys wanted a place of quality yet within the budget. Brochures only caused unanswered questions needing answers where sought was a telephone book.

Finding a booth, the book offered many choices but such only helped to complicate matters where upon Dave's suggestion a stop was made at a clothing store to get some answers. Putting together what the sales people said along with opinions from other people outside provided places for as well as those not wanted. Deciding was not simple as ach was fully aware the place chosen would not be another cheap motel but the guys only knew they wanted something better. Already into the dinnertime, choices narrowed to three places where flipping coins was used as the simple process of elimination.

Hotel Warwick, located on Locust Street was where the crew ended the eighteenth of June. It must have been an Indian hideout, Stan uttered seeing the name yet, the place was not one of the lesser hotels. Just from the outside it should have caused the four to at least telephone first for prices however, being in a hurry to get a shower the no thinking syndrome had set in. Once inside, the crew questioned the clerk on the various services offered where it was just what the crew wanted except there was the cost issue. Hearing the rates Stan and Dave attempted to generate a deal intensely, one by one picking on the matters with the clerk. Simply discarded were all suggestions even as Bill and Larry added sob stories regarding the various problems encountered in reaching the place.

While all pleas fell on deaf ears attempting to push, Dave and Bill mentioned how they had driven all the way from Pennsylvania just to stay at their place. After quizzing on where from and why, the man's attitude turned to curiosity where admitting from hearing the radio broadcasts he had some idea of what the crew had experienced. Although the clerk showed interest, all of the guys' pitching fell short. Room for one was about four to seven dollars then with double occupancy it was six to twelve dollars. And since two rooms put the amount well over budget they walked away. Holding a conference it was considered how other nice places would probably charge the same amounts.

Neither wanted to spend time driving around or wasting time on the telephone attempting to find lower rates where again the team went back to the desk. Attempting to coax the clerk for lowering the rates but no matter what was stated, all fell on short ears. While the four started to leave the clerk made a phone call where quickly, a middle aged attractive woman joined the clerk. Upon hearing of the guys' story, the sharp woman at first showed little hope then surprised the crew was when instead of being negative woman asked if she could help. Immediately the four taking turns explained about the small budget while requesting help in reducing costs but like the clerk, response from the woman became the same. Inquired was if on college break her staring gave the impression that the four were loonies. Hearing the woman express how the hotel wasn't sold out alerted the guys to know there were rooms available but, when she asserted they couldn't change the rates all efforts were dashed.

Pressing the matter of having driven all the way from Pennsylvania to stay at the place raised the eyebrows but noting the need to save every penny fell short. While the woman explained how they didn't have any authority to change the pricing policy other customers walked up to the desk. Immediately the crew was asked to step aside. Such was since they had to take care of their regular customers. Having resigned itself of not being affordable, the team started to leave when at the outside doors a discussion erupted. Another decision had to be made as to which other hotel to try plus when the looking would stop. Unexpectedly, the well-dressed woman again approached the crew requesting the guys to come back inside smartly identifying herself as the assistant manager.

As she led the four back into the foyer the manager was waiting where he looked into the matter. Apparently the assistant must have had words with him because he wanted to hear the whole story of where from, where going and why plus why not a bus. As the frustrated team obliged, immediately taking control looking amazed the man expressed his interest of wanting to know even some details.When Dave stated how such would take time, the man simply replied how he had all night, then when asked of each one's ages the manager's jaw dropped hearing not even eighteen. Showing understanding of what the basis of trip was for along with why his place, the manager pulled the four away as he asked if he could ask a personal question. Stunned the team was when he queried how long it had been since each had a bath. It seemed everything the man found out only pushed his self getting involved.

Shortly hearing the manager's discussion the assistant seemed captivated where she pursed another path as if the team was a group of gangsters on the run from robbing a store. Shortly, showing their being emotionally drained while having enough of the go around from the woman, the four shook their head while starting to leave. Recognizing the guys being fed up with all the badgering the man stopped all questioning while requesting the four to wait until he returned.

Returning to the front desk the woman aided the clerk in caring for other customers leaving the four only waiting in suspense. Meanwhile, unknown to the four was that the manager simply had to see Nashie for himself where upon his return the man stated how seeing the vehicle he had a clearer picture of what the crew had been through. Returning to the group the assistance's persistence provoked the manager as she pressed to know why the parents weren't there and wouldn't help.

Upset, Stan boldly asked why she needed to know all that personal stuff suggesting for the guys to leave. Showing concern the man sternly noted how he needed to be aware of the kind of people his place was catering too, yet asserting his willingness to try to help. While serious looks determined the scene as the manager released the assistant to her duties all smiles the man asserted how he wanted to show the hotel's way of helping the guys' celebration. Lowering the cost of a large room to an off-season schedule the manager noted his appreciation for stopping at his place also providing a slip for a non-holiday special discount on food.

Joyously, the four accepted while showing much gratitude for his generosity where acting like gentlemen there was much hand shaking. While the man showed his good character the dirty clothes being worn as well as unshaven and dirty told the story. With Stan and Bill completing the registration, the other two brought in the bags along with a few beverages where as far as the crew knew they had signed for a plain large room.

Boy, oh boy, was all Larry could say upon entering the room when surprised the team was that instead of a regular room, the manager had provided a luxurious suite big enough to hold a large family.

Perhaps not the Chrysler building but, the place had the amenities which showed it was above the average with the plush carpeting, chandelier extra sinks and air conditioning, While one grabbed a chair another stretched out on the bed as Larry and Stan fell on the floor content to spread out on the cool carpeting.

Following a turn soaking in the tub while the others used the two sinks for washing clothes short tour of historical places was made. Dinner at another diner rather than the restaurant was had to save money for the next day. Familiar with the bar scene, any pretending to enjoy such was put out of mind as the foursome returned to the room. With Black Jack being on everyone's mind the large table was great for practice and although fun for the three, to Stan it was serious matter. At times it was almost like a classroom scene even until everyone retired for the night

Nineteenth day of the trip, when it was the morning where the team headed for some grub at another diner. Not wasting of time sitting in a booth it was fried egg sandwiches of ham and bacon with onions along with home fries, biscuits, toast and large coffees to go. Stan was behind the wheel with Larry making up the driving team showing a pioneering spirit as the crew connected the various sites with what history education had provided. Each able to combine what was seen with their imagination along with what was learned in school elevated the value of the historical sites.

Even recalling some of the western movies seen helped where conversations became heavy regarding the days of cattle and riverboats. Soon the brochures led the crew to Fitz's Root Beer. Here having the appearance of a typical tavern it was actually a diner of capability. Just the place! Good burgers, fries, sodas, and ice cream really hit the spot. Demonstrating an improved outlook, Larry took over the driving even hamming it up putting on the act as a chauffeur in a travel package. Various stops allowed seeing pictures and displays of the old time means of transportation, tools and industries. Then combined with seeing the formal attire and various work clothes it became a day of full educational entertainment.

Bill mentioned how it had to be with a regular cloth covered dinner table. Smiling, Dave uttered, for him to order one made out of baloney that way he could eat everything. Considering the place they were staying the crew agreed to having a sit down meal but, no sandwiches, hot dogs or meatloaf. However there was the concern over the funds causing a change of plans again and again as each showed some displeasure. Stopping on a corner Bill and Dave looked in the telephone directory, then back in the car notes were compared with the literature. Having his fill of the money situation knowing it was driving everyone batty, Stan hollered how the guys must be nuts since there were too many places to look plus the crew didn't have the time. Some short discussion then it was decided to stay with what the Warwick had to offer.

SEGMENT 10. Curiosity pushed a walk to the hotel's ballroom restaurant where after seeing the luxury a short stop was made at the front desk. Understanding the crew's pressure being strapped in a budget the clerk suggested using the alternate dining room. Amazed the four was hearing how familiar the clerk was about the crew especially since none of the four had mentioned any details with him before. Beyond the crew's budget, the hotel's prices dashed all thoughts of the formal dining room since any meeting of such prices would mean causing minimizing of other places to celebrate.

Settled it was to use the alternative room so everyone could enjoy from the top of the menu without any worry about the cost. At the moment everyone feeling good even felt better that common sense prevailed. Minutes after returning to the suite there was an unexpected knock on the door. Surprise it was when Bill opened the door where standing was the assistant manager wearing her classy business attire. Uh oh!

WARWICK HOTEL — ST. LOUIS, MO.   7A-H1493

Thinking the worst, Dave mentioned how they probably needed the four to move out for some dignitaries. Not knowing the reason why she was there the other three simply mumbled their agreeing. A suttle smile from the attractive woman as she looked the four over by her questioning whether the boys were truly doing some sort of celebration. Back to his self, Larry responded how the guys were at least trying to have a happy time with a cause. When Dave inquired why she was so nosey asking such person stuff, showing some arrogance Bill asserted how the manager knew all about it the day before. A pause of silence, then Dave blurted out asking what's up and why the questions. Accepting Stan's invitation the woman came inside and while leaving the door open sat down while pressing why the four were there. Amid the wonderment atmosphere, lively Stan replied how the place marked the spot of importance being the designated half waypoint.

Expressing her suspecting of something she responded with a short, oh come on, really? Displaying a full grin of disbelief, the woman pressed on how being so young such a large project could not have been started. Just what the four didn't want to hear. As angry looks took over where Dave and Bill advised how it was planned even over the objections of the parents while coping with the negativity of their friends. Right away Stan demonstrated his dandruff being ruffled by suggestively showing the woman the doorway.

Asserting having been riled by one of the local town's Police Chief along with other unpleasant occurrences the guy added how he was no longer interested hearing any more cynical words from unassociated people. Standing up, the woman exclaimed how she had heard enough while in the doorway she asked the four not to leave for a while. After closing the door mad as all get out, Dave jumped on Stan asking what that was supposed to be all about, asserting how he did it getting the woman all upset. Bill also jumped on Stan asserting how it was then they would most assuredly force the four to leave. With made decisions up in the air, the team passed the time playing cards as misapprehension escalated. Feelings grew thinking to get ready to leave because Stan had caused a rift where management's concern would change to, too much fuss without the full suite price.

But later came the knock on the door, the four didn't want to hear where the assistant manager had showed up again. Even more powerful she was accompanied by the presence of the manager where seeing both, erroneous negative thoughts prevailed as each expected was to be thrown out. Big time surprise it was as the manager while not saying a word simply smiled as he presented Stan a hand written special discount note on all meals. Quick the note was passed around for review, where the crew responded stating how it was highly appreciated. Then as the four groped for words, the manager advised how the discount was so that a true celebration could be enjoyed but there is an exception where it was only good in the main dining room.

Offered a chair by Larry, the manager waved it off noting how the hotel was interested in assisting to make the stay enjoyable plus for some personal reason while motioning with his arms, the man asserted how he personally wanted the time to be so worthwhile that it would even allow the staff to remember it. Shaking their heads while wondering, the team stood, not fully knowing the full impact of what the man had said. Following some shaking of hands along with the crew stating their gratitude the manager departed leaving the team not knowing what to expect next.

Facing the assistant while anticipating some not kind words Stan shook his head while stating, "what you again with more questions"? Softly, as the woman smiled she replied of their being happy how their place was the team's choice. Then she advised about use of the manger's note while inquiring about dress. Disappointed hearing the four not having any formal attire but only sport coats and ties she surprised everyone with a small but joyous laugh while asserting for the guys not to worry, as long as each had a dress shirt to accompany the jacket and tie. While receiving a resounding thank you she asked for the place to be remembered to people the group met once the team departed.

As she walked away, she left the four wondering what all of the stuff meant. Since the note was void of any numerical figure discount, what was going on was the question especially about the dress in their formal dinning room? All charged up, Bill mentioned how it was time to forget about the dollars especially since the manager showed how they were looking to help. Unanimously the team decided to forget about the other places as well as the alternative room. Soon comments about what should have done flowed as a running stream noting of bringing a formal suit or, rented tux. But soon it was to stop, as no one had any interest in discussing hindsight.

Not only was it to be a complete change from what the four had been wearing but also they would notice a change of attitudes. During one moment while dressing, Dave looked at Larry asking in jest who the heck he was, while Bill all excited asked where the heck the guys came from? Meanwhile the team had no idea what was in store or just how high class the customers would be found dining in the formal area, but they would surely find out.

As the team entered the dining area they did enjoy the frowns and piercing eyes that caused a not so good feeling, yet among the staff the four had the feeling as though the crew was actually expected. Smiling, the maitre de asked for the names of each as he greeted the crew along his introduction that was accompanied by a most unexpected generous smile. But more surprised the four was when he made known his knowledge of the past weeks of horrendous weather. Then noting a few words of encouragement the man expressed his congratulations for making it as far as the team had traveled.

Not expecting such understanding the four was also not expecting anything out of the ordinary as the crew mumbled assumptions of being seated somewhere in a far back corner. However, contrary to all thinking the man led the four to a table that was not isolated but relatively close to the center of the table's area. Seeing the placement, shaking his head, Dave mentioned how he could not get over their having showed such interest in such a group of small time guys.

With a cask of flowers on the table, the attractive waitress distributed glasses of ice water along with the menus while taking requests for beverages. Falling into the atmosphere, the team was soothed by the semi and classical music, even whispering where soon the four found their selves looking at each other as if a bunch of strangers. Responding to the specials, the team advised the waiter of needing time but what was really needed, was time for getting some composure. Far from the kind of life style the four were used to, overhearing about state dignitaries being present, Bill suggested that those type of persons should provide some level as to the high quality of the place. Each one took hold attempting to show some above normal mannerisms but, the present situation was of a different level.

It was where each felt a little out of place. Smiles from some of the people helped calm everyone down while Larry mentioned how Bill had got his wish of not only cloth table settings but with matching cloth napkins complimented with goblets, decorated glasses and genuine dishware. The crew's sit down formal celebration had truly begun with Duck and Bison being at the top with the steak items with prices of everything, including the coffee beyond the anticipated reach. Momentarily a silence took over when all elated, Bill unexpectedly forgot where he was as he blurted out a yell of yahoo and wow-wee.

Showing his face from behind the large menu, Bill looked around the room attempted signaling with his hand but receiving stone face stares from some of the other guests. Along with coaxing from the rest of the crew Bill quietly stood up while motioning quiet apologies. Even the maitre de with a straight face surprised him when he looked over but then smiling gave a short hand signal of, thumbs up. While enjoying a simulated quiet form of clapping from the other three, Bill sat down quickly moving his face so as to hide behind the menu.

Moments later Stan uttered, "now it is you guys asked for it, and now you alls is gonna gets it"!

Quietly without Stan knowing, the waiter had come to stand in back of him while displaying a huge smile but, misunderstanding the other three's motions regarding the waiter, Stan continued quietly stating that Da Ceelabreezson was officially on so, get with the program!. Moving around looking at Stan while nodding his head showing some appreciation, the waiter took everyone's order. Meanwhile, all smiles, Larry advised Stan of the waiter having been in back of him where Stan busted out in a laugh. Responding, other people at neighboring tables having seen the action showed they were not mannequins. as laughs from the close-by tables sounded.

A short time after the waiter brought over a full pot of the coffee, smoothly while reaching into his coat pocket with one hand Larry slowly waved his other arm over the table in circles acting as if looking into a crystal ball.

Wearing a smile from ear to ear, Larry brought out his mini flask of whiskey then inconspicuously after adding a little to his coffee he passed it around under the table. A welcomed surprise to the threesome it added some zip to the coffee while Bill suggested a toast where Dave responded, yes sir friend, you bet. Toasting was done to Tom along with to each one helping each other, and having good luck in Vegas. Then as each became like serious robots, the four offered a joint prayer of thanks to God for the helpful manager, food, everyone's safety, their families and friends.

Soon the happy composed group enjoyed the appetizers and loaves of different breads when as if he hadn't eaten in a week, Larry eagerly ate causing the waiter's eyes to bulge. By the twinkle in the boys' eyes along with happy faces, the waiter must have suspected some alcohol was probably brought along, yet he only smiled while saying nothing. Shortly having agreed of being at the halfway point while noting of the atmosphere, there was no further talk about costs or prices during the meal. Although trips to the restroom brought some frowns from other customers, the matter was dropped as neither wanted to talk about things that could ruin the joyous moment.

Although the steaks ordered were not the most expensive, they were of quality and size that satisfied each one's appetites. Plus having seen other people's dishes it was noted that the chef had added much extra to the vegetables and side dishes where during the second serving Larry's plate had been built up so much there was almost enough for two. With the food perfectly prepared to each ones request along with the pepped up coffee, excellent desserts, easy music and formal atmosphere the entire crew enjoyed a high level of euphoric enjoyment beyond anyone's wildest imaginations.

Later causing a fuss among the four was the waiter setting unexpected rounds of deserts as he noted how they was provided by the management with best of wishes. Then as time went by the maitre de made an appearance at the table when unexpectedly he inquired if he could announce the team's presence, along with where from? Whispering to each other it was taken to mean, he would be speaking to an individual customer that inquired. Late in the evening, the maitre de rang a little a bell of which the four had no idea what was to happen.

Announcing that the hotel had special guests, the maitre de all smiles mentioned a teams presence celebrating their high school graduation. Then responding to a statement from a patron he added how that was right, ladies and gentlemen their not even eighteen yet. Of no consequence, his announcement sounded as if speaking about graduates from one of the local schools but then again the man rang his bell. Loudly he noted for the audience to remember that the four had driven all the way from Pennsylvania where amidst a few moans and sighs, the man belted out each one's name.

Then again, he rang the bell with more enthusiasm while showing a stern face requesting everyone to recall the weeks of deplorable weather where immediately it became quiet when if a dime had fallen on the carpet it would not have been heard. Strongly the man asserted of the having battled the weather while on the way over from one state to another to get to his hotel. Motioning with his arms, the maitre de urged the crew to stand where an excited atmosphere moved everyone hearing how the team was from Chester Pennsylvania.

Unexpectedly the room responded with resounding cheers and much hand clapping from the patrons where such was as if at a sporting event. While one of the patrons questioned what large city the town of Chester was near another inquired of what school had been graduated from? Then a bomb fell when sarcastically another asked whether it was daddy's cars or of the mother's money? Such a question caused Stan's temper where he responded how it was neither but from the crew's hard work and own paid for vehicle. Then, so what is it a fifty-five or fifty-six something, another person inquired? Swiftly caught up in the negativism, Dave sarcastically replied of it being a 48 Nash Ambassador, why you want to trade? Immediately feeling out of place hearing all went quiet as if some terrible words had been spoken the crew sat down.

Thinking was that the manager would be asking them to leave but about that time someone from across the room yelled, hey guys that's great, and good luck to you men. While the maitre de ringing his bell requested the team to stand up again and take a bow. Wow! As if a cloud of bliss erupted from people holding it in, right away nice salutations from other persons filled the room one after another where seeing the maitre de raise his arms, the teary eyed four stood up. Awesome was the response as the room exploded with multiple bouts of applause along with shouts of here, here and yeas. Enjoying a moment of complete euphoria, Bill all smiles mentioned how he wished his mother could have seen the incident.

Instantly surprising the crew was a well-dressed woman at one of the nearby tables who offered a toast to our celebration asserting she had some idea of what the four had gone through. A ripple affect among the crowd ensued where persons at other tables enjoying the woman's words also stood up to participate. Almost that quick, it was everyone in the place ended up standing, clapping, cheering, giving off words of encouragement or waving some signal.

All protocol manners of formality seemed to have vanished and whether the management anticipated the unexpected outburst or not it was obvious for the moment that the customers had taken over. But shortly, with everyone smiling, it was back to business as usual where everyone resumed whatever they were doing. After four hours had gone by, the waiter arrived where during his congratulations he surprised every one as thought was he would be tending with Larry. But instead he presented the book containing the check to Stan where as he opened it, a cough was heard then passing it around.

Heartily yet softly, the four started singing happy times are here again, when upon the words by other patrons, rather than frown some actually nodded with smiles while others waved. All bleary eyed, Larry caught up in the euphoria again passed his small bottle around but only a little of the spirits remained, yet only a few drops for each along with the emotions flowing such was used to allow one last toast of simple good luck with raised cups. Rather than the usual of each paying their-own, the team agreed to split the amount with an equal share of the tip.

As Bill stuffed the book with the money he added the manager's note inside where once the waiter picked it up he quickly left the room leaving everyone wondering. Thinking the party was over the team started to leave only to be stopped by the waiter who had returned. Handing the book back to Bill while extending his thanks for our presence he extended special compliments from the management, adding his wishes for the team's good luck on the way to California. Almost stunned Bill looked to the four unknowing as amazed each was of how the man had remembered what we were about. Then while he walked away the maitre de came over thanking the team for an enjoyable evening. Surprising was his loud tone which was enough for most people in the room to hear.

As if the whole room was waiting for a cue they responded to his arm waving where rounds of best of luck wishes, claps and cheers resounded. Opening the book showing his astonishment found was a large portion of the tip along with almost half of the amount of the bill that was paid.
Surprise it was that the manager had excluded the cost of the desserts with a written note of good luck. Then on the way out the four stopped to question the maitre de about the note where he advised how it was a surprise from the manager. Slowly the man turned ringing his bell as he formally addressed the people, ladies and gentlemen can we have some applause for our guests from Pennsylvania.

Immediately many of the customers stood while waving along with others that hollered good luck, hest of luck as well as other niceties. Hamming it up, Dave and Larry stepped forward taking a bow then while the four waved, emotions soared as the whole place engaged. Even the chefs came out joined by the waitresses, waiters and maitre de where everybody had joined in clapping and hollering with some women even yelling some niceties. It may have been only a single moment for the other people but for the crew it was a moment in time no one ever forgot. Walking back to the room there were few words as each as overwhelmed by what had taken place. Sadly no one thought of calling the local papers to give them the scoop on the great hospitality of the hotel that went out of its way to help with the celebration.

Friday morning of the Twentieth dawned already nearing the end of the month where before checking out the team paid their respects to the manager.

Each noted the professionalism of the staff along with his generosity. Then the assistant manager with teary eyes thanked the team as having received compliments from some of the customers. Nobody ever forgot the people of the Hotel Warwick for it was to the crew the place and time had become a true meeting of friends and not just another building.

Switching time it was for team partners where from then on the teams were made up of Dave with Stan and Larry with Bill. After checking the car over and refilling the ice box, feeling perky Dave's team started.

Finally visiting a few places not seen before the crew stopped at a diner for brunch. Arriving at the table just like any other waitress, she looked on as Dave all excited expressed his cordial welcome of, "hello and good morning gorgeous"! Instantly heads were shaking as the three could only wonder what would follow. But the attractive looking waitress in a business tone ended the scene smartly mentioning her being married with a family and to drop the charm nonsense.

Afterward a stop at the Post Office was made. As Stan filled out a post card he had obtained at the hotel to send home, the others noting it a good idea did likewise. With Stan behind the wheel conversations funneled on getting to Las Vegas where driving westward a push was maintained being restrictive. Stopping only for needed food or nature callings, get to the west coast was the enthusiastic mental calling. From the back seat unexpectedly. Bill hollered for the driver to quick, stop the car! While Stan pulled over, Larry all concerned asked what the matter was as thinking that perhaps the guy was sick. But Bill was all excited where he jumped out of the car yelling how it was noonish.

With innuendos flying, Bill was pressed if he had lost his mind or just sick? Waiting for the right moment, Bill stated how it was time for another celebration as the crew was standing on the highly important road of history. Being the famous, Route Sixty-Six highway, it was originally known during the early thirties of the dust bowl where people used the federal highway as an exodus to travel westward. Showing his history awareness Larry noted how it subsequently came to be known as "the road to opportunity". And wow, did the others climb on the phrase.

Generating spontaneous conversation it was also making toasts for the crew being on the road of opportunity along with the other usual reasons. True it was only a short time since the big celebration but for sure it was noticed a change of how the four were not the same teenage boys that had departed Chester only weeks before. With the weather having turned bearable along with the improved road conditions the crew was soaring. Although there were isolated thunder showers from time to time the group was really appreciative that it was no longer the rain and down pours.

Rolling along on the famous highway, while not highly religious often heard were expressions of prayerful thanks for the improved weather forecasts. Rolling along on the famous highway, while not highly religious, often one expressed sporadic feelings of prayerful thanks for the improved weather forecasts. Shortly while noticing signs along the road that mentioned of specific places such as the hideouts used by the outlaw gang of Jesse James anxiously the crew stopped at a place availing of visitor's information.

Loaded with brochures it was on to Stanton where once arrived excitement stirred. Seeing many artifacts with descriptions relating to the living conditions, clothing tools and weapons set the atmosphere where looking at original clothes, weapons, stores, banks and farm materials the guys became fascinated. Descriptive conditions of the times had struck hard into the intrigue parts of the minds allowing easy relating to the times that advanced the educational level. Then drawing on conclusions along with what was remembered from history classes many comparisons were made even using matters seen in the western movies. Having just had the great experience of the previous celebration time at the Warwick, along with the sites that were seen, the occasion at Stanton was just what the four needed to put their minds back in previous century.

Back on the road, shortly the crew entered the town of Rolla having history of an early highly used railroad spot during its time period but it was not one of the planned stops. So only a quick drive thru was done where afterward, with many miles have gone by, needing some space a stop was made at a diner. Following a walk with some trotting to loosen up it was cold sandwiches and sodas purchased to go then once again, back in the wagon. Making good time the miles went by until a tiny roadside appeared where curiosity grabbed Larry who yelled for the driver to park it.

At first sight, thoughts were of a vegetable, fruit or candy stand, but the small shack also had a bunch of flags waving which read fireworks. Once Dave and Larry got to the stand it was found to be all about fireworks. Evidently, the empty fruit crates and vegetable boxes had been just a front where the small place offered everything except military missiles. Being about the upcoming Fourth of July only weeks away yet none of the four had given any thought to the holiday. At first there were no intentions to buy anything but Larry started buying some torpedoes and Roman candles.

Dave seeing what Larry had bought he jumped in where inquisitively Bill raised the question to Larry and Dave of what their intentions were, but only received smiles along with the response of, don't know yet. So, Bill not wanting to be left out did the same leaving Stan standing around dumb founded.

No doubt the stop in Stanton had somewhat affected the minds when minutes later the three surrounded Stan while resting their arms on his shoulders. Displaying happy grins they uttered kind words of being buddies and friends until they persuaded him to join them in buying some of the items. But, it was not his idea, stating his feelings of not worth spending money for. Yet it was all about the guys where Stan gave in buying a small amount similar to what the others had purchased. Then he also purchased some blockbusters where responding Dave had to do the same. Of course that caused the remaining two to do the same. Stan was not happy about the stop or the spending of money on such items where he belted out how the guys had turned into a bunch of childish hoodlums.

With dangerous toys it was wasting money they might need later. Meanwhile Larry suggested having a contest where Dave and Bill suggested it sounded great but, shaking his head Stan only countered for the guys to stop some place to pick up some taffies or rubber duckies. Miles down the road, Larry suggested a war of two against two where Bill all enthused replied how the four could have their own shootout at the, Ok Corral. Bursting out in a laughing frenzy, Stan asserted how he thought the three was ready for the funny farm.

Perhaps the visit to St. Louis and then the outlaws' place allowed some wild thinking, but whatever it was the crew had become a bunch of unknown character. Seeming it was the crew lost in the past, didn't know how to handle their selves. About then a place was spotted of a very high dirt mound a little over fifteen feet high. Due the conditions of the area, it was understood to be the result of road work.

Right away, Larry urged Dave to pull over and park where immediately Bill and Larry jumped out, yelling as a couple of loonies of them being the Americans with the other two being the Russians! Upon reaching the top, Larry and Bill wasted no time in starting to shower the other two with the roman candles. "Take cover"! Dave yelled when just then along with tossing a few of the small fire crackers Larry yelled for the two to give up. Dropping behind the side of the car for cover, Dave looked at Stan as he commented how he thought it was their turn!

Grinning while lighting one item then another, Dave all hyped up blurted out to go get em, where violently as Dave threw his firecrackers at the top of the hill, Stan joined in as it became one volley after another. Amidst the action, Stan stated how it appeared that the other two had been contemplating such a situation when agreeing with his partner, it became as quickly as Dave lit a few different items he tossed one after the other. At one point, Stan remarked how he was pretty good at that, suggesting how Dave may do well in the army! Right away Dave replied how it sounded good so let's do it like the army taking turns so as not give them a chance.

Before long all four were handling the torpedoes along with the blockbusters as if tossing hamburgers while shooting birthday candles. One time a few went off closer to Bill than what he expected causing a scare where loudly he hollered for the guys to take it easy as what the heck you guys trying to do, kill us? Mayhem had taken over where responding, Dave yelled back at the top of his lungs, how it was their idea calling them dummies while asking if they wanted to give up? Suddenly the few minutes of fun blew up into a situation way past what either had intended.

All craziness had let loose as Stan yelled for Dave to watch out, as one of the torpedoes exploded close to the underneath of the car. Although it was not near the gas tank, both understood the dangers. Seriousness had stopped the fun. The situation changed into something neither had thought of. Upset at what happened, Dave shouted for the other two to be careful as the gasoline area of the car was off limits. However, thinking only of their strategic position, Bill demanded that the other two reds should give up. Angry at the reply Dave stated, bunk to Stan noting it was their idea so, lets let them have it. Upset at what had taken place, Dave all fired up stood up confronting the other two yelling back for them to give up. Right away, Stan yelled out that it was blitz time, throwing stuff at a faster rate.

Throwing while ducking, the Americans wildly threw a few of the projectiles which went over close to the highway. Unexpectedly, one of the cars swerved then pulled over. As the two on the hill started laughing, all funny stuff stopped when a man suddenly jumped out of the car displaying his rifle. Startling the four, the man took aim at the two closest. Immediately, Larry yelled for the man to hold up. Appreciate your understanding he hollered, where there was an accidental misfire of a firecracker. Quickly attempting to help, Bill yelled how it was a Roman candle gone wild. In reply the angry man replied how he thought that he heard gunfire where Dave responded being from a torpedo type firecracker.

Quickly Stan followed mentioning how there were no guns while offering an apology. As the man walked closer he questioned the age group where seeing the four he asserted criticism advising how the team wasn't far enough away and to be more careful. After unloading his rifle in full view, the man drove off. Realizing how the small episode of fun could have caused someone to get hurt, a happy mood of destruction took place ending the occasion of fun. Maybe a lack of adult supervision but who's to know an adult wouldn't have joined in.

With Dave at the helm, and the two in the rear asleep the crew reached Springfield in late afternoon. After a quick drive thru the city and picking up of literature it was another time at a diner. Later more places were visited including a historical railroad museum with an old restored caboose. However, the peak entertainment was the site where Wild Bill Hickok had his first shootout. Reviewing photos, clothes and guns sparked the imagination where visiting an ice cream parlor all excited Bill mentioned about robbing one of the casinos. With places similar to Philadelphia and Chester it was back on the road.

Arriving in the tiny town of Carthage a visit was made at an ancient county courthouse then with nothing else of interest it was back on the road again. Although thunderstorms had been forecasted only an occasional short down pour or burst from drifting clouds were experienced. Then as the weather improved the team continued to downplay any negative talk about the weather. At the next city the driving team switched seats where Bill took over. Joplin was a big but quiet lead and zinc ore mining city that the notorious Bonnie and Clyde couple had routed. Old buildings along with an old hotel allowed savoring of the rustic atmosphere.

Displays of many old photos along with the clothing people wore in those days and guns along with the couple's young age trapped the crew's minds in the times of the era. Then being at an actual location it allowed use of the crew's imaginations. Car chases along with the bank robberies recalled from history along with what had been seen at the movies enabled terrific forming of mental pictures. The history bug had really set in where it could have caused a stay. But at an ice cream parlor recalled was not to deviate from the plan so, with cartons of bulk ice cream, soda pop, chips and pretzels, in good spirits it was back on the highway. So fired up was Bill and Dave they wanted to go to Wichita Kansas but the other two declined. As Nashie rolled west into the sunset another day of exciting education came to a happy end.

The Twenty-First day of June when easily noticed was how each had showed a change in attitude. Dave's team had taken the wheel with Stan his copilot. Travel literature and maps allowed understanding of how far behind schedule the crew was. Coming to grips with the problem changes were forced where places had to have time reduced while others needed to be eliminated, but which? Originally traveling time was based on averaging 55 mph on the main highways with the assumption of clear weather along with good road conditions. After all it was summer time.

No one anticipated the adversity received once past the central part of Ohio. The flooded road conditions often kept speeds in the 20- 30 mph range. While in other instances of very high water traveling was limited to only 5 - 15 mph. Lost travel time makeup just was not happening. As if at the races Dave drove, till he reached the town of Miami. Contrary to the usual way, he went past the first diner suggesting that it being a big town they didn't need to stop, But not so sure, Larry asked, what if there is no place on the other end. Then passing a side street a restaurant was found which happened to be the last eatery on the route going out of the town.

While enjoying oversized hot biscuits along with large sized omelets there were also choices of side dishes. All excited by the moment, Dave stood up displaying smiles as he uttered how with good friends, great food, the weather improving and everyone healthy, what more could we all ask for. Instantly the four let loose with a barrage of clapping that drew interest from others. It was only a small matter to the others but to the four while departing with coffee and Danishes, the Chester Eagles Boys Club had experienced a state of exuberance.

Then traveling southwest on the highway nonstop, Nashie ran smooth and with the weather improved while passing around a couple of beers along with snacks the miles went by. Often mentioned was how it was noticed the land changing as if in a different country. Although Tulsa was originally selected for a stay over it was changed to a short visit. Short stops were made at entertainment places and eating establishments but museums along with Indian and other stores of historical matter were observed from the outside.

However, the retailer, Lyon's Indian Store caused the crew to venture inside. A fascinating time of education on life styles and means was enjoyed as fully described was the dress, tools, housing means and weapon varieties of uses. Also the described living conditions helped understand the emotional feelings and traditions as well as the peoples' strong character. Such information along with the crew's firsthand experience with the land and weather allowed the team to truly relate to what the living past may have been like.

Once Stan took over the driving holding steady on the accelerator, the miles went as well as time until relief demanded a stop. Observing the area, Stan started waving his arms along with yelling out a few chants while doing some sort of a Indian dance. Full of expression while doing a turn he pointed to the wide-open spaces while suggesting for everyone to look around. Not having any idea what Stan was about, the other three only blurted out innuendos of his being out of mind.

All serious, Stan responded how there would be no going until the three did a full turn. Finally with Stan refusing to budge, Dave turned then so did the other two. Seeing no reactions Stan asked if the area appeared like that which may be found on the moon. In a flash while the three pinned him against the car suggesting he had put one over on them, showing his fist, Larry asked if he would like a shot to the moon. But Stan all confident quietly asked if some of the things visible resembled meteor craters. Once Larry and Dave took another look admitted was seeing the possibilities where the comradely took over. Subsequently discussions started on meteors, volcanoes and even space travel where Bill mentioned that being two thousand miles from home to him it seemed like driving on the moon.

Stopping at an auto station while a full check of everything was done the heavy straight fifty weight oil was added to curb oil consumption along with helping gas mileage. Tis a shame but, neither of the four gave any thought to bother with the oil filter. Back on the road, stops were made at eatery places but everything was bought take out. Then when all was going well Stan pulled over seriously noting about not feeling well. While pushing the three away he went to sleep where they decided to wait and see.

As Bill's team took over Dave hollered, ok, let's go guys! In a hurry without thinking Bill attempted to pull back on the highway. Whoosh, it was when suddenly a vehicle traveling at a high rate of speed with horn blowing swerved to avoid Nashie. Immediately as Bill turned back off the highway Dave mentioned how it was a good thing there were no cars traveling in the opposite direction. While Bill was trying to get his breath, Larry shouted out, "driver, follow that car"! With the three laughing Bill replied, ok boss, but with what? How funny, Stan yelled adding how he wanted some peace and quiet. Heading for the metropolis, it was believed the road may have been originally used as some sort of boundary or dividing line separating the Indian nations of Osage and Cherokee.

SEGMENT – 11.   Oklahoma City, where cowgirls were attractive women, then with genuine cowboys along with the good looking, true Indians, all were part of the population. Some visitors' places along with materials from Tulsa allowed usage as a time saving guide. Wow! Was all the four could say feeling they had truly arrived in the old west. As Larry assumed the driving it was thought the city in size was close to that of Philadelphia. But fro dinning to the shopping places, nightclubs and historical sites were all different from those seen elsewhere. Indian stores, grilles and steak houses were not only different in style but also in food preparation and service.

Suggested by people regarding a good eatery was the Cattlemen's Steakhouse but it was located on the outskirts town. With the aesthetics, foot stomping and yodeling along with the good music, snacks and cold beverages created were happy dancing periods everywhere making each place enjoyable.

At the Iguana Lounge sampling everything on the menu was done while saving the appetites. Then seeing the guys sampling of tacos, enchiladas and Chimmychangas along with the side bits the waitresses noted their curiosity that livened the meal. Seen were enough motels, cottages and mobile home parks where it was guessed they could have housed the entire city of Chester. While the temperatures climbed into the high nineties the residents took it in stride with their humidifiers or air conditioners. Having parks back home none were visited saving time. Then aware of the long drive ahead a service station stop was made for performing a double check of everything.

Then it was on to the Cattlemen's steakhouse where Bill remarked how the people weren't kidding about being almost out of the area. Back in the old west it was a cattle-feeding area originally known as stockyard city. Used as a storage and holding area it was also a market place for the cattle. Seeing the place divided into several dining areas, Bill suggested the building was larger than an opera house.

While Stan signed the log book for customers to put the names, city and state observations of other customers' tables were made. Initial thoughts were keeping costs down but Stan wanted a full meal where after seeing other customer dishes it was decided on taking full advantage of whatever was offered. Large menus required thinking because spelling was the same but the meanings were different. Choice of sizes was the children's, small, medium and big man's size or large plus there was the extra large. How much bigger, could large get, Dave and Bill needing to see took a walk looking at other customer's plates.

Also, the waitress advised that a medium was about the size of a very large steak back east. Larry having ordered the large was surprised seeing how his cut of meat took up the entire plate that was large enough to hold a dozen large sticky buns. But there were no complaints as Larry was happy as a rat in bacon/cheese patch. Meanwhile the other three was in seventh heaven with their medium size. Then with the large beverages, biscuits, onion rolls, home fries with onions and peppers, sides of vegetables plus chips, and dips the four had their hands full.

When the waitress stopped by watching Larry dismantle his last bits, showing her wide-open big eyes the two bodies eyeballed each other. Bending close she uttered politely how he must have really been hungry, huh big fella, where the three broke out in a laugh. Using his napkin to wipe his chin while looking up Larry, in a gruff tone of southern draw blurted out a simple, yepper sister, why sure enough babe, that was some real good grub, just like back on the ranch! Startled, the waitress backed up with her face aghast. Softly, she questioned if he really had a ranch in the area. We knew he had her going, looking for some fun, but Larry replied how it was just a figure of speech.

Later contemplated was getting back on the road however, unbeknownst to the team, the eatery had its own mind regarding when new customers leave. Returning with the check, the sociable waitress suddenly became the leader of the band. While raising an arm she semi turned to the other customers, almost scaring the daylights out of the team. Unaware of what to expect all the four could do was watch. Loudly while clapping her hands she hollered if the customers were ready. As the place went quiet she gave the team a short look then belted how the four was going to Amarillo all the way from Chester, Pennsylvania.

At once a customer responded singing how it was a long, long way to Amarillo. hen others joined in where shortly the whole place was singing the tune. But smiling, Bill mentioned how it was only two thirds of a day's drive. Sudden a unexpectedly, his remark seemed to be a cue as the place had transformed into a fun house. As the gorgeous waitress hollered out reminding of going to Amarillo a customer yelled that he was from Scranton. Shaking his head Dave responded, oh well guys its doozzen it again as here wees goesss again. Several people started dancing.

As if in a parade, clapping their hands while singing using another melody of it's a long way to Tipparraree, But they also replaced it with Amarillo. Shortly a huge applause erupted where the waitress put her book away as if something contagious had affected everyone. Cheerful people suddenly gone bonkers they sang, it's a long way from Chester Pa, it's a long way from home connecting with it's a long way to Amarillo, it's a long way to go, etc., etc. From a time of all quiet with low music the whole place erupted singing, while stomping their feet or toasting as the place maintained a state of joyous mayhem.

Our waitress had joined with other waitresses and waiters swept away dancing with a couple of patrons. While some customers were chanting while standing and clapping the place was wild with people dancing around tables and stomping their feet in rhythm. Caught up in the joyous frenzy of the crowd's momentum the team's emotions were almost close to flying. Amidst the pandemonium, after several minutes the eatery returned to some sort of normalcy. Then while leaving a few customers hollered, God bless you guys while others yelled out, good luck men. Full of smiles, the four returned their acknowledging with much waving of hands and clapping.

Decided was that non-stop driving straight through should be the way with driving limited to three and half-hours. While Larry started the driving, knowing there was no other big city until reaching the center of the panhandle a stop at a grocery store was made. Luncheon meats, cheese, bread and fixins to make sandwiches along with sodas and chips were purchased. All hyped up Larry yelled his expression of hi yo Nashie, away big girl! Then some miles later Stan caused Larry to pull over where the road was of higher ground. Hollering for the guys to look, standing in awe the crew saw one of those magnanimous spots in the universe as if a person could almost see into forever.

Speechless, the land being so flat seen were the clouds hanging, hinging like to a curtain edge while the very large sun put on its show as if sitting on the very edge of a stage. With the rays of the sun reflected on the clouds the only thing missing for the show was music along with the hymns. While staring, Larry suggested how he could not imagine anyone not thinking there was a creator. What allowed the superb majestic view was that there were no obstructions such as tall buildings, or factories. Later while making a stop, Dave's team took the wheel. Having interacted with real people showing down to earth earnest feelings was a help for the crew to relate to the people. However considering the weather and land conditions, to live in the area was definitely not in anyone's thinking.

Awhile after Stan had taken over the driving the crew reached the small town of El Reno. Begun as an important railroad town it was a crossroad of route sixty-six and the Chisholm Trail but there was no visiting. Later with Bill driving it was the same in the town of Clinton where it was passed through. After Bill it was Larry behind the wheel then, later the two teams exchanged seats. Past the two a.m. hour noticed were sections of large cities that had became totally dark while certain businesses and houses turned off only some of their lights. It was similar to being on a train due to the tiny lights in the distance going by swiftly. Later with Stan driving another day of the trip had ended when for safety so not to push it, found was a place to park and get some sleep.

The new day was the Twenty-Second Day of June. While the midway had been reached minds was about the car's age along with the weight it was carrying. Maintained was the odometer held below the fifty-nine mile per hour mark while occasionally a stepping on the gas, was done for the purpose of blowing out the smoke, preventing the spark plugs from getting fowled. During one of those times the Burma Shave signs started to appear again. While they took the bore out of the co-pilot's seat times of high entertainment was watching a vehicle go passed at such a high rate of speed where Ole Nashie would shake from side to side from the breeze of the car going by. Void of any streetlights along with no moon, it would get absolutely pitch black dark where being unfamiliar with the road all driving became a chore.

Reaching the town of McLean the guys changed places where Larry resumed the driving. Founded as a train watering and switching spot during the war years it was used as a World War Two German prisoner of war camp. While the three quarter point was reached the evening had passed into the night. Then in the morning with Stan, then driving he yelled that brake time was over. As Bill took the helm he remarked how Stan was a slave driver having no pity, only wanting to keep moving. Later having reached the outer city limits the driver hastily parked the car where the four zonked out.

SEGMENT - 12.   Early morning, the anxious crew drove into Amarillo Texas the Twenty-Fourth. A Catholic Church was arrived at just in time for Mass where the service had already begun. Besides a historical religious experience it was also an antiquated church that enabled some learning of older times. Afterward it was to take advantage of southwestern meals at one of the several grilles. Known as the center of the Panhandle it was the largest city on route sixty-six.

Then it was off to Canyon where noticed were the various automobile camps plus cottage type motels and countless motels of all different sizes plus lodging and cabin camps. America's second largest canyon had cliffs several hundreds of feet high containing various granite and other metals such enabled the cliffs to give off a glisten in the sunlight. A visit to an enormous historical museum was awesome having everything from geology and history to archeology and artifacts regarding Indian and western art.

Although the main profession was still the cowboy, cowgirls were also found to be in the trade. Then with rodeo and amusement places, numerous antique and material shops filled the city. Later visited was a place that had an early genuine chuck wagon luncheon. Naturally with each hankering for a true western experience the team enjoyed an out on the range type meal event. Of wooden construction with a canvas top, the old vintage wagon matched the meal.

Portrayed of being on a cattle drive it was just beans, coffee, beans, bread, bacon, more beans, slices of steak or rabbit, biscuits, home fries and onions with more beans. Then while eating on metal plates with metal cups while being in the outdoors enhanced the atmosphere. Seeing many cows and horses around plus a horse drawn wagon it became evident that in those days there wouldn't have been much to write about if on a cattle drive. Larry all stuffed, retook the whee where it was seventy miles to the border with another hundred miles to the next targeted town.

Constantly it was to push, drive, mush, and go, go, go. Time passed where

Stan assumed the driving until later when Dave took over. At some point upon reviewing the maps the team discovered they had made an error. Rather than a hundred and seventy miles it was figured to be another three hundred miles to Albuquerque. At one point the guys were asking whether the inside of the car had gotten smaller. With the three hour rule on driving in play the miles went by at a steady clip. Only stopping at a gas station, a diner for the personals or to change crews it was a steady diet of driving. Over the dales up the hills and down the crew traveled the highway. Spectacularly different dazzling scenery not seen elsewhere put the crew into a spell bound mind from time to time. When the highway took the crew into the mountains the team of Bill and Larry took over.

Arriving in Tucumcari, New Mexico hot weather was the call. With highs in the mid to upper nineties any place with air conditioning was welcomed. Yet the area did provide morning lows in the high sixties which allowed good sleeping. A small town with a small diner but for the team it was allowing some mental relaxing. Not expecting anything out of the ordinary an interesting time it was seeing new names of some items. All smiles, Bill asked whether those things were some form of building blocks. Done with sampling, the team couldn't wait for the basics of large tasty omelets, potatoes with onions and large biscuits along with good coffee. Then how nice it was that the cute waitress of Mexican descent with a great personality helped the enjoyment with some humor. Missed pronouncing Chicharrrones since never having heard the word before it was all up to the imagination. Although bland, the dipping sauce helped the taste but the tortaleedes were better tasting where the culinary delight for the crew was a nice change from the driving drudge.

Back on the highway Nashie rolled until reaching the town of Santa Rosa. Visiting was limited to reading the historical signs also making a thorough check of Nashie. Sometime after Stan and Dave's team took over it was up, around and down as the crew went rocking around inside. Occasionally it was like being in a sixteen-foot boat out in two-foot ocean swells. Originally designed to be used for the average roads Nashie was not but like a tank for taking to the mountains while being overloaded where the first big mountain was a true adventure of itself.

Finally, as the crew reached Albuquerque pulling Nashie over, Dave mentioned of his feeling dizzy. With him and Stan in the back resting Bill and Larry's team took over with Bill driving into the city. A great place for American history founded in the early seventeen hundreds, the American Pueblo Indians were the primary people. Of very distinctly attractive features the proud people, mostly wore plain clothing. The Indian center enabled communication where the close by Indian village allowed some real comprehension. Good bar-b-q places along with other places serving steak and other southwestern foods alerted the team of the general appetite. Many historical signs told of its significance where some of the city's buildings hadn't changed since they were first built centuries ago.

With Larry behind the wheel visited was the El Patio Café and then the El Sombrero Restaurante where enjoyed was the delicious Sandia wine which name was derived from the Mountains. While Stan was a Vodka, Jack Daniels, brandy, Ballentine Ale and Pabst beer person, the others enjoyed the sour mash, bourbon and named beers, yet all appreciated the good cool wine. Great Burritos, Chimmychangas and tacos were enjoyed but during one moment, Dave had everyone rolling in hysterics when referring to the Chimmychangas as some sort of barber tool. Later the crew retired at a reasonable motel where each enjoyed a fresh shower along with washing of the dirty clothing. Ending the evening was to practice with the Black Jack card playing.

Sporting clean attire, with Stan behind the wheel it was breakfast then on to the Laguna Pueblo Mission followed by a visit to Rio Rancho. After observing petro glyphs, drawings and other written materials along with enjoying the warm people it was back on the road. Reaching the town of Grants the crew pulled into a truck stop where afterward traveling took the crew through a mountainous area. But Gallup was a challenge coping with the temps in the very high nineties where riding became very uncomfortable. While much use of the ice was made often noted was how driving through the days of constant rain compared to the heat was a picnic.

Crossing the continental divide the big event caused a short stop where a toast was made commemorating the occasion. Generated was much discussion relating to the area having been crossed by covered wagon trains, horsemen, scouts and those on horseback. Later the crew ventured through the Navajo/Pueblo Nation area where seeing sites not expected was at a trading post. Fascinating was the crew's discussion of their experience having to pick and crawl just to get their journey developed. Along with getting Nashie which helped their being able to relate to the Indians unfair despicable treatment.

If all the pictures were squashed together they would never do the Indian people justice. Not only beautiful, but the Indian people were found to be of great character, good looks and stature as well as having great personalities. Often from the radio was heard a chance of severe thunderstorms with warnings of strong winds. However, no credit was given to the high wind warning as assumed to be something found in a thunderstorm. Alarmed? Not the crew as what did the teenagers who hadn't been in the area before know?

Unexpectedly the crew found it-self caught in one of the windstorms. Somewhat like being in a sandblasting tunnel but the four had no idea what they were about to experience. It appeared suddenly like a cloud moving allowing the sun's rays until it hit. Combined heat along with the voluminous bits of sand-dirt moved by the wind it was not a time of comedy or enjoyment. No such thing as stepping outside for clearing the windshield. And forget any turning on of the wipers as it was muck all over or stepping outside to use the hand for clearing the windshield. Of course driving like walking was impossible then after the exciting period passed, it was noticed the paint in spots had been removed clear to the metal while in other spots it had been left tissue paper thin. Easy it was to realize how such weather would affect persons as well as property and what really catches people by surprise is the lacking of any real warnings.

Hot weather was one thing but, wherever the team stopped to eat it was also hot food such as hot beverages, hot peppers, hot sauce, hot plates, and hot cups. During one stop Bill mentioned how he was beginning to feel like a hot sausage. New Mexico with its quaint towns and historical Indian villages combined with its scenic wonders kept all four fascinated. Humorously Dave exclaimed how he would never again speak against cow manure odors as it was great people in the newer ole west. Leaving New Mexico was done in a sad state of mind as much heart emotional joy was felt with really good and soft people

SEGMENT 13. Rolling along on the famous Mother Road highway heading into Arizona, Larry commented on the beauty of nature and there being no charge for the view. Just before the town of Holbrook a stop was made close to the Petrified Forest National Park. Fossilized wood of millions of years in age along with the displays of ruins from human's that had lived thousands of years ago took time that caused making a mistake in planning. Time was wasted traveling to the Painted Desert because nobody gave any thought about needing sunlight to create the activity of the sun reflecting the rock changes shape and colors. Then arriving at Geronimo's Trading Post was also a waste of time since it was closed. With other places closing it was decided not to wait around till morning.

Miles later, the crew arrived in Winslow where after asking people for suggestions it was on to the Falcon Restaurant. Hungry while looking to shake the blues Stan decided to have some fun exploded by Bill's efforts. While sampling everything, an older but cordial waitress provided service where upon seeing she became inquisitive regarding the switching portions of the foods she inquired if there was a problem. Speaking with authority, Bill formally introduced everyone gaining the waitress' full attention of bulging eyes. Short of a speech he focused on security and how they were unable to divulge details because it was a secret government project. Attempting to ask a question, Stan interrupted the attractive waitress asserting the team was from the University hall of codified biological warfare studies. Displaying a face of intrigue she blurted out suggestively asking that we were really not kidding. While Dave added how the four was a special operations team working on the top secret project Larry and Stan whispered about sensitive material. Surprisingly the curious woman raised her arms while blurting her query of, what out here? Yes, Stan replied because of the place's location.

Shortly, Dave and Bill stood up attempting to rectify the joke asserting how they had said too much. But struggling with her curiosity the woman responded being sorry as she should have minded her own business. Feelings turned sour where Dave and Bill attempted to tell the truth wanting to rectify the wrong that was started. But, the harder they tried the harder she rebuffed their attempts. Feeling bad almost beside his self, realizing how misled the woman had been taken, Stan in an apologetic tone admitted they had been feeding her the bull. More remarks by Stan followed of pleading, almost begging for her understanding along with the other three commenting. Moments later that seemed like an hour she finally mentioned of her understanding. Then turning a mad face she showed a large frown while she angrily exclaimed that it was not Halloween and her place was not a zoo.

Giving Dave a wicked stare she asserted how it was not a nice thing to have done. Almost in tears she snubbed her nose walking away while the four noted their bad feelings. Upon leaving, as the waitress provided the check, Stan complimented her on the professional way she handled the matter. Then as the other three gave adulations with smiles displaying a smug the waitress noted being impressed by Stan's gift of gab but that she had taken all in stride. Following a silent pause by each, a moment of gleeful laughter ensued with clapping by all four. Feeling a closeness Stan threw her a kiss while stating of her being a terrific lady.

Traveling, the crew headed for the nationally known meteor crater but when arrived seen was a large hole in the earth. Made by a meteor thousands of years ago the crew saw, and disappointed as not having technical necessity departed. Drive and sleep became the routine where keeping Nashie moving was the priority. Even talk had been reduced as focus had switched to Vegas when shortly another day had gone by which had been most interesting as was sleeping in the car.

Early morning started by making a pit stop where the teams' seating was changed to Larry's team. The off, on, sleep and drive was taking its toll where everyone moved as if in a semi stupor yet, it remained to keep Nashie moving. Up and up then down and up again through the mountainous areas the four drove but forced to stop from time to time as the views were simply awesome.

Totally worn out, the crew pulled into Flagstaff Arizona. Fueling up at the Cannon Padre Service Station while inspecting the car more used motor oil was picked up. Then as Bill drove on a tour of the city it was considered comparable to Upper Darby in size. Following the tour a stop at the Lumber Jack cafe allowed enjoying cold beverages along with washing up where cooling down helped to put everyone in check.

For lunch it was at a place where enjoyed was a new delicacy, the Sonoran dog. Found was the new being similar to the old corn dog as constructed of beef franks wrapped in bacon with pinto beans, tomato, onions, mustard and mayonnaise. Yet, along with the city's Flagstaff Beer the meal became a true pleasure. Expressed was renting a motel room as the four were beat but being so close to Vegas no one wanted to needlessly spend money. With happy spirits and Bill at the wheel, he and Larry enjoyed doing the driving because of the challenge. No nonsense application of driving skills became essential due to the ongoing windings of the road.

SEGMENT 14. Time having passed it was also passing through the town of Williams. Then shortly the crew stopped in Seligman at a place called the "Snow Cap". Original thinking was only to accommodate Mother Nature but the sights and smells of the food was too much to resist. Good chiliburgers along with yummy milkshakes, and ice cream sodas got everyone refreshed. Also it was educational since with numerous pictures hanging on the walls it was learned how the town was the home of actor Andy Devine.

Inquiring it was found the town of Oatman being the famous actor's residence was only a short detour. Caught up in the hype all beverages and food were changed to go to be finished in the car. Ole Nashie hadn't even reached the second gear when the crew was greeted with signs limiting the speed that caused a slow down. Moving along but in the slow gears unable to see any reasoning the crew could only think it being a speed trap. Suddenly, unexpected several attractive, good-looking, handsomely dressed Indian women appeared running alongside the car. Smiling while vocally making their pitches where the four understood the opportunities presented.

Being leery not knowing the area or what might have been lurking in the caves behind the women's intentions plus not having extra money, no stop was made. Politely smiling while thanking the young women with waves of goodbye, the crew moved on. Heading for the actor's residence everyone was in a state of anticipation. But, a time later disinterest surfaced when mentioned that none of the team knew him. Considered a waste of time Nashie was turned around to head for the town Oatman was only of two city blocks where the old, gruff and shabby place was at one time an ongoing mining town. However it turned to be a great time to be there since contrary to the shiny towns painted in Hollywood it presented a realistic version of what the old towns used to be like. Just in time we pulled in as high entertainment started with a shootout. A wild western type gun battle in the street had started. Acted by players wearing attire worn relative to the respected era along with the conditions of the buildings helped to present a true state of reality. Great acting along with real guns using blanks rather than live ammunition was great. Although the literature didn't give it as much credit as it should have the concept was impressive, well above stage acting and better than most movies.

Rolling along, how sad the team was leaving the states of Arizona and New Mexico. Route sixty-six the Mother Road of Main Street of America where Barstow was departed heading for the gaming city. With Dave driving, the crew departed then unknown why but, a stop was made at Kingman. A short recalling of their sticking together seemed to matter as the guys were aware of what they had left behind. Savoring the moment a toast of much affection was made to each other with special wishes of success. Only a few minutes in time but, to the four it was truly special as emotions of comrade exuberance flowed like water. Even a prayer was offered in thanks for the team's health and safety.

Then it was proceeding on Route Ninety-Three where the convenient road led directly to Boulder Dam. With the sun beating down, the temperatures inside of the car felt as if close to boiling. Comically Larry commented his understanding of how a roasting chicken felt. Parking was off the road located on the bridge top of the dam. While the three stayed on the lakeside, Stan went to the other side curious about experiencing the slope. Feeling the moving air dynamics, he generated some thick mucus then spit it over the side to see what would happen. Although the wet wad fell for a long distance, not knowing what to expect Stan was surprised when suddenly feeling the air current reverse direction.

The updraft on his face became similar to having his head sticking out of a moving car window. Stunned, Stan could only watch as the fast moving updraft carried the saliva batch over the dam's top. Unfortunately a man was standing a few yards away wearing some sort of a fruit hat occupied with taking pictures. Totally unaware of what was taking place, the glob sailed well above the heads, finally dropping directly on top of the man's hat. Astonished at what had just occurred while feeling terrible Stan thought of trying to explain to the man. But, having considered his own young age and not interested in any animosity he said nothing. Quickly he took a picture of the man for any future reference then returned to the other side for rejoining the other three. Obvious it was at lakeside that the fishing bug had bitten yet, passing up a day of fishing the four headed inside.

First was the walking tour of the huge inside structure visually reviewing its awesome dynamos connecting electrical means and operating mechanical apparatuses? Then along with seeing the film, the tour enabled a comprehensive understanding of how complex the place truly was. Much more sophisticated was realized than what any person could understand by viewing motion pictures or photos.

Knowing it was only about thirty miles after the dam, a rush of adrenaline was pumping where feelings of anticipation turned to high expectation. Closer the crew got, a person could have thought the four was a bunch of five year olds expecting Santa Claus. While the air was hot so was he car that had the crew boiling. How much more heat could there have been? Shucks, Bill hollered it's a dry heat, so they say, where Dave responded asserting how if there was the humidity the crew would be like eggs in the pan.

Strike up the band! Hurry up, call the army, alert the police and notify the gambling halls as the ornery, boisterous and wild youngsters of the Chester Eagles Boys Club were on their way! All the way from Chester Pennsylvania, the team of seventeen year olds was anxious to engage the money town.

Although the two had practiced playing black jack daily having realized the team was going, for Dave and Larry it was just another means of having some fun gambling.

Due the lack of funds cautiously the guys tried to think of every thing so not to lose their selves in the atmosphere. Little discussion there was but it was heavy where it was agreed that any stay in the area would be limited to overnight. Although the boys assumed they were ready for a normal day little did they have any idea of what they would actually do.
To them it was new, different and a place they had never been to or any place like it. But each had their own ideas as to what they would be doing. So much for human thinking.

SECTION III

THE HEAT,

DESTINATION

AND FESTIVITIES

CHAPTER SEVEN

POLICE ESCORT, SIN CITY, HOLLYWOOD AND MONASTERY.

Afternoon when Dave sounded the alarm belting out, "oh crap now what"? Unexpectedly Nashie had been forced to come to a stop. Flagged over to the side of the road, thoughts ran wild as the other three asked him what he did. A couple of motorcycle cops had blocked the way a good distance before the town's entrance. One of the cops talked on his microphone while walking to the car, where the other looked inside while asking the driver for identification and driver's license. As the one on the passenger's side ordered everyone to get out tempers flared. As the cop was asking Dave where going, Larry, all irritated assertively asked what the heck the problem was. Just about then an unmarked police car pulled alongside the motorcycles. Showing strain, Dave had forced himself into the patrolman's face asking why the stop. Perhaps the cop could have taken it in stride showing some understanding but, instead of being courteous he chose to blow up where in an angry tone he started demeaning the young man.

Meanwhile the officer in civilian clothes was waving his arms hollering to stop. Reaching the patrolman the man pulled the cop aside putting a halt to the patrolman. While the officer took the document papers with us seeing the patrolman being questioned, it became obvious the officer had authority being in charge. Temper showing, Stan sarcastically questioned if such was the hospitality they provided all new visitors to their city? Introducing himself, the Lieutenant showed his credentials. Then politely asked what the guys' alma mater was where noted was going into the military. After that it was where the team was going and for what purpose. Boisterously the four responded, showing their anger wanting to know what the driver did wrong or what the problem was. All calm, the officer seeing the four overheated, sweaty and angry explained the town's policy. Their job was to check all new visitors, as intended was to keep any potential troublemakers out.

Walking around, the Lieutenant looked inside the trunk as Dave angrily pressed whether he was searching for a place to plant some false stuff? Understanding the insult, the officer quietly replied of him only doing his job where Bill replied asking if they would like to look inside the shoes. Right away one of the patrolmen arrogantly asserted how the boys really thought they were so tough and smart. If the man intended on starting something physical he definitely hit the right note as it caused Larry and Dave's tempers to move them in front of the patrolman's face. Quickly as Bill and Stan moved to their two partner sides, in a flash the officer seeing the situation out of hand yelled for everybody to shut the heck up while moving in between the group.

Angrily, Dave provokingly asked whether all the town people were stupid like them? Responding, one of the patrolmen stated how they could not allow the four within the city's limits in their present appearance. Almost boiling, Stan followed with the assertion of what the hell kind of inhospitable inconsiderate animals are you freaks anyway. As the patrolman approached Stan, immediately the officer hollered that's enough. Assertively the officer positioned himself in the middle while yelling for everyone to shut up, not say a word and calm down. As if mannequins all seven stood their ground.

Noting the cops had nightsticks Larry mumbled for Stan not to say another word. Repeatedly the officer questioned of what kind of car the parents were driving or where staying. Almost in unison Bill and Stan replied how he had already been told, as back home. Not leaving well enough alone, one of the patrolmen uttered how then smartest which hotel have they a checked into. Amid the tense situation the officer escorted the cops to their cycles. Noting how each had never received such unkindness, thinking by the four was to figure out a way of returning the favors.

For some reason the lawmen refused to believe that there was no adults or supervision. Having questioned about the school attended he noted how the guys had a lot of guts traveling such a distance with all the weight, especially in such an older car. Finally displaying a smile the officer asked if anyone knew of a Stacky's sandwiches. Causing a lowering of tension the officer mentioned having friends when in Chester visiting they had gone to the small sandwich shop. When he quizzed if the guys had a lot of money or limited funds Dave unhappily responded how it was none of his business then, followed asking if he was blind as couldn't see what was being driven.

With patience tried, Stan asserted how regardless of what opinions the cops had the crew was not some rowdy bunch thought of. Quietly the officer replied of getting the message then mentioned of being under age where there was to be no gambling and no alcohol drinking. Sternly he gave everyone a look over while he instructed to follow him with no funny business! A short with the patrolmen then inside his cruiser he led the caravan with Nashie following.

With Stan behind the wheel the crew followed. Red lights on, the patrolmen rode with one cycle on each side until just before the close entrance to the town where the cycle cops changed to one in front with the other in back. Through the city the vehicles drove even going off the main road a few times. Slower than the posted speed limit noticed were the people on the side walks waving. While Dave and Bill waved back, Larry uttered how it was something to remember how the crew was getting a police escort. While thoughts were of the crew being escorted out of town or being put in jail Stan suggested thinking of the free meals.

Then with occasional siren toots the caravan never stopped at intersections where Bill uttered how they were providing a good tour. Various lighting methods were seen from colored and flashing to blinking lights of size small to the large where mentioned was such could light up the city of Chester. Surprise it was, as the officer must have had the place planned the whole time. Stopping at a hotel's main entrance located at the very end of Las Vegas Boulevard it was the Hotel Hacienda. Sounds of horns tooting along with bang and more bangs from guns were heard but the team assumed it was for other persons. Yet almost a half dozen costumed cowboys approached the car while yelling yea and hollering yippee. Suddenly it was New Year's Eve as several young highly attractive women were joining the fiasco.

Wearing scanty mini skirted cowgirl outfits including hats and boots they danced around hollering greetings of, you guys having some fun tonight. Joyfully, one woman was hollering something like, hello from the Hacienda on the fabulous strip while another was yelling, welcome as the Hacienda greets you all. Stunned at first, not knowing how to react it was only moments later it dawned on the crew who the excitement was for. Amid the madness the crew was provided token bags of cookies, candy, coupons, hats and other novelties.

On the Fabulous Strip

Las Vegas

HACIENDA

LAS VEGAS · NEVADA · DUDLEY 2-7800

ESCORT BY POLICE THEN 3 NIGHTS STAY
ORIGINALLY TURNED AWAY BY POLICE
AT TOWN ENTRANCE. CONSIDERED AS BUMS.

Pandemonium set in as the four jumped out smiling and waving. Then each went up to the officer sitting in his vehicle, seeing he was tending to business they paused. Seeing his signal one by one they thanked the man for his understanding and help while the others joined in the hoopla. With a serious grin, the man replied for the team to remember no drinking or gambling or all would be swept out of town. Turning, the officer waved to the business-man standing on the steps while the crew also shook hands with the two cops bidding good byes.

When one of the hotel men asked Stan for the keys so to park the car he was advised that the team would take care of it mentioning it being touchy having mechanical problems. Attempting to sign in Bill and Stan learned of the room prices where it was decided a no. Walking out, the manager showed up with questions of where from, how long staying, where going and why. Then hearing the answers the man pressed about his busy schedule but desired to see the car.

Mentioning about his town growing prompted Dave and Larry to quiz the man about the police experience. Holding his chin the man walked to the rear staring at the license plate then observing the automobile, so fascinated he was, the man couldn't stop looking at it as he walked around the car again and again, even stopping to inspect the rack. Noting how he understood while putting his hands to his face it appeared as if he was about to cry. Twisting his head it seemed he may have thought the whole thing was some sort of a bad joke.

But sternly the manager asserted how he heard a lot of stories about people with their problems but, this to him was really beyond any thinking. Suggesting how it was probably the parents who made the plans for the trip as well as matters of the rack all but moved the crew to leave where Dave mentioned finding another place. As the man's voice changed he acknowledged seeing of the guys being insulted. With compliments the man asserted how for once he had come across something really genuine. Being overwhelmed, he mentioned how he had worked on a project, but not as risky. Following a short pause he added how he was really impressed by the guys' organization.

Escorting the four back inside, the man pulled out a batch of papers from his suit coat pocket. Providing complementary passes covering whole dinners for two days at any restaurant he took Stan and Bill to the check-in desk. Without advising what was intended he handed specific keys for two certain rooms. Smiling the man asserted his wish. Displaying much expression he mentioned how he hoped for the crew to stay at his place. Demonstrating as much excitement as the three he noted that he slashed the rates of the rooms to a third. Excited over the turn of events the four thanked him while adding how his hospitality was appreciated. Concluding the meeting he asked that in extending the hotel's hospitality when returning they would spread the word about the hotel's kindness. Furthermore he asked the four to behave like gentlemen suggesting that if anyone wanted a job he could use a few talented men. But, the four with thanks, noted having plans with the military.

Elated, was the team when found they were two large rooms next to each other. With all the action of the day along with the high temperatures taking its toll it took time for the four to shower and get their selves settled. From all the events of the day, the team was so uptight they were almost afraid to be themselves. Later, all was confusion as how to restart since original thinking had been dashed. Amid all uncertainty fun time was put on hold where it off to a diner. After the meal it was enjoying ice cream sodas, pie and cake, trying to put the pent up feelings behind them.

Unsure of what to do the crew returned to the rooms where at their young age it was not that simple as the ugly episode kept creeping back into the conversations. Shortly it was out they went but concerned about the police, to make the car inconspicuous parking was always far away from the streets. Having canvassed the second one, the four split up into teams of two for observing only. A limit of five minutes was set where outside they could compare notes then move to the next place.

Fremont Street was taken as a good omen since it was where the original town's history began with the old Binion place, Golden Nugget and the Golden Gate. Times wearing the new western style hats were spent only looking around for things that would give our ages away such as the guards, security cameras and persons observing customers in play. At one of the small casinos it was back outside as fast as they went in because smoke from the people was too overwhelming. Late, playing around a little with nobody having won while Stan and Bill having lost a little it was time to quit.

Stopping for a draught in one of the small bars provided some cheer where soon it became a pattern of drink, talk and out the door from one bar to another. But at the last bar it was noticed how the bartender hung around listening to the talk. Uninvited intrusion by the bartender agitated the guys where as stern glances by Dave and Larry were made the bartender asked for identifications. Finishing the brews without saying a word the four headed for the door upsettingly the man. Upon asking where going Stan and Dave turned asserting how neither was yet eighteen. As the bartender noted their kidding at once all four blurted out, not kidding, so stuff it, for at least we have manners! Outside Larry smacked Dave and Stan on the back suggesting to grow beards while putting on some weight, which ended the night.

The next morning the team prepared for the gaming matters in a full discussion. Next was the big business of saving dollars using the coupons where it was time to leave. A surprise, it was hearing a knock on the door. As Dave opened the door, standing was some gorgeous young woman. Staring as if she had found her targets, the four assumed she was some kind of a hostess. But, paying a cordial hello she introduced herself, smoothly demonstrating some modest gyrations. Use of the woman's arms along complimented her moving hips. Then in her early thirties being very cute wearing a happy smile she simply lit up the morning. Each of the guys had seen burlesque at its finest at the Trock, and it was that she was that good.

Gyrating while making conversation she moved inside while keeping the door open. Her mini sexy tight fitting outfit along with womanly features while grinding whisked the four mentally off guard. Speaking with a Spanish accent she presented such a site the woman aroused the men's senses where Stan uttered how it was a hallucination.   B r e a k i n g everyone out of their trance, Larry blurted for the team to wake up where they were seeing a live action billboard. Each aware of the Mustang ranch politely advised her of having plans which would not allow any detouring. With her act squashed, she presented literature regarding events at various places plus, even offered opinions where good food at decent prices could be had. On her way out, Larry and Bill commented how it was a hot way to start the morning.

After having the woman's knowledge of the eateries such was relied on where it was one of the diners she mentioned. At the place, received was a coupon for a free breakfast or lunch at another diner. Also there was a free roll of nickels but unfamiliar with such practices each thought the roll was accidently left behind by a previous customer. It was only a couple of dollars but to the four who were pinching pennies it had value. Later the team was advised how the roll of coins was marketing ways of promoting business. Emotions pumped with caffeine the feeling of joy bloomed were Larry asserted, is this some kind of celebration or what"?   Feelings of happy abounded where upon leaving Dave, mentioned how the woman may have been an angel.

Another review of the town was taken until about midday. Time for another diner caused thoughts of saving funds. Then at the eatery, two grabbed unattached booths waiting for service. As the waitress took the orders, Larry hollered, inquiring of Dave if that was him. Having picked up twice as many coupons along with two more rolls of nickels the team felt fate was in their favor. All excited Bill commented how his mother would have appreciated the way the crew was not spending foolishly. Back to the hotel for a nap where later, Bill banged on the wall yelling, yo guys, wake up, it's go out and gets em time.

SEGMENT - 15.   Wearing sport coats with the western hats, it was off to the restaurant located inside. Using the complimentary tickets for dinner emotions ran high. Then while stuffed to the gills it was off to the Riviera. Having a good atmosphere its glass doors gave the feeling of being inside without even leaving the sidewalk. Table game denominations ranged from ten to twenty five cents and dollar to even hundred dollar chips. While some people dressed as if they rode in from the range, others appeared ready for the opera. Then cute attractive cocktail waitresses of various ages wearing sexy costumes presented real distractions for players. Yet, the girls' mingling was still a treat.

Shortly, the team stopped at the Flamingo where intended it was to be of only minutes. But as it turned out it was anything but short but who knew? While Stan was greeted with a string of good luck such action caused all plans to change. Although the other three departed, thinking was to return soon knowing Stan was not a professional. However, as time passed the situation got strung out. Stan was amused watching people come and go. Some people stayed after hitting while others left having felt the sting of the game.

A few players not appreciating Stan'methods often provided some choice words. Inferred was that he was taking their cards. Then other times it was about him passing. Complained was about cards that he should have received. Although nerve racking, Stan only ignored them so not to draw attention from the dealer. With his sunglasses on he kept his head facing the cards so not to arouse the dealer.

Refusing to respond to the bullies tried his patience but, to Stan avoiding being carded was more important. Although often responding with a semi smile one time he suggested for them to provide expert opinions when situations arose or showed his favorite number finger. Then while holding down on his play, he kept his vodka on ice watered down, only sipping while enjoying the coffee. Frequent glances by a woman in her late forties while sitting a few seats away later had the dealer move her chips where she took the seat next to Stan. Soon the two often conversed until the atmosphere grew tense when one of the other men busted yelling a sly remark at Stan. Quietly as the woman responded letting her feelings known. How they were bothering her, she mentioned the same to the dealer.

Soon while going to the rest room he passed by Larry at a slot machine. Coughing twice gave the password for restroom where understood it was agreed that no one would come around while he was playing.

Later the two uttered a derogatory where Stan finally responded by giving multiple short waves with his favorite finger on both hands. Soon easily noticed was that Betty was a good player since knowing the game while using high value chips. Respecting her chip values while noticing her wedding rings and casual talks with the dealer it became apparent she was also a regular player. Then what helped Stan was when she gave a return of angry sophisticated lingo to the men in suggesting them to go scratch.

During one hand the woman whispered to Stan how she could have liked him as her partner but knew he was under age. Softly she whispered how his secret was safe with her. As time passed Stan realizing his lucky streak, didn't care who said boo, focusing on the game. One moment, the woman offered help mentioning for him if going to the men's room to be careful since the two men had been drinking while losing a lot of money.

When the two men had lost several rounds in a row they verbally came down on Stan tired of his reckless playing even taking their cards. Showing her being mad at the situation, Betty stood up alerting the dealer to their antics. Then in one hand, angrily while clapping she showed the two men her sophisticated finger while loudly stating, way to go Stan. Needless to say it was just what Stan didn't wish hearing as the outburst drew a crowd. But at least they were watching the woman and the two men, but not him.

Time passed where one hand caused some excitement. While the dealer had eight showing Stan with four cards had a count of which amounted to nineteen. Decision for the player while several people had gathered around voicing their notions such as for him to stay, are you crazy, or you can't hit that. Inquisitively the dealer seeing the crowd gather had assumed the player would be staying pat. Surprised seeing the player's motion he asked Stan whether he was sure. Pointing to the cards with direction while repeating himself in a stronger tone, Stan feeling his oats, indicating to the cards uttered yes, do it, go ahead, but hit it softly!

Suddenly a moment of quiet took over. Loud comments followed as the dealer turned over the card. Into a small frenzy the crowd went seeing the two card. As voices rang out yelled were phrases such as look at that, or did you see that. Sadly, the other two players, livid as if getting ready for war uttered their negative language. Fascinating it was hearing no response, the crowd was clapping while sending out cheers. As some spectator women

spoke to Betty indicating they knew each other, she spoke to the dealer causing him to warn the two men. Good ole Betty had become Stan's friend without him even trying. One time the woman stood up while sticking her thumb on her nose pointed to the two players.

Being the lowest price wager on the table left Stan feeling almost out of place, yet the dealers showed they were having a good time. Fun was when Betty angrily responded to the dealer who raised his arm in a motion. Immediately, two good size guards out of nowhere approached. And easily noticed was their being ready for the rowdies to give them a cause for some action.

Although the atmosphere quieted down Stan knew his game was going nowhere. Approaching midnight as if a door opened, another good luck streak started which caused Betty who was having a good day to display a spurt of jubilee. But also, about then the team showed up all played out. Dave without thinking put a hand on Stan's back while glancing at the woman. Quietly he uttered how the three had enough where Stan replied of needing another quarter hour but, smiling Dave responded hollering, hotsie totsie what is weez to dooz, sit around waiting for your royal highness?

Seeing the act, the dealer questioned of him knowing Stan where Dave in a squeaky tone answered them being old friends. It was all the dealer needed to hear where he required identification. While Dave attempted to fudge the other two approached where showing an angry face the dealer belted out for the three to get off the floor or be escorted. Right away as he asked Stan for his identification he was replied of the player leaving. The dealer noted enjoying Stan's play but also called for a guard belting out for the boy not to come back until he was of age. While Stan was picking up his chips, Betty gave him a kiss on the cheek where both exchanged good luck wishes. While the evening hadn't cost a penny, with the excitement and socializing there was even a bonus. Besides ending up winning Stan felt he had met a friend in Betty.

Outside, as the team hassled Stan for staying so long he promised to treat breakfast the next day also neither of the three had lost any amount to be concerned about. Dave having hit a small jackpot it was agreed not to add another day because serious thoughts were that one may have gotten hooked, losing a bundle. Back at the hotel, while walking along side the swimming pool Dave asked to try on Stan's sport coat. Suddenly showing all smiles while quiet, the three acted fast. While letting Stan know of their congratulatory feelings on success and his treat for breakfast, as if practiced, while holding him down the three removed his outer garments. Then in one motion while hollering, "here's toasting to you", they threw Stan into the pool. So much for good old friends.

SEGMENT 16.   Just another day, Thursday the Twenty-Sixth of June. Bill started as the first driver where at breakfast it was decided to have some fun. Not to throw away what funds had been conserved but thinking was about the first day of insults. An urge was felt by all to carry on mischievously the way young people do to have some revengeful fun. Yet, how and where were the questions? Finally a plan was developed back at the room, based on timing strategy lasting until time to leave. Unexpectedly a knock and when Bill opened the door to everyone's surprise there stood a scantily dressed woman. "It's Cinderella", Stan all excited hollered.

Smartly the highly attractive young woman displayed her huge smile. Initiating her cordial introduction with displays of modest swaying of hips and arms Larry murmured for the guys not to get excited. Look at this way, Larry asserted, it was probably another mirage. Staying in a rhythm she inquired of the reason for the team's trip. Of French or Greek descent, she presented an appearance that would have short-circuited any man's brain waves. Shortly the team advised in amiable voices of being fully savvy but, was leaving town. All attempts by the woman failed even as she suggested of running from the law while offering assistance.

Slowly while rebutting, each made aware that such pleasures if wanted was always available back home.

Displaying smiles from ear to ear, the four grabbed their bags as the team moved through the doorway all eyes glued on the beautiful moving statue. Gracefully observing the bags in hand, all she could do was state, "oh my gosh, gee you guys really are leaving, well good luck". Ss the four watched the woman strut down the hall Dave was heard uttering of, my, my, what talent.

A stop at the manager's office biding a thank you, then to the desk clerk who inquired which direction going. Hearing of the team's lack of knowledge of the area he made a call. The kitchen responded with instructions while the cooks stuffed the containers with chunks of ice and cubes boisterously asserting about being careful of the heat. Dave raised issue of their removing the beer and soda bottles where the cook queried asking which was more important to die drinking sodas and beer or live enjoying quenching water? Of course the guys not knowing, thinking was they were exaggerating.

Then it was on to a gas station where another voice was heard repeating the same matters of the heat. What, more mention of the heat but, the guys only assumed they were able to handle anything. So, the crew moved on with their revisiting plan. Causing havoc was the intent. Feeding on what the casinos didn't want patrons to experience was the plan. Frolicking in between two slot machine players, Bill and Larry in different rows set the mood acting as if drunk. Simultaneously, Dave and Stan in other rows put on their show as if on drugs or drunk, singing off key with slurred words, the tune of home on the range or I come from Alabama.

At different places the four even switched partners where during the course of the episodes each was escorted out. Behaved beyond reproach yet causing the police the guys were never caught as bouncing around from one end to the other. Being the last day nobody really gave a darn, as the performance was so good it caused more chaos than anticipated. A winning morning of victorious humorous episodes of high emotions was for each genuine innocent fun with tons of laughs.

Following the last place, the crew stopped at a diner where the waitress raised the level of joy with an amiable sendoff. With good food along with the nice waitress the crew recalled their action on the strip especially the Golden Nugget, Flamingo, Desert Inn, MGM, Sands, Pioneer and Horseshoe. Dave all hyped up it was driving with a cloud of dust and a hearty hi yo Nashie of pounding horses as the jubilant Chester Eagles Boys Club headed west. A great place for a vacation or recouping from ills but noted was not anyone's idea of a permanent home.

On route ninety-one the excited team traveled arriving in the tiny town of Jean. A bunch of signs intrigued the crew about an article for a good souvenir but paid little attention. Called "Pop's Oasis" or "the Oasis" was similar to a large town's corner mom and pop store. However the place was not in a large town with people hustling about. Rather it was smack dab in the middle of nowhere. Smokes, beverages or fuel were not the big items but rather canvas water bags.

Taking plenty of ice, the crew felt that such item was not needed plus not wanted to spend money on some stupid empty bag being a new gimmick. However speaking to other customers finally realized was it not some trifle but a necessity. Porous though a solid container it was that as the car moved forward the air passing through the porous bag kept the water cool. Also was that if a breakdown occurred where people might be stranded, the water was also drinkable.

Back on the road, intelligence set in. Soon it was desert to the left, desert to the right along with nothing but desert in front and back. Ouch! Bill yelled as he brought his arm inside from touching the burning hot roof. Comments such as turn down the air conditioner or turn up the heat were quickly quieted as the crew gripped the situation. Down the road, a short detour was taken to make a pit stop at the Sidewinder Café. With no way of cooling down as Bill stepped out of the car he laughingly belted out that the drive was not one he wished to make daily. Meanwhile it was understood that the area's enormous problematic drain on people by watching movies or looking at photographs could not be comprehended.

With added ice the crew headed for Baker and, while the scenery was seen as new and different its affect on the mind body was highly noted. Desolate was the word Dave mentioned while Stan noted how if their experience was anything like hell, it was not the place he ever wished to visit. Originally it was to go to Barstow but reading the brochures, it was a detour to Daggett, an old mining town, yet recalled from history classes the place didn't mean much. A live education it was when actually seeing the area's surroundings along with first hand experiencing the extreme elements. The entire situation enabled a true picture of the past.

Aware of the kind of clothing worn along with the tools used during the time period along with experiencing the weather allowed a full and true comprehension of the early prospectors' hard times books and pictures failed to relate. While Stan mentioned feeling like a turkey in an oven, jokingly Dave suggested taking a tour of the famous Death Valley. In jest, Bill suggested keeping the vent and windows open to experience the cool breezes. Other responses were slow coming as simply too hot to even talk

A refreshing surprise Barstow was where after a visit to a tavern haven gotten cooled down a tour of the town was made. But beat from the heat each lost interest in site seeing. After giving Nashie a quick check it was Stan driving back on the famous route sixty-six. Larry having driven in the destination area gave him an advantage since having been to California, with his parents by way of flying. The area seemed similar to New York with all of its people, and traffic. Hyped up aware of getting close, the crew acted like a bunch of cheerleaders urging the driver onward.

Shortly seeing traffic while not familiar with the area, as not to lose time Larry became the driver. Enthusiasm combined with nerves being strained from the past pressures then the intended area close at hand caused emotions to exploded. Slowly tears formed, pushed by the success of reaching the destination. To the world, the feat of the three was not news worthy but, then the rest of the world wasn't aware of the boys' overcoming of obstacles or their accomplishments. Not only did they over come negatives from people and the formidable weather but, survived more mental strain than either had ever experienced.

SEGMENT - 17. Finally, the moment arrived as Larry pulled on the emergency brake. Thursday the Twenty-Sixth of June while the two in the back seat rested their Fascinating it was hearing no response head in their arms on the backs of the front seat the two in front had slumped forward. Nashie was parked where it was so quiet the hearts could be heard as the moment had seized the minds. All choked up, Bill belted out, "Oh God, we're here, we made it". All at once, each joined in prayer giving thanks for allowing the crew to arrive safely. Momentarily, the four sat as frozen in time where it was as if someone had let the air out of a big balloon.

Emotionally showing tears the four started shaking hands feeling a relief from the strain that ended up giving each other semi hugs. As the atmosphere was strained with notes of how they had done what everyone had told them would never happen, Bill started yelling yahoo and yippee with Stan and Larry hollering out a few Amen's. Last it was Dave mentioned a few yeas ending with assumptions of how it would be easy going from then on.

Located in Granada Hills, California, a northern part of Los Angeles it was good for Larry to drive being a weekend with heavy traffic. Although aware of Larry's upcoming visit the family had no idea as to what day. Since, Larry had forgotten to contact them, the arrival turned out to be a surprise. Stunned the family was when first seeing the guys. Sitting in the car no one moved, even as the family was shouting hello. When the man tapped on the roof it was an alarm. The sound sort of brought everyone down to earth.

Larry's family's friends showed joyous expressions of clapping and hand shaking as Larry introduced the three that helped the three to relax. Following a social introduction time with cool liquid refreshments it was time for dinner. With Dorothy, the mother demonstrating her gift of gab she commanded the center of attention. While all four questioned wanting to know everything from why to where, the daughters pushed the discussion.

Excited about the new guests it was Fred, the father only seemed amused with the whole scene. Soon though, the mother crossed the line wanting to know how each spent their money. Right away the guys clamed up looking to Larry and Fred for some help. Minding their personal business Larry amiably let Dorothy know how her third degree was not nice. Timely, Fred pressed his need to get a look at Nashie where, out went the family.

Looking it over he expressed disbelief in seeing. A far cry from the clean waxed vehicle when started what he saw was paint removed down to the metal with other areas of greasy grime and dirt that covered the true color. When told of the dust storm and weeks of heavy rain Fred comprehended what was explained. But the humorous moment was when he lifted up the hood. Showing concern the man noted how it must have really been babied.

While the older sister was two years younger than Larry it became noticeable of her interest to win him over. As was found out later, Larry's mother and Dorothy had lived in the Media area. Noted was often they joked about their children growing up, possibly dating each other. And there the two were trying to catch Larry. Although she had been to Vegas several times Dorothy couldn't resist questioning on the group's casino efforts regarding where and how much money each spent. But shortly it played on the guys' nerves where even Fred and the daughters hinted to Dorothy about minding own business.

Later with the team leaving for some sightseeing the parents allowed Larry to borrow their 1957 Chevrolet. Condition was needing to be returned with a full tank full plus before the sun fully set. What a relief to ride in some comfort then, with Larry playing tour guide it was off to Los Angeles proper noting the bars, cafes and nightclubs. His knowledge, combined with that of back home, beach towns, parks, historic and military places help discount places saving time. In Hollywood it was at Universal Studios seeing the various set of props, material things and music. Then learning of the many stages allowed a quick understanding of the place.

Hollywood Boulevard ended as a quick bird's eye view where reading of the various billboards, informative signs and literature enabled a grasp of what would have been seen. Though many lots such as Warner Brothers, Paramount and Universal offered tours such was not considered. Often seeing beautiful women in sexy outfits along with a few major actors made the tour enjoyable, especially for Dave having got his wish for seeing some of the women. Although a drive thru Burbank, Studio City and other places allowed some understanding of the enormous size of the area it was too late. Time running out, the four stopped at a café where the three gave Larry a send off of good wishes.

Then later it was back at the house for another surprise when Fred offered to put the three up for the night. Disturbing the goodness Fred attempted, Dorothy in front of all made known that he had not asked her for approval. In an apologetic tone Fred mentioned his assumption how he thought she would have allowed it. No body said anything but it put a quiet into the atmosphere causing everybody to tread lightly. Since Larry's presence required sleeping arrangement adjusting took place where the young one moved into the older sister's room. Then as Larry and Stan occupied the room Bill and Dave slept in the living room making use of the two sleeping bags over the pull out sofa.

Next morning Dorothy and Fred had put together a huge western type breakfast for a get together. Following much discussion and cleanup, Larry again took the part of a guide. While historical buildings, old monasteries and mansions allowed educational touring. Sunset Strip provided some fun. Following the seeing the beauty of San Bernardino valley UCLA was passed up where Larry was to attend. Since Larry had promised to return the car by sunset touring was cut short to allow some socializing as the four had become a chummy very close-knit special bunch of friends.

Upon finding a Mexican/American establishment it was agreed that intended was to be a short visit to return promptly. Yet, it all started with a simple salute and toasts to each other. Suddenly, Dave in an excitedly joyous mood jumped out of his seat yelling yes, yes, we did it. Throwing one arm in the air he raised the other with his glass. Then screamed out, "yes we did it, really did it, we're here". As the surrounding customers looked on, Dave let out what he had been holding in. Meanwhile, the three were surprised as had never seen Dave so pumped before.

Shortly as other customers found out what was being celebrated they started yelling out hooray with other cheers. Before long patrons at some tables were hollering, hey or yo, over here, we're from so and so, or other places from cities on the east coast. Then as some people yelled, hey those guys drove across the whole country it was as if a siren sounded where a rush of music took hold. If a person understands the melodious tempo of southwest music along with the cordiality mood, they would understand how the rush was definitely not the norm. Even as the team tried to quiet things down the efforts only seemed to heat the atmosphere. Engaging with the crowd, the band became alive with increased rhythmic volume.

Responding to the customers clapping stimulated the atmosphere as the place turned into a chorus of a joyous people singing in Spanish and Italian. With the singing, clapping and added feet stomping the place took on a different atmosphere. Prompted by the atmosphere of hearing yells of congratulations or good luck, the teary eyed four stood up singing while also saluting the crowd. Perhaps the Chester Eagles Boys Club was only boys of seventeen in age but with the dialed up peoples' hype the level of the party escalated.

Feeding the frenzy was the band playing its soul reaching medium non-stop music tune to tune. While customers stood on chairs while clapping, others danced around in between the tables where some customers even grabbed waitresses to dance with. Meanwhile as Bill blurted out how ain't this something, not in the least bashful, Stan joined in the dancing by grabbing hold of a female customer. Cheerful, while not thinking, Stan had actually interfered with a couple as was dancing with one of the women who had been dancing with her male partner. Yet as the other three joined in hopping around unknown to each was that a problem had grown.

Beyond Stan having a weakness for Italian and Spanish women his dancing was too close yet it seemed nobody minded. Shortly seeing stern faces Bill and Larry grabbed Dave letting him know of getting Stan out of harm's way. While the three recognized Stan's semi intoxicated overly happy state they excused him while pulling Stan away from the woman. While doing so they were surprised to see the man and woman smile while noting they enjoyed his dancing.

Once back in his chair Larry was forced to partially sit on him while Bill advised Stan and Dave about the troublesome scenario. Finally having regained their composure the great farewell of social fun soon ended with sad joy of true meaning. The four had accomplished so much and traveled so far yet neither had the words of respect which they were thinking of each other. Upon returning,Dorothy expressed concern about the three's condition along with traveling on roads not familiar which resulted in the three staying another night. The final day among friends had slipped by.

SEGMENT 18. Saturday the twenty-eighth where showing their appreciation the four helped with the table settings along with carrying the food and cleaning up. While loading the car with the cooler of ice cubes, sodas and bottles of water there was also snacks and fresh sandwiches the woman made. As Fred offered traveling suggestions, everyone realizing Larry and his friends may never meet again, teary eyes appeared even from Dorothy as feelings had grown. Larry being left behind was hard to take where the three departed in sorrow knowing their crew member and teammate was no longer.

Now! Let us return to those exciting days of yesteryear where the original three club members were again starting out. So, Stan the first driver with his loyal companions Dave and Bill inside their ever-reliable car Nashie hit the road running. As the trio departed, Larry was seen jumping up and down while waving his arms. Then while the family of four was also waving it was in a cloud of smoke and thunder of driving pistons where the wheels turned. The celebrating trio almost in a state of uphoria drove Nashie off into the sun.

Some short distance later, Dave had Stan stop the car as there was another wish to be fulfilled. Dave wanted to drive on the notorious L.A. Freeway. Thinking was that later to be able to tell people that he had actually had the experience. All hyped up Dave quickly grabbed the wheel. "And their off", Bill yelled when out of the gate running at semi maximum speed the driver without whip or crop pushed Nashie for all she was worth. A fast roadway with multiple lanes yet, Nashie was unable to keep pace as the cars zoomed past. Speeding cars were neck and neck with Dave hugging the inside wall. Zoom and zooming past they went where frequently passengers in some cars waved while others tooted their horns.

Not quite was it as driving in a derby but Bill and Stan did have an enjoyable time. Watching Dave respond to the other cars was almost like being at the movies. As a couple of sport cars went flying by Dave asked whether they had wings forced as he was forced to keep Nashie content in the far right lane. Watching the driver cope with the slowness along with his temper, knowing Dave was used to driving his father's fast Buick was amusing. When some going by waved with their favorite number finger Bill hollered for Dave to get ole Nashie in super drive. Calmly while laughing, Stan mentioned that the car was already moving fast just that the other two didn't know it.

Shortly, the driver hollered out," ok you guys, so it's excitement you wants, well its action plus excitement tis what yous all gots" as look out the rear window. Trailing with the red light on after a few toots of the horn it was the siren. All Dave could do was pull over close to the wall.Out of the car, while Bill sarcastically asked Dave if he had his thrill driving on the highway the young highway patrolman did a visual of walking around the car. Then while he reviewed the identifications Stan noted for the two to remember how they drove on the highway even escorted by the police.

Doing his job, as the officer lectured he got agitated when cars passing by tooted their horns. Angrily the cop asserted of the car going to slow where following a short discussion of where from going, etc. he noted how he could have given the driver a ticket for obstructing traffic. Minutes later, after informing the crew about the minimum speed requirement that was posted the cop asserted the choice of either getting off the freeway or he would issue a citation causing the car to be towed. Initially, Dave thought to be smart ensuring the car to stay at exactly the minimum speed but the two seeing the antic advised that if given a ticket he would foot the bill. Then after following a short distance, the cop pulled up alongside while showing a hand signal as he proceeded onward.

Once off the freeway Stan retook the wheel heading North on route 101. While the cold sodas and pretzels helped ease tensions the three kicked their opinions around it was how interesting to have traveled across the entire country, only to find it wasn't the buildings or places that mattered, but all about the people. Passed up were highways leading to Fresno and San Luis Obispo which had restored missions and Victorian homes. But the crew was aware that Cape May, New Jersey had similar places.

Interest had been mentioned regarding the wineries, rain forest and Yosemite National Park but watching water falling, taking up bird watching or looking at large Sequoias was not for them where they had other plans.. Following a long drive, the crew arrived at San Jose where with Bill curious about the Rosicrucian order a visit was made. While Stan grabbed a post card to send, the trio saw, read and discussed about all of the major religions. On the road to the monastery, recalling the Rose-Croix order generated much interesting discussion that helped in thinking about other religious orders.

After stopping for an early dinner the crew soon arrived at the Jesuit Seminary. Father Dunnion of Saint Michael's Parish in Chester knew one of the brother's relatives at the high school of which he had taught two of the team. Unknown to the team who were members of his parish he had notified the brother in California of the three. The old three story building of late twenty era having a cement exterior was of plain design. Yet the arch contained a window that was different from the other windows of a rectangular shape. Inexperience with the religious order was overcome by a short-guided tour.

But not known was that the priests, Dunnion and Lenahan back in Chester helped to lower all formalities. Smartly introduced as brothers since not having taken their vows as priests it was for the three where choices had to be made. Offered their hospitality of staying overnight there was the matter of time. With the brother's regimented schedules decisions had to be made regarding which parts would not be wished to participate in.
Although plans did not include any stay at such a monastery their offer was

accepted. And to the brother's astonishment the crew made no objections to participating in any chores, prayers or any of the daily activities. Somewhat curious, the three had no idea of what they were in for. Nothing was lacking in the meals or sleeping quarters, except for the rooms being as large closets were very small and plain. And while television was available in the central reading room it was never watched since the social activities offered plenty of enjoyment. Meditation, prayers and rosary times were worthwhile however the class times provided challenges where arguments by the three had credibility which led to heated debates. Then easily handling the crew in pinochle and darts they suffered an impasse as unable to win against Stan in shuffle board or him and Dave on the pool table. Morning of the last day it was the brothers provided a festive breakfast as a send off celebration where if it hadn't been for the military reporting date the crew would have stayed as long as welcomed.

Coasting, the Chester Eagles Boys Club arrived in San Francisco the last day of June where those extended stays at the last two places caused the crew to conserve time. No sit down meals where it was mixing the sightseeing with food to go. Following a visit to a gas station giving Nashie the once taking a trolley ride was found comparable to that in the town of Jim Thorpe, Pennsylvania.

 Then the visit to china town was all its own where appreciated was the oriental snacks along with seeing their mixing of the multi story row houses with various businesses. Such ingenuity fascinated the three where such was discussed later over a few burgers. To avoid riding up and down the hilly streets driving across the tops of the streets were done. Allowing with saving fuel and time it provided the viewing advantage of seeing from a distance places such as Alcatraz, the Golden Gate Bridge, the vineyards, Fisherman's Warf and the navy yard. Since the Maryland, Delaware and New Jersey coastline offered similar places seeing close up was not needed. Also looking downward the tops of the telephone poles along with the tops of buildings were readily seen.

 Located on a bay while at the ocean it was understandable about being called fog city. Then depending on the time of day the bridge seemed to change tones. From an orange to a pinkish orange the structure change, but to the three, the bridge was and as a bridge it was not crossed where Oakland was passed up. Fun time was seeing the city preparing for the upcoming holiday where at the Hollywood and Vine intersection with the heavy volume of traffic and pedestrians with obvious sightseers trying to cross six lanes it was absolute mayhem. Later on the outskirts with only three in the car and less luggage it was better sleeping.

The next day after much visiting along with sampling of snacks in diners of different nationalities the town was departed. Later under a clear sky with a brisk night and a cool brew the night ended planning the distance to be covered the next day. Day two of July, where the morning was greeted using the melted ice along with the bottled water for a small splash wash. With the brisk weather matched by Bill who excitedly took the wheel, the crew in a state of bliss headed for Sacramento.

As the awesome panoramic scenery went by it almost seemed majestic. Hungry, the trio wasted no time eating at the first diner they came to. Fully enjoyed the place which had kept the old western type atmosphere. Furthering the old style was the full breakfast aroma which gave an extra lift of western realism. Joyfully, Dave uttered how the only thing missing were the horses and steers. Afterward, it was Dave driving as the three enjoyed education from the older city. An old baseball town having the title of, "big tomato" there was much farmland. And along with the ritzy section of hideaways for the Hollywood were old trolley cars and buildings with ginger bread fronts. Such matters indicated the town had resort prominence, plus produce as well as manufacturing means. Relatively easy it was to compare to Chester, and Cape May. After spending the day it was a short ways outside the city limits where the three sacked out.

Anxiously the next morning, the crew returned to the old fashioned diner for another western breakfast. Subsequently with Stan driving, it was on to Reno where traveling through the high mountainous terrain the crew felt confident noticing the difference in the car's performance.

Missing the person of two hundred and thirty pounds, luggage and tires, Nashie moved with more ease. About three hours duration, the drive with full stomachs along with the extra coffees allowed an enjoyable ride of breathtaking scenery.

Awesome as it was, the three made comments how compared to God's creations, man's big inventions were trivial. Plus Stan added that his only regret was not having the piano where he could have played some rhythm as the beauty went by.

Somewhere down the road, all excited, Bill took his turn in anticipation, knowing the little big town was getting close. Lots of wishes and hope was expressed for some good luck as the crew approached its last part of the plan. "A big bang of a jackpot would really give the trip something to remember", Dave suggested. Sure. Stan replied adding how such would be enormous if such was enjoyed by two of the crew.

Hearing the cheerful words Bill showed his enthusiasm adding how he would have enjoyed seeing all three hit just some small ones. The atmosphere was one of ongoing excitement as the weather was cooperating with the vehicle acting as though it was renewed.

CHAPTER EIGHT

COOL CHANCES, HEAT AND THE WILDERNESS

Amid feelings of joyous anticipation the three arrived in the tiny but big, large and yet little town on the Third day of July. Bill stopped the car as the trio gazed at the large banner hanging across the main entrance. Seeing that it stated, "The biggest little city in the world" fascinated the crew wondering how the town could claim to be so large, when the maps and literature indicated it was really tiny in size.

Without knowing why, upon reaching the entrance, police standing in the street caused Bill to stop where a few officers looked inside. "Hey, what's going on", Stan and Dave hollered where they instructed the driver to pull to the sidewalk. Moving quickly under the sheriff's direction a swarm of uniformed men grabbed hold, helping the three out of the car. After informing the three they were under arrest the Sheriff started to read their rights when other officers stopped him stating how they had heard enough.

Completely baffled the guys were blurting out asking what all of the stupid action was all about. Not manhandled yet each was subdued by the strength of the men. Meanwhile as some legal jargon was exchanged between the Sheriff and his deputies a judge showed up dressed in a black robe. Displaying an angry face while standing in the middle of the street having heard the remark, the judge responded giving Dave a hard stare as he asserted being in contempt. Right away the other two yelled at Dave of not needing any more of their stuff and for him to keep his mouth shut.

Unexpectedly the judge hollered how the culprits had resisted and due the bad actions, the three were guilty of vagrancy plus contempt of court. Then waving his arm he directed for all three to be sent directly to jail. Instantly the policemen reacting escorted the trio only a few yards to a cell of metal bars. Not even behind closed walls with people gathering around waving closed fists where one of the policemen yelled out asking if the punks were having fun.

To the three it was unbelievable but there they were out in the open among the public. Fixed atop a flat bed truck the jail cell was initially hidden from view by a truck that was parked behind it. The cell of metal bars may have held four people but, not more unless they were skeletons. Who the heck ever heard of a town having a jail cell that was open to the public, Stan hollered. Once placed inside, the police gathered around where it was assumed a ring was being formed to keep the people away. But oh, how wrong it was. As Bill yelled out how crazy the people were, Dave added being more like sickos.

While the crowd of smiling faces looked on amid the officers displaying their angry looks it was as if a bell had sounded. More people came out of the casinos where soon the ruly mob began showing signs as if being after blood. Some were yelling such as, "yeah, lets ride em out of town in a barrel" with others hollering, "string up them varmints" while others were yelling, "it's lynch time for those gangsters". Seen was one person waving a rope with a hangman's loop. Alarm time it was realizing that instead of keeping people away, the police waved to get closer.

Shortly while denied any means of escape, the sheriff made a political speech of harsh words spoken as if the three were some gangsters they apprehended. Right away the mob responded yelling to break out the tarn and feathers and have a party. Wow! The more the judge spoke the louder the crowd got. Following the judge was the sheriff using a bull horn to mentioning how great the community people were with accolades for the judge. Hearing the words, while seeing the mob excited where some shouted cuss words of what to do to the bad guys Stan got worked up. Fully expressing his self he hollered how the crew gottsta gets the hells outta there.

Meanwhile as the three attempted to force the bars apart the judge was using vote getting phrases while waving his arms announcing that the criminals had been found guilty. His short statements about not wanting such outlaws in his town heightened the chaos where angrily, Dave kicked at the bars attempting to dislodge them. Also it was the other two showing their hostile defiance as had joined with similar kicking while adding angry profanities. Something just didn't seem right yet, neither of the team could figure out why the madness was going on. But one thing was sure, which was not having any part of the rowdy crowd as some fear had set in.

Soon while waving to the crowd the judge surprised the team climbing onto the platform. Then while smiling the judge explained how he with the other men was all members of the Reno Jaycees. But in the dark Dave denied the judge to explain, angrily cussing how if the three had any guns they would have shown him some eastern Jaycees action. Perhaps if known about the Jaycees, the trio could have played along but up till the moment only anger was of the minds. Then while waving his arms and hollering for the crowd to settle down, the judge explained the cause of the event.

However, the trio aware of how rowdy the crowd was, along with seeing the fists and rope in the crowd each paid little attention. Again the judge repeated himself about the Jaycees also adding how if a donation was made charges would be dropped letting them out of jail. Not thinking, Dave hollered back how what he meant was to pay a fine. Adding to the tone while displaying his hot temper, Bill blurted out how the team ain't gonna pay nuttin. Stan angrily added that the team ain't done nuttin wrong, ain't payen nottin, where you tubby and your cronnies can go stick your head in a toilet.

All thinking had gone to the clouds, as who would have believed the entire matter was staged. Even the town people became participants as the crafty setup was done for a worthwhile cause. Once back on the sidewalk where finally learning the three understood where a donation of fifty cents each was made. While the normal questions as to where from, going and why was answered with minds clear it was comprehended of the good cause. With a shaking of hands, making merry followed. Actually being a part of the scene provided not only action but being fully engaged as participants was truly educational allowing feelings and emotions to be felt.

Shortly considering what had been read or seen in other towns having western history thinking was how every city should have something similar. Its educational benefit was awesome allowing direct experience that books and pictures don't allow. Following a trip to a gas station for taking care of Nashie a short tour was taken. With minds in a tizzy from the jailing event little was thought about the upcoming holiday of the fourth. What could possibly be so special about a day they have every year was thought.

Hungry the three were where a great turkey dinner with all of the trimmings at Lee's place turned out to be just the thing to get things started. Following a two-dollar holiday special with all the trimmings, Bill noted about Lee's being the right place at the right time. After visiting the Harold's Club it was the Primado, Silver Dollar, Frontier and the Horseshoe. Finally trying other smaller places such as the Nugget club tapping penny and nickel slot machines conserving play to save gaming money for the next day it was late. Totally exhausted the three stopped for the day. Referred to by a few people a room at Harold's Pony Express Motel enabled bedding to sleep plus, being on the outskirts it had a less expensive room rate where the trio finished the day.

Supposedly heavy gambling was the plan for the whole day, but after a filling breakfast, the team got sidetracked. Early a parade started and though not as long as those on the east coast, it was exceptional. Consisted of dozens of flags and banners there was flag waving by even the bystanders. Along with steers, bulls, dogs, horses and ponies in the parade were displays of other animals on wagons but in cages. Also there were the bands from commercial to the high schools and college with their majorettes, baton twirlers and musicians moving with their instruments.

All about people the parade was of all American ethnicities and ages displaying their history, ethnic groups, magnificent dress and sizes with the Indians putting on the best show. Because temperatures exceeded warm there were printed signs abound reminding people of the fire hazard resulting from the heat. Water buckets, fire hoses and fire extinguishers of every size were found in various locations everywhere. Plus there were signs for people to be careful with their cigarettes and matches. Elbow to elbow were the rows deep with the crowd that turned into cheering spectators.

Making a showing was a miss somebody who was a beauty queen along with other persons of talent, bulls and other animals that received decorations and or prizes. Several politicians along with the mayor, governor, many entertainment female and male celebrities and contest winners made presentations. Actor, Glenn Ford took the Silver Spurs award as the Hollywood Star having made known his gratitude for the peoples' appreciation of his entertainment value.

Afterward it was a short lunch with plans for gambling but such sidetracked by who would have guessed but it was time for the rodeo. Reluctant at first since having such on the east coast but, the trio had to see. Thrills and spills highly entertained the crowd beyond what had been imagined. Then tired from all the standing, sitting, only to stand while cheering, the three enjoyed some refreshment with a little slot playing until dinner. What a day it was.

Seeing an advertisement for the Bank Café, in keeping with the holiday spirit the trio made the most of a Fourth of July T-bone steak meal. The special really was something special as included all amenities the entire serving amounted to under three dollars. Dave and Bill mentioned their being in heaven aware that in other places the prices would have tripled. While events of the day had taken away the best time for gaming, with boosted spirits the three managed but limited the gaming fun.

Supposedly to have departed that evening there still remained some of the money each had set aside for gambling. Making the most of their time, the eastern cowboys decided to stay another night. Failed to consider was the increased number of people due the holiday where in some places it was wall to wall with standing people gambling or waiting. Finding a place over the holiday weekend turned out to be an impossibility where thinking was to end up sleeping in the car.

SEGMENT - 19   The last place was tried. Aware it could not be afforded, the crew had to try. At the Hotel Riverside quickly the trio was told, "sorry but we're all sold out". So, it was turning off to another motel, but while walking away, the clerk stopped the three, inquiring whether we were the ones greeted by the Jaycees in Vegas. Quick, the clerk made a telephone call while showing all smiles stating how the whole town had heard of the trio's episode.

Swiftly, a uniformed guard came ordering the three to follow him where it was anticipated being escorted out of the hotel.

Not wanting to create any trouble but Dave and Bill inquired to know why being hassled? Right away the guard answered not to break any of the minimum age rules but just follow him.

Inside the big office after a short introduction, like everyone else the manager wanted to know about where from, going to and why. Displaying a straight face the man gruffly mentioned how he heard about several men having routed Vegas asking if it was the crew. Then adding how it wasn't funny, he mentioned how the Vegas police had been run ragged with phone calls for assistance. Various casinos along with many of the customers had complained about being disturbed by the bothersome drunken men and men on dope. Neither of the three could hold back, And when the big man saw us with smiles, surprisingly the man noted his being amused stating how he would have liked to have been there.

Then he questioned of the three intending to gamble where Bill replied how the only interest was the show. Right away Dave added about being too low on funds not able to afford a room let alone gamble. About then, after inquiring where the car was parked the manager had the guard remain while he left the room. Shortly having returned void of skepticism the manager pressed on the Jaycees episode, as he was a member. Since he heard the Vegas version he wanted to hear what the trio had to say where surprised he was when the three advised of their good feelings about the whole event noting how to them it was a real life experience even providing education.

Following the third degree on the Vegas matter and Jaycees he showed sincere interest in the car and also about Chester where a long conversation ensued. As if searching for something, the man pressed to know why such interest was mentioned regarding the show. Then hearing of Bill's accordion playing along with Stan able at the piano he offered a thank you for not making a big ta do about the Jaycee's fund raising situation in his town.

Although polite, Dave interrupted asserting of the lack of time and needing to be going where the man requested some patience.

While he answered the telephone of no conversation but only short one word answers the trio assumed the content was about them thinking he would asking them to leave. Surprise it was when afterward the manager offered a small room at a very reduced rate that cut the price to a fourth. Then pulling out free passes to the show along with the sandwich shop he inquired about our future working intentions. Finally the man brought the meeting to a close while advising the desk clerk of the rate reduction. Thanking the trio for their donations the day before, it was with handshakes he belted out, no gambling guys, and understand that he meant no gambling. Displaying his piano playing high entertaining talent, the genius of Jimmy Durante highlighted the early evening. With Bill and Stan having musical instrument ability the two were fully able to appreciate the talents of the snozz. Then after some short gaming action in other places it was a return to the big hotel to appreciate good bedding.

With good weather starting the morning hopes were ringing for some good luck. An early start along with a good breakfast the trio was ready feeling that luck was on their side. Off to the Fun Room at Harold's place only disappointment greeted the team. Off to another a casino trying again, then another but, as time went by with all places tried it didn't matter. Not even a tiny pot, as neither one could get lucky. Whether table games or slots, the unlucky slump couldn't be dislodged. After lunch extremes of silly things were put into play such as after entering a place it was immediately to turn around then walking out only to stop for a minute then walk back in.

Simply it was to exchange their dollars for other dollars where no matter what was tried, neither was able to make any gains. A struggle to hold on to what each had started with became the challenge. As it turned out it was a most long frustrating day as all means to generate some luck simply failed. Each had ended up only a little less than breaking even from what was started with. But aware that there were no other cities or gambling places to go to, the guys not wanting to quit, the trio agreed to stay another night sleeping in the car.

Sunday the sixth of July, where after services it was during breakfast, no feelings expressed but only hopes for some luck. Then noting the places neither wanted to stop at it was onto gaming time. But as life goes, the three were unable to make any headway. Rather than fight the absence of luck each stayed within their monetary means while taking advantage of the free snacks and beverages to at least make a day of enjoyment.

Later following an early dinner with several salutes to each the team drove a good distance to a spot way out in the middle of God's creation. After enjoying some beverages and snacks while recalling the fun of the day before, the three went to sleep. Where Vegas was faster paced and larger with much lights it was the people in Reno were just a bit nicer and food a real bonus. Then being of a slower go while being more sociable the place was always times to be enjoyed where the few days spent was realized a higher level of fun.

Although the parade, rodeo and food specials really hit the spot, it was the fascinating worthwhile occasion with the Jaycees that exceptionally topped the stay. While Dave wanted to go to Carson City, Bill suggested the north road to see the salt flats but neither wanted to add miles or time.

Stan pushing the direct route it was heading for route fifty where to allow Nashie to keep moving the driving was limited to four hours. At end of shift the driver moved to the copilot slot for four hours then, slept for many hours. With Larry already dropped off, the destination reached and the fun gaming towns visited, there was nothing left except happy memories. Homeward bound the crew traveled over the wide-open spaces in all its glory. Awe inspiring scenery mile after mile helped but it was just keep going.

Reaching the town of Ely it was a stretch of the legs then after some grub it was back on the road till close to midnight. After parking well off the road it was sleep till the wee hours of the morning. Continuing on the way without the usual social, driving had become an obsession. Several hours later the team arrived in Spanish Fork where a stop was made for a meal. Then on with driving it was needed. Enjoying lunch in the wet city it was overheard that people can't sink in the lake. So, hearing not the same as seeing while being curious about the big attraction, the trio went for a dip.

Taking a swim in the Great Salt Lake was amusing but also quick when found how salty it was. Yet fun was watching other people where laughs were generated by seeing people walk out of the lake where the water dried left swimmers looking as being a salty dog. Naturally, those of the darker color of skin it was more pronounced where it seemed they had comical makeup on preparing for a stage play. Fascinated, Dave commented how the floating might resemble the feeling of weightlessness as being in outer space.

Afterward while refreshed by a shower then having found a

newspaper lying on a bench Stan held on to a part of the front page. Then enjoyed was a change from the usual diner by eating in a good restaurant. Well rested and fed, the team drove out of the city until reaching another deserted area where the team sacked out for the night. Wednesday started with a breakfast then after visiting "This is the place" monument having historical significance about the early pioneers, it was to see the Trolley Square and a place called Temple Square.

A bistro for a luncheon change, then a coffee house helped to relax while looking to depart the area. Indian communities, parks, lakes, shopping areas, and other small restaurants though present were of no interest plus with showers about, it was to hit the road.

Route Forty was the direction where heading eastward it was on to Colorado where again it was through the mountainous area. Leaving the high ground it was on to the frontier where traveling through the Oupay Indian Reservation the crew was provided more education.

The next set of mountains presented more of some awesome views, until passed by Fort Duchesne but, being dark it was too late to stop. Amid the ongoing push the drive continued until finally the state line was crossed.

Somewhere around midnight a secluded area was found where the air got down to the fifties. Full of confidence the happy threesome was not anticipating any problems but thinking of a continued simple drive heading home, from where the guys started.

All played out looking forward to the next day, it was a night of no worries as only good sleeping.

Chapter Nine

HIGH UP SPRINGS, DIVIDINGS AND KIND SHARKS

Well, how about that, Dave noted while crossing into Colorado. It was early morning of July Ninth when the crew arrived in the settlement of Dinosaur. Thinking was how it must have been a large city however, once at the first place it was coffee to go. Having no atmosphere it was anticipated that only a short distance further would be found another diner. Driving under erroneous assumption was not fun knowing that food could have been had at the previous stop. Another error as the crew traveled almost two hours.

Finally, the crew arrived in the town of Craig. It was at a good size diner that served good food also having a splendid view. Sitting in a booth next to a window seen was the clouds drift by.Dave suggested maybe some angels would be seen. Since catered to horseback riding, hiking and skiing of which the three had no interest the trio continued on its way. A stop was made at the small town of Steamboat Springs but with no places to visit it was continuing on the road.

Then it happened where not seen in any literature but, a peak had been reached which actually caused the excited crew to stop. Such absolutely staggering view caused Bill in awe to express his thought of being able to see the magnificence of the creator's handy work. Right away, Stan added how no artist or painter could put the emotional feelings generated by such beauty. Following a short discussion it was driving on till a visitor's center was reached. While obtaining some souvenirs another awesome sight was enjoyed.

Resuming the ride, it was along the Continental Divide where the Colorado Mountains attacked the car. Such rugged terrain prompted the trio to acknowledge being amazed by Nashie's dependability. Another moment it was where the driver patted the dashboard while recalling how the people back home suggested the car not being road worthy. Through the swamp and flooded areas of the mid part of the country then it was forced to cope with the mountains of the southwest along with weathering the cold. Also there was the ongoing desert heat all the while carrying the extreme heavy weight of the people along with the rack containing the baggage. Plus there were the beverages, food and tires as well as the mechanical stuff for the car. Even though the car's back part actually sat directly on the frame due all the weight, good ole Nashie kept right on trudging forward. All those miles it was without even giving off as much as a belch. Plus while providing thirty-five miles to the gallon on gas the three figured they had more than received their money's worth.

Suddenly, unexpectedly while up in the clouds Nashie started giving off periodic different stuttering mechanical sounds. Unfamiliar with such noises attempts to guess were made by stopping from time to time however, the noise refused to occur when stopped. The crew pressed on passing through Berthoud Pass where a stop was made for a little snort to celebrate the event as another landmark was crossed.

As the crew arrived in Idaho Springs a quick stop was made for some enjoyment of delicious milkshakes, ice cream sodas, cake, pie and cookies. After spending enjoyable time it was to visit the Narrow Gauge Train Depot then on to Stella's Café for some liquid refreshments and fresh snacks. Finally, a stop at Mickey's Conoco Service station was made for a check but Nashie's noises refused to happen. Coasting along downhill the city of Denver was reached. Though a little larger than Chester it was not even close to the size of Philadelphia.

Mountain climbing, skiing and rodeo were the main attractions and although blocks of stores for shopping, restaurants, cafes and coffee shops were available, there wasn't anything of historical interest. Close to the dinner hour, Dave called for another celebration. It was big matter as having successfully crossed the great divide. With many Mexican, Latin and Spanish restaurants available it was decision time. Each wanted a sit down dinner but at some place different that resulted in much discussion.

Finally, the Buckhorn Exchange was chosen that caused a change to good casuals. Feeling right in style it was a western style American restaurant serving cold Coors beer on draft along with serving good meals at a decent price. The huge place was complimented with good-looking waitresses and tables by the dozens. Since reservations were never made the trio was put on a waiting list but, time was pressing where Stan made an effort. Assertively he mentioned of the three being junior reporters working on a story. When the host merely pointed to the line of waiting customers Stan responded stressing their position of not having time to wait around.. Flashing his wallet as if containing credentials, he pressed for the manager while   mentioning to the other two for making like newspaper reporters.

Quizzitively, Dave asked whether he was joking but, right away Bill understood where all serious, he noted being junior reporters on assignment checking out the quality of the eating places. Quietly, Bill went to the car swiftly returning with a few souvenir tablets and several pens. Just in time when an older well dressed man showed up. While speaking to the host, the manager also addressed the trio. Over hearing, a few people in the line, the manager and host began showing curious interest about the newspaper guys. Shortly, the atmosphere became tacky where again Stan flashed his wallet in an evasive motion showing his identification while mentioning the team's duties of taking notes on the major restaurants.

Smiling, the manager nodded his head where Dave questioned him regarding the building's age, size, capacity and whether the aesthetics were original or fakes. Shortly, customers in line started hollering their being interested in the article. Timely utterances moved the manager into questioning the three being associated with the Bulletin and Inquirer. All serious Bill responded how the team needed information regarding the place's influence on the city.

Quietly, Stan interrupted stating how the team's time was short, interested in obtaining a meal but if the place was too busy the host might recommend another restaurant. Startled, the manager's face showed he didn't want to lose the chance of having the name of the place in a newspaper. Whispered to the host was that a table should be made available, where quickly Dave insisted that although on assignment there was to be no special treatment.Shortly seated, it seemed as if everyone in the place was aware that the trio was from an eastern newspaper.

Decorated similar to a hunter's trophy room, the place had stuff of the west placed neatly over the walls. Then with the attractive waitresses in their western attire the atmosphere of the west was set. Noticing the manager and host often watching, the team gave showings of taking notes. Also Dave and Bill took different strolls questioning the people where from or why that particular place. Finishing the meal, the manager showed up, noting his being thankful for the visit where Bill noted their being associated with the Inquirer through a printer.

Also, Dave added how the other two team's business had contacts with the Evening Bulletin. Several stops at the table were made by the manager after that but seeing the guys often in discussion while writing descriptive matter little else was said other than offering his thanks for selecting his place. As the manager gave Bill his business card while inquiring as to the team's position noting he had a friend that worked at the newspaper. Then when he questioned the trio's being in casual attire where straight faced, Dave asserted it was the call. Adding some details he noted of formal clothing drawing too much attention interfering with getting accurate information. Having received full interest, Stan added how under the rules the notes were confidential but would be translated into the newspaper's story with him receiving a copy.

Outside, the trio noted how each became enveloped in the pretense created where puffed up, ego had rose to new levels. Stopping at Lyon's Conoco Service station the road to Pikes Peak was discussed where it was found the toll road was not necessarily the best road conditions. Afterward the newly appointed reporters were back on the road until the evening where Nashie was pulled into an area near a tree for a good night of sleep.

SEGMENT 20. Twas the ninth day of July when late morning the crew entered the town of Manitou Springs. Feeling adventurous the crew headed for the famous landmark. Yet neither paid attention to the warnings the car was giving. Going up Pikes Peak was found to be easy, until after some long distance. Although started as paved, the roadbed had changed to either gravel or dirt/gravel mix. Able to feel the changes in air temperature also noticed was how the breathing became somewhat laborious. Not like going up a hill in the Midwest it was where the hill didn't stop for a long while. Up gradually and then the incline started getting steeper. Up may have been going around but it was always up and up, where about the halfway point another took over the driving.

At times steep inclines actually forced the car into first gear. Fascinating was when able to look over the side but, wow it was when reaching the top. About fourteen thousand feet comments abounded such as being up with the birds and wanting parachutes or renting a set of working wings. Awesome views along with the cooled hot coffees made it difficult to leave. Then on the way down the view was fascinating but also had a plus. Thrilling it was to say the least where most of the time it was necessary to keep Nashie in the lower gears. Excitement abounded during some of the turns where the driving went to being even challenging where at about a halfway again, the drivers were changed. Constant rolling from left to right was the action all the while able to look straight over the side. More than steering, the exciting driving taxed the skills of each of the drivers as total focus was necessary all the way down to the main road. Probably, there was more wear on the brakes than had been used across the entire country yet, it was definitely a most unique fun experience.

Reaching Colorado Springs a small automobile shop was found where Nashie was pulled in for a check. A man working on a vehicle hearing Nashie pull up, without even having spoke to the driver made his presence known. Stepping close to the driver's window the mechanic gave a quick hello while asserting how it was the timing chain. Stunned by the man's quick statement Dave asked how he could have known what the problem was without looking or driving? Smiling, the mechanic replied how it was his trusty ear and experience. Soon the mechanic lifted up of the hood.

While he requested the car to be started, then after working the accelerator he had the car shut down. In a mild tone he explained what costs were needed for making repairs while also suggesting buying another car. Tongues tied neither of the trio knew what to do. While Bill mentioned there being no funds to buy anything the other two attempted to get the man's help asking him to cut the costs. But the mechanic only responded how no matter what repairs were done, there could be no guarantee on how long the engine would hold up. Unable to communicate as having no experience with such matters, neither of the crew was prepared for what was being heard. What to do? The situation was monumental where the three felt helpless. Just what the heck we needed and, look where we is, Dave angrily screamed. Any attempt to buy another car for a hundred dollars was felt to be foolish as it could result in receiving similar problems. Also knowing funds remaining would be needed for fuel and food, the team found itself behind the eight ball, struggling with indecision.

Intensely, the man listened to our money situation along with the military date obligation finally offering what help he could. Formally noting he was running a business he offered to provide the parts at cost. Also he would reduce the rate per hour. For the crew it was either pay or get the bus. With ego in the picture, taking the bus was out of the question. So after hearing about the type of parts, kind of repairs and costs along with the crew's location a heavy discussed resulted. Finally it was agreed to have the man perform the work. Standing around watching, the three became depressed.

So, having nothing else to do the three walked to a close by grille. "Geez, it was worse than being at a funeral", Bill uttered as the three were unable to carry on any conversation. Men in the cafe showed their capability on the snooker table being either pros or sharks. But as the talk evolved hearing about where from along with the team's pitiful situation it became a real friendly game. Then with the bartender showing consideration the entire place helped the trio feel welcomed. Not a real match, the trio only presented a challenge where the men didn't win all the games.

Sometime later the three returned to the shop where seeing engine parts in various pans lying on the ground each knew the worst. In detail, the mechanic explained while showing the bits of chewed up metal pieces, where at the man's mercy it was necessary to trust him. Again it was back to the café where realizing the heavy pay out meant the last of the big spenders it was decided to have a last celebration. The three made the most of some tasty tap cold brews served in half moon shaped mugs along with sandwiches and free snacks. Two of the men gave opinions of taking a bus home while the others mentioned how they respected the adventurous spirit and to finish what was started.

Meanwhile, taking a break in the men's room, Stan found an official state health notice, thinking it being a unique souvenir where he kept it as a remembrance. Later it was back to the garage where the kind mechanic provided information on the cause along with showing the destroyed chain. After noting the various costs Stan started Nashie up. While the mechanic worked the accelerator it was all heads under the hood smiling. Each readily saw how proud the man was of his work hearing the purring sound. Then sadly, he mentioned how the new parts would affect the old ones strongly noting there was no guess how long the engine would hold up. Slowly, the trio departed no longer having access to a kitty of substance plus there was no real private money remaining. Shortly a stop at an ice cream shop was made as needing a mental up lift. Having to cope with the man's warning, the balloon of being able to do busted.

Mentioned was to call home for funds but such was shot down. Under the parents' orders was not part of the plan. Getting back to some normalcy on the road became a struggle. Into the early evening a stop was made at a small market where the change of pace helped in allowing some relief of the stress. Bought was cold cuts, bread, spreads, sodas, chips, pretzels and cakes thinking of the long drive ahead. Only a short drive to route forty yet, although the roads were connecting the three weren't.

Heading east through one small mountain the crew came to Kit Carson but by then the venturing spirit had evaporated. With the lack of money along with Nashie no longer dependable it was too much of a mental burden where conversation became limited to bunches of words.

Seeing the land flat as a board, Dave suggested how the prairie must have been where the creator ran out of ideas. Even then there wasn't any response as upset the three were thinking only about the negative occurrence.
With each feeling miserable about their situation sometime around midnight in a secluded area the trio pulled in for the night pondering what to expect next.

The next morning, constrained by matters out of their control the trio was desperate to show something positive. Fate had its moment but, no matter what, the three were determined.

Well, come on guys Dave blurted out let's get rolling. Would time help the crew? Would prayers help? Would being young help?

Would anything help the three were asking their selves? Neither one could offer assurances of doing anything.

 Aha! Another experience to be coped with that which wasn't planned. Just what the crew needed, a financial wreck! What a mental mess!

SECTION IV –

NEW WAY TRAVELERS

in OLD MEANS

CHAPTER TEN

A MYSTERIOUS WOMAN, REALITY, ANOTHER BEGINNING

In school there were classes on both geography and history but, who ever heard of Wallace Kansas? Overcoming hometown adversity then successfully avoiding gaming losses in Las Vegas, while reaching the planned destination having meaning, was great. Even forgotten was the short comings of Reno and Colorado Springs where the thinking was smooth sailing the rest of the way. Feelings grew that there would be no problem in making it back especially if Nashie was babied, so it was slow but steady.

Important was that slowly the guys had cleared their minds determined to make a go of it. Yet, without realizing it the three had again been bitten by the ego bug. From time to time, mentioned was of being in the middle of nowhere where looking in any direction the view was the same, only wide open country space. But then, with the land being so flat it helped ole Nashie move along easier which helped keep the three in better spirits. Having crossed the border, the crew was aware of being out of Colorado where under false pretense the three assumed that the worst was over. Jesting, Dave asked what a guy would do when on a first date a tire blows out.

Then when showing some spunk, Bill added, yeah, only to find the spare tire flat it caused a few laughs. Seeing no population around generated some interesting thoughts where feelings grew strong that with only five states to cross along with the mountains behind them the rest of the trek would be a piece of cake. Such thinking allowed comments to flow regarding what folks and friends were going to say when we returned in ole Nashie. In high spirits the crew drove across the wilderness where at some time they stopped where Dave had taken over the driving. In the wink of an eye, the trio unknowingly passed thru the town of Sharon Springs. Enjoying the ride, the crew didn't have a worry in the world as the old feelings of able to do had returned.

Unexpectedly without any warning, there was a sudden loud bang along with sound of crunch. Instant sounds of metal chewing up metal could be heard as Nashie came to a stop. What the heck was that, Bill belted out? Bashing the steering wheel, Dave angrily yelled how he thought it just threw a rod. In a flash of one motion the three were out of the car and under the hood. As the crew searched, hoping for whatever, repeatedly heard was how this couldn't he happening again. In a shaken voice, Stan while banging his fist on the fender hollered of, what the hell, way out here whatsa you guys alookn for, as dere's nutten to see.

Biting his lip while slamming his fist on the fender, Dave got behind the wheel attempting to start the car but, all that was heard was a click, click and click. Although it had juice, the starter was unable to turn the engine over. Instantly all bliss was replaced by disappointment. Yet, hoping it was stuck in a position Stan got a hammer, then while tapping the starter Dave turned the key but, only a big nothing. With each hoping for ole Nashie to get some life, turns were taken bashing the engine block then the starter as the three tried again and again. But finally the trio realized from all the effort that the car was at its end.

The not so happy threesome stood dumbfounded. Boldly, Stan yelled out his anger hollering, "oh God, why now". Looking ugly, Dave's face displayed his sadness as he yelled out, yeah Lord now what the hell are we to do. Then other similar expressions were made as the three coped with the time. In a release of frustration, Stan laughed as he kicked a tire while yelling how the situation was just terrific, just great. But no replies were heard as the three just stood looking around in disgust.

Soon the three became a ware of the car blocking the eastbound side of the highway. But, in a contrary mood the disabled crew looked on without as much as taking a step. Perhaps seeing the little traffic go around it, had given the guys some feeling of revenge. Whatever feelings each had became part of the predicament. After some time, the crew seeing their futility reluctantly pushed the car to the side of the road. While doing a good thing, adding to the joy was that it started to drizzle. Of all things, the three were forced back inside the very obstacle they were having trouble coping with.

Inside the shelter of the car, so upset was Dave, reeling in anguish he sarcastically attempted to sing happy days are here again but, couldn't pronounce the words or put the melody together. The worst part was, there wasn't anyone around to speak with.For the first time in their lives each was truly not only alone, but actually isolated. Slowly, the strain started showing its claws as more comments of anger erupted. Out in the wide-open spaces and on the wild frontier, except that the Chester Eagles Boys Club's reliable horse Nashie had died.

Before the crew had been invulnerable but now only a day later it had been reduced to an inexperienced, indecisive and uncertain trio wallowing in chaos. Time dragged as the afternoon slipped by with tempers reaching boiling. If there wasn't the banging on the doors there was the punching the ceiling or seat backings. What else, as at their age they were in a mental position of being totally lost While consumed with anger amid the hapless situation, Stan uttered how the guys couldn't just sit like a bunch of morons, as needing to do something. Hearing the response of the other two of doing what took his mind off the car.

Loudly he pressed for them to get the thumbs out! Surprised he was when void of argument he saw movement. Not to get soaking wet, turns were taken whenever it was just lite drizzling. Watching cars approach it only added to the frustration as they passed by so fast it seemed as if in a race or attempting to fly. Other times there were no cars but, what really preyed on the minds was there were no highway, federal or city cop cars seen passing by. Each had thoughts that they couldn't just sit around listening to the radio yet, having lost all interest that's what the three did. Spurts of thinking did occur but it all amounted to nothing as each was aware they couldn't carry everything in the car or carry the car. What to do was the big question?

Dave mentioned to stand in the highway to block one of the cars. However, the speed of the cars caused too much fear of ending in a hospital resulting in simply putting out the thumbs. More frustration amid the anger as time passed realizing not one person ever stopped to ask if anyone was hurt or even needing help. Actually seeing the high speeding going on each was aware that the drivers couldn't have stopped even if they wanted to.

Get a ride in the opposite direction was considered but not knowing how far backward, it went nowhere. Then to catch a bus or train except there were no buses, cabs or trains, plus there were phones around to call anyone. Everything was beyond the team's experiences. Yet, for some reason the word blame game never got started. Later on, a false sense of calm soon took over, as each was aware of the other person's feelings, not wanting to say anything or cause mis-feelings. During one moment, Bill acted weird, waving his arms yelling how it was excitement time and for everyone to step back.

Meanwhile, as the other two watched, not knowing what to expect Bill mentioned how he had enough of it where he was going to put Ole Nashie out of her misery. Demonstrating a clenched fist, he yelled for the guys to say good-bye to their Nashie, as he was going to shoot it. Quickly Dave went hiding where he laid on the back seat. Then as Stan watched, Bill drew his arm up in a continuous motion. It was along his side as if drawing out a pistol he pointed with his arm while using his finger as a gun.

Bang, bang he belted out while simultaneous smashing the fender with his foot that gave off a good sound. Hearing the sounds, Dave yelled how the man was going crazy where Bill sarcastically responded of, yes sir general Davy chumpski so now there's no reason left for any complaining. Pathetic how each groped for words that just would not develop. Stan mentioned for the guys to thank God that neither had become critically ill and count the blessings. Afraid of stepping on each other's toes there was little conversation then, when evening turned, hope was that upon waking all would be realized as a dream.

Thursday the Tenth of July greeted the guys with nothing new. As morning pushed, the team found itself all alone and really up against it. Missing was traffic normally found about towns as it was truly the wide-open spaces. Missing were the telephone booths or commercial buildings plus there were no houses, farms or any other structures within sight. Then seeing only space as no trees, light poles, horses or people the trio faced their dilemma. Reduced to a team of mayhem seeing the cars go passed without even slowing down it was guessing the speed was all we could do from going bonkers.

Of course, who could blame the drivers for not slowing down as it was just like the racetrack of nonstop riding on a straight highway with no speed limits. Of course Bill's brilliant suggestion of how all luck was probably used up in Reno didn't help any. Eventually, left without options, the three stuffed their pockets with anything of value when it was decided to walk east. Having participated in school track and football along with weight lifting and a good swimmer, Stan was in great shape. He suggested trying some trickery to slow the cars down. But the other two fearing danger, simply wouldn't hear of it.

How dense, when even looking at the map the three only focused on east of where they were. Actually the guys could have walked west to the town they drove through the day before but, being of upset minds each was void of any real thinking. Just about ready to start walking unexpectedly it happened..

"What's happening", Bill yelled, as a small truck pulled over. Who would have guessed, that of all people, it would be a woman who would stop. All excited Dave hollered out, "thank God for you lady", speaking through the small truck's window. Almost in shock, a moment of curiosity hit the trio as each had already assumed that no woman would ever stop seeing the three dirty looking men. Especially was thought when seeing no women were around, but shaking his head, Bill uttered how it must be someone's guardian angel. As the woman quickly questioned of where going, how come and what for, the team stood in awe.

Quietly she alerted of the town of Wallace only several miles up the road while out and walking around it was after seeing the tires were okay the four lined up the woman's pickup with Nashie. Slowly the woman gave the car a push until on the road some speed was made. Almost in a trance from receiving such unexpected hospitality each was. Unable to believe what was happening, while Bill told the woman details regarding the trip Stan steered Nashie along.

Finally reaching the determined area, she let the car coast to a stop then as the three got out they made attempts to thank the woman offering a few dollars of thanks. Smiling while shaking her head the woman hollered her need to get home. Then as she wished everybody God speed along with good luck she moved back on the road. As the three watched her truck disappear into the distance all the three could do was wave back while blowing a few kisses. Afterward, emotionally overwhelmed by her kindness the trio flopped on the ground trying to reason the event. Discussed was to go into the center of town but how surprised the trio was being already in the town.

Humorous comments abounded in the strained atmosphere. Only several states away from home yet of no transportation, with the kitty of no consequence and only the few dollars each was mentioning of being in another time zone, Having hallucinations or suffering from some weird time event. Getting mentally reorganized was primary. So, Bill was elected treasurer where all personal cash was combined to restart what kitty money remained. Right away a spending rule was made where no money would be spent without total agreement by all three. Then Dave was elected the leader while Stan was voted to be the politician representing the people. Dave's first decision was to remark how it was a Ripley's believe it or not time and make the most of it. Then looking to beat on someone the two bombarded Stan with innuendos, pressing him for a plan to get them out of their freaking mess.

SEGMENT 21.   Wallace, of historical significance had become a living ghost town. Started as Fort Wallace, it was also known as Camp Pond Creek. General Sherman had the fort built during 1864-65 for enforcing the white man government's intended takeover of the area. Along the trail known as Smoky Hill, the outpost provided settlers, stage coaches and wagon trains protection against the Indians, outlaws, bandit gangs, surveyors, hunters and pioneers who had set out across the land. Later, President Andrew Johnson formally declared the Fort a military reservation in 1868 providing quarters for over five hundred regular men while also housing the officers and their families.

Soldiers endured daily extreme hardship during the harsh winters until 1875 where bathhouses, an icehouse and a new corral were built. Abandoned in 1882 it was by late 1885 settlers began removing lumber, stone and other materials for their own use. During the time period a good carpenter could earn up to five dollars a day, where foremen would bring sixty dollars a month while a blacksmith and store clerk earned a hundred dollars. Painters realized eighty dollars a month with laborers hoping for forty-five dollars a month while cowboys and trail persons were at the mercy of the owner. Having control owners set their own pay and benefits scale while offering a place to sleep and good meals.

Inside one section of an old run down building was the mayor's office along with the general store while in another was the post office and police department. With other signs of titles about there was a residence located next to a junkyard. And that was the content of the entire town. Seeing the town's layout presented a true out of mind experience where the three actually felt for a moment as being in a different time zone.

Shortly a man came out waving while hollering, hello, hello there. Walking close, the well kept older middle-aged man introduced himself as George Lock. Terrific as was not only owning the junk yard but, was also the government and post office. Smiling, the man told of his watching the car being parked. Yet he noted of not seeing any older truck doing any pushing leaving the three in wondering. Along with answering questions of whose car, where going, and the problem, it was noted of what transpired in Colorado.

Shortly at the car, with Dave turning the ignition on and off George was under the hood trying to get the vehicle started. Finally, the man asserted of the starter being fine but, the motor was finished. As the three gathered around he gave the good news of with the car's age and its mileage, it was worthless. George offered five dollars being used for scrap but attempted was to haggle with the man pleading even into his office. When Dave asked for ten dollars the man responded how it was a matter of business.

Showing a quizzical look, he questioned how it was the three were so broke and upon hearing the response the man suggested about the three not telling the truth. Quickly each displayed their empty wallets while they mentioned how if the team had any money they certainly would not have been driving the damaged vehicle. Slowly displaying a change in attitude

George showed some kindness providing fruit juice beverages freshly squeezed. Then smiling he offered for the cooler an extra five dollars plus ten for the sleeping bags. With no options and the team over a barrel the amount was agreed.

While Mr. Lock wrote a short note giving his name, and the amount he stated how the note was a receipt and proof of the sale in event there was any later questioning by someone. Spiteful thoughts were later mentioned about flattening the tires, putting salt into the gas tank or other mischief but, such revenge just wasn't of the team's character. Since George was going for his own business he provided the trio a lift to the railway freight station. So it was back to the car where each bundled their clothes. Not wanting to be bogged down with any luggage or a bedroll each took what they wore plus held a change of sox and a handkerchief.

Having stripped the car with pockets bulging, thinking was locked into being only a few states away where it should only be a couple of days before reaching home. Surprise it was when the three realized how close they had been to Sharon Springs. After the railway agent gave the trio small bags for each, he took care of Mr. Lock as being a freight depot where it only handled packages, no passengers.

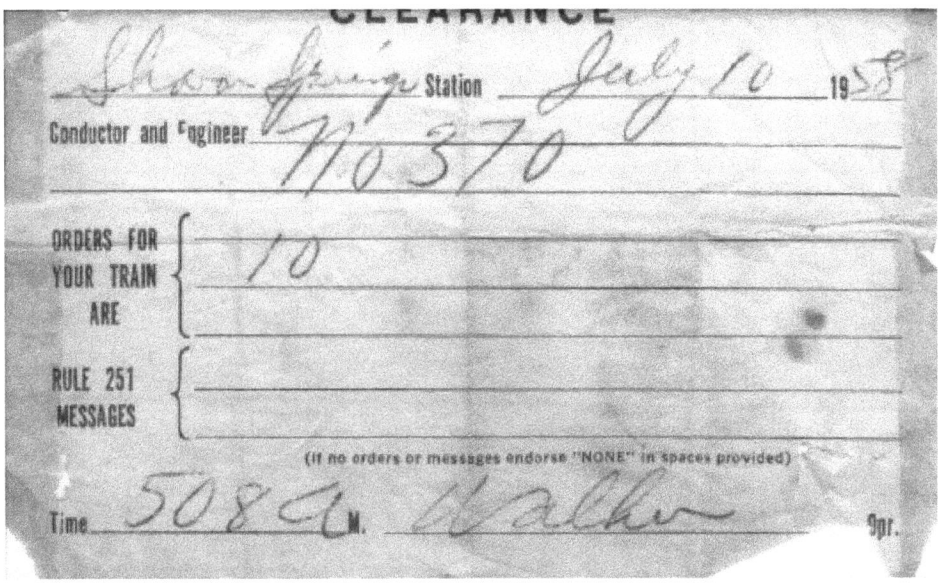

Once all personal items were put in the small bags, those were wrapped inside the bundled clothes and put in large bags. Last it was with all tagged with names, all the large bags were put into a single large box where it was shipped to Dave's home to be divided once returned.

While Bill paid the clerk, the man offered suggestions on how to hitchhike adding not to even think about jumping on one of the freights. Quickly Bill replied how the team wouldn't think of doing such while Dave added that neither had any experience anyway. While exiting, the man hollered that if education was wanted on how dangerous, they should speak to the yardman. Unknowingly he had reignited the thought Stan h+ad mentioned earlier. But walking to the road another debate ensued regarding calling home for bus or train fare. Such would have been the intelligent way but not wanting to hear from anyone about having failed or given up ego was in charge where it was not considered. Also there were feelings of getting rides of fifty to a hundred miles at a time where the team anticipated arriving in the east in just a matter of a few days. The Chester Eagles Boys Club was looking to do but a struggle had risen as neither wanted responsibility for making sole decisions.

Curiosity had Stan bent on needing to find out but, at first the yard worker all skeptical was reluctant to even speak to the trio. Alertly, Dave advised that the agent suggested for hearing of the dangers from the yard man where at least he listened. Hearing of the ages and not having funds or travel means along with home being far away the man mellowed. Interjecting shorts of his experiences the good sized African American laborer provided useful information where the visual of him only hid the man's kindness and wisdom. Easily apparent by the worn skin along with the man's speech his knowledge of life was such that books with all of their words could not illustrate.

Understanding his cautious willingness to help, the three respected the man's goodness where they promised that if ever caught, it was they never spoke to him. As the trio listened his changes of tone along with repeated words, drove home the ways. Yet, constantly looking around it was obvious of his concern knowing someone was watching. Noting his needing to get back to work, the man strongly asserted hard safety tips. Then while smiling, the polite man mentioned which train to hop while pointing to where and why to be at the time. Further he suggested that if no boxcars were available, to try for the rear of the caboose.

After a pause he lastly mentioned a Ho Bo camp located some miles away. Smiles with good handshakes abounded acknowledging the team's loving respect for the older man's superb good nature. Then whispering, he added, that if having any problem to mention Charlie. But as Dave questioned who was Charlie, all the man did was put his finger across his lips uttering hush. Turning he went back to work where feeling to avoid any trouble the trio walked away. Short turns were made gving the man a saluting wave. With good feelings it was agreed where the trio was to at least give the rails a try.

A short distance later the trio found their selves waiting in the very spot the man had mentioned. Feeling good about the moments the team waited for the train back in the brush. Nervously, Bill mentioned how he was having second thoughts since the practice was surely dangerous. But all confident, Stan responded how it should only take a little learning. Hesitant, Dave noted how not having experience it was pressing the team's luck. Cooped up in the trench while not knowing how long to wait, along with not having any training thoughts of the dangers brow beat the three.

Shortly a freight train approached causing the hearts to pound thinking about what to do. Disappointment was short as it only slowed down, giving off only toots of its horn. Named the Pawnee and Western Railway, on the local runs, used were the old steam coal engines. Shortly, a small freight train chugged into the area where several men dropped off boxes along with picking up packages. While the yardman spoke with the brakeman, the brakeman waving an arm blew his whistle. Just like clockwork the trainmen boarded as the engine blew its whistle in response. All excited, crouched with hearts pounding the three watched the monster start up.

Immediately thoughts sprung out on which car to grab and when to run. Blowing its whistle the engine was also letting out a large burst of steam as the engine blew its whistle. One toot then two toots huge smoke puffs filled the sky as the stream from its stack puffed out. Seeing the large wheels start to turn being so close, while huge puffs of black smoke emitted from the stack and steam pushed out from the side, the team became mesmerized. As the boiler pressed hard the train moved forward while Dave hollered how hyped up he was.

Moments later Bill yelled about his heart blowing up as anxiously the trio waited looking for the right moment to move. Like three mice in fear, caught in a trap looking to jump out, tense as rubber bands stretched to the max Stan hollered how he was scared. Chug, then chug, its speed slowly increased as so did the chugs. Slowly as the approaching moment peaked hearts pounded so hard it was as if we had just ran the mile. Each body was trembling where the three had gotten next to each other actually leaning on each other for support. There wasn't even enough space to put pencils.

After various types of work cars passed the three jumped up ready but, there were no open boxcars. Suddenly the caboose approached leaving no choice, as it was the last car. The off color red caboose was at the spot in front where excitedly Dave blurted out, "ok guys here it is". Instantly as Bill and Stan hollered, "yeah, so lets go", Dave yelled, "holy crap guys". Running alongside the moving caboose in a dash Dave jumped onto the bottom step. Then while he moved up a couple of steps the train was gaining speed. Bill easy followed jumping also landing on the bottom step. But, just at that moment the car rocked from side to side.

Both overtaken by the car's sudden swaying were forced to grabbed hold of the railing becoming stationary. Meanwhile in those few moments, Stan had lost his chance. Stopping on the skinny stairs with the small train steadily gaining speed, the two had blocked Stan from jumping on. Unable to jump on with the other occupying the skinny stairs, Stan only inches away, was prevented access. Still running alongside the car started passing him where grabbed on to the fence at the rear.

Responding, Dave and Bill were only able to holler for him to hold on. Meanwhile running in a daze, Stan had flashbacks of racing against his schoolmates. However such sporting was on flat land while the roadbed was anything but flat. With all thinking about safety gone to the wind, Stan's mind was recalling his past leg injury as the railroad ties presented an obstacle of which he was not prepared. Clickety clack went the wheels where the rhythm pushed Stan's concern on being scared of falling. Alarmed at losing his balance he was squeezing the lower fence rail with all of his might as if to keep it from blowing away while letting out a screeching prayer for help.

Shaken by the moment Dave and Bill had moved up the steps to the platform. But frozen as statues the two simply responded for Stan to hold on. Fear seized the moment as the runner screamed for them to help and do something. Yet, with the engine chugging, along with the clickety clack of the wheels, chills went over the three only thinking of the worst. A capable runner having run the mile in twenty seconds over the state record didn't help Stan. Also recalling his left leg giving away playing football causing torn ligaments at the ankle twice as well as behind the knee didn't help. Timely switching his running to a trot helped Stan keep his balance but, the speed of the caboose steadily pumped his adrenaline to stress levels. All self-confidence slowly disappeared since Stan had never known such fear.

Attempting to reach the top bar of the fence Stan tripped causing him to slip and bang his head. Although accessible, the top bar became out of reach. Running while holding on also coping with the ties, all being dragged at the same time denied any means of jumping. Fright was all he felt as Stan's eyes caught sight of the roadbed going by under his feet. Terrified, Stan screamed out his lungs, "for God's sake guys, do something, help me"! Almost in shock by the unexpected occurrence the other two feeling helpless were perspiring like squeezed dishrags.

Pounding out its energy while dragging the train along, the train was also pulling Stan. Sweat of his hands on the warm metal caused a loosing of his grip where he was forced to wipe one hand to gain a good grip then the other. Meanwhile, running on the roadbed his mind was going berserk where stress hit the beyond stage. Stamina being taxed to the limit while perilous by the minute, thoughts of dying raced through Stan's mind feeling his loss of energy. Pull him up Bill and Dave wanted, but why weren't they moving to help. "What the hell's wrong with you guys", Stan yelled.

More difficult by the minute, totally frustrated he was able to feel his body getting weaker as time passed. Angrily feeling alone, Stan screamed at the top of his lungs for the guys in God's name to help him.

Unexpectedly the train's motion caused the car to jerk forcing Stan to scream in pain as he bounced against the turnbuckle. Amidst the fierce pain in his side, he recalled where even the breaking of his nose in football or the tearing of his leg ligaments didn't cause such pain.

During his sophomore and junior years he participated in weight lifting at the YMCA often pressing over 290 pounds while also able to hold his breath over five minutes swimming. Yet, such flash backs provided no support. Banged up and hurting while overwhelmed by the situation, Stan was losing his spirit where depressed by his inability, moments of hopeless uselessness led to thoughts of simply letting go. Yet, out of nowhere a burst of strength allowed him to hold on. Semi dragging his body while straddling the turnbuckle with teary eyes, Stan's feet banged against the ties finding their spots.

Stumbling off balance then recovering allowed a moment of sudden energy enabling Stan to regain his trotting. Reaching in between the spokes, grabbing hold to secure Stan's left arm, Dave hollered for Bill not to stand there like a dummy but quickly grab the other wrist or arm. With good holds, swiftly the two moved in panic realizing their friend's hapless situation. Easily perceiving Stan's vulnerability terrified the two beyond their senses as they were put in such a heavy situation of instant responsibility for a person's life. Excitedly, Bill hollered for him to hang on while Dave yelled for Stan to know they were doing and just hold on.

Amazing it was that Stan hadn't slipped breaking his neck where death would have been quick. Fully aware of how close he had come to fracturing his head, rib or breaking one of his legs, absolute terror had taken control.Stan was frightened out of his wits. Never before had he ever thought of dying but, floundering about the turnbuckle while holding on caused Stan to pray for help like he had never done before. Hearing his words the other two was only able to reply amen and amen. Give us a hand Dave yelled to Stan, while hollering for Bill to hold him steady.

Constant thoughts of being helpless falling like a rock bashing his head or breaking his neck kept Stan's mind raced in a state of fright. Slowly the two having a good hold yelled to each other pull, pull, pull !

Simultaneously with the two pulling at the runner's arms allowed Stan to move his hands up the spokes but in a frenzy close to the top rail Stan's sweaty hands slipped. Instantly limited to only holding on as he slid back down the spokes, hold on, Dave yelled. Also urging Bill to keeping on pulling while stooping, Dave stood being able to reach over the top railing with one arm. As he reached with the other arm, Bill did the same while holding on to Stan's other arm. Both guys took a pause together where again they tried.

Dave grabbed hold of his friend's pants and belt where Bill and Dave together lifted at the same time enabling Stan to grasp the top railing. Whew and whew were the guys' sounds over a moment. Following a few moments pause it was with Stan's help where he was able pull up till able to sling his right leg semi over the top. Aware the metal could have torn his skin with eyes bulging, his heart hit new poundings. Responding to his awkward position instant pain caused a momentary loss of control of his right arm. Unexpectedly, Stan slipped leaving him partially straddling the fence top.

Stan almost in tears the two grabbed his leg then with both arms fussed to help him regain some balance where another pause allowed Stan to get a grip on himself. Asked if he was ok, already half dazed Stan could only reply, you betcha your betchum. Moments later he hollered ok guys, let's do it. On any other day, Stan could have jumped over the rail by his self but, at the time he was exhausted, weak and helpless. While securing their hold on him the two hollered one, two three, then pulled but Stan couldn't make it. Too weak, the spring had gone out of his legs where he ended remaining laying half over the railing. Subsequent to another pause, the two pulled and tugged. Then with Stan also doing it allowed himself to flop over on to the platform. Instant sighs of pain erupted as he hit the steel platform floor. Although relieved from the precarious position, momentarily Stan remained lying on his back not wanting to move.

While seeing Stan in prayer of thanks the other two joined in as they helped their wounded partner to pick himself up. Realizing how upset he was, the two guys attempted some humor. Uttering it being a close call and not to try another stunt like that again may have been of good intentions, but the innuendos only irritated Stan where he showed to engage his clenched fists. Struggling with pain along with his temper Stan's verbiage was sluggish but, the two comprehended where they felt hurt having said such things. Fumbling in frustration the two blurted out of not knowing what to do which only drew remarks from Stan such as, stupid idiots and morons. Moments later while in anger he asserted for the two yo yos to jump out there to let him have some fun watching them being bashed around. As three understood the ugly situation being beyond either one's control slowly a calm settled the threesome down.

Emotions between the three flowed like water in a stream when unexpectedly the caboose door flew open. A brakeman was standing with a facial grump while waving his club yelling in a ruff tone asking what the hell the guys were doing there. Not giving any chance for a reply the man shouted how the next time the train slows down the three had better not be there or it would be the police for the lot of them. Meanwhile seeing Stan dusting himself off while using his club he pointed at Stan questioning whether the guy had fleas. Shaking his head no, Bill mentioned how there was no intention of causing problems as only trying to get home.

Sternly the man responded in jest asking if the three performed such stunts on a regular basis. Immediately the other men inside the car hollered how the trio was a carnival act. Irritated by the lack of consideration, showing his displeasure, Dave hollered in response how he thought they were a stupid carnival act. Seeing the animosity building, the brakeman yelled for the other men to shut up while he pressed how the three came to be on the train. With finger to lips, Dave replied how such couldn't be told because it was a secret. More subsequent attempts to trick the three were tried but each fell on deaf ears since to the team a promise was a promise. Seeing Stan peeked, the brakeman advised him to sit down while he reached into a cabinet.

However, thinking the man was reaching for a gun the trio reacted in a state of alarm moving for the door. How relieved the three was seeing the man pull out Band-Aids, iodine and a small cloth. While Stan tended to his bruises the man asserted how the train would be slowing to less than twenty miles an hour, where the three better jump off.

Meanwhile having heard the team's story, he explained how things were easy on his side.Then moments later not having success with the quizzes he added how the further east traveled, the more difficult things would become. Such was because of new rulings where railroad men could end up losing their jobs or even sent to jail if proven they provided assistance. Aware of the train slowing the social ended when in a rush, the men provided information regarding the highway along with noting a diner.

As the men waved, the three jumped off where reaching the ground, Bill blurted out, "heres weez goes doozzens its agains. With grease spots while scratched up Stan and the team full of dirty sweat, walked desperately needing a shower. Often they were forced to stop due to his sides hurting. While the two inspected his ribs Dave made reference to Bill regarding the huge big black and blue mark. Determined there was no brakeage or cracks, a sigh of relief from Stan was heard with smiles.

From then on, it was over hill, over dale through the dusty dirty brush where the trio went trudging along where Bill started singing a jingle with the other two joining. Then Dave started singing it's, hi ho, hi ho, yo ho, ho ho, it's on the road as the trio goes bumbling along. Later showing some resiliency Bill noted how Stan was one of the few that could actually state how he pulled up the rear.

Then in other moments shouts of screaming words were heard as the three simply tried to relieve some of their pent up anger. Never forgotten, the event's affect had visibly shaken each to the bones where a difference in attitudes was showing. Sometime later Bill exclaimed, after all that and losing Nashie, what else could possibly go wrong.

It took some time but moments later, Dave responded about being due for some good luck. Gee whiz, Stan hollered, for the guys to stop it as he had enough.

Without realizing it, the three had gone through changes in their personalities.

CHAPTER ELEVEN

OLD WAYS AMID THE NEW, NATURAL FURY, SCOUNTING AND PENNIES

"**H**ey guys look, there it is", Bill yelled seeing the tops of trucks going by. Shortly reaching the highway it was facing the oncoming drivers with the thumbs out. Rides were scarce considering the volume of traffic. Even when picked up the rides only traveled short ways plus the team was often let out at spots either around dirt roads or of no major intersection.In frustration the three took a break making use of a fallen large tree trunk to rest the limbs. Jesting, Dave commented about getting home in time for Labor Day but, no matter what, it was stand, walk and take a break since little else could be done. With night falling, found was a grassy place where the three dozed off under the sky till morning.

Getting going that Friday it was a long time of the thumbs till finally a car pulled close. Hearing the passenger ask if looking for a ride, the trio was stunned by the question. Standing out in the middle of nowhere each failed to comprehend how such could have been asked. Anxiously replying with a few yes and yeses the woman noted of only going a short distance. Breaking out in laughter the team shouted great and terrific. Once the man headed into the traffic he advised how it was not a good time of day to be looking for a ride while the woman mentioned of their turning off. But, at least it was at an intersection.

Afterward it was no more rides, but walk and walking then, after some time seen was a diner. With lifted spirits the three actually jogged part of the way to the place. Following a mad scramble to get cleaned up it was grabbing a booth. Just sitting, was before taken for granted but then it was a big deal. Able to relax the trio fumbled to plan ways to stretch the food. Amid grumbling of not calling for money it was discussion on ways of saving money. Not of a good attitude the team probably made it difficult for the waitress to feel wanted. Attempting to sell the usual stuff she was rebuffed as not interested. Having a difficult time accepting we had come all the way from the east sociability was hindered.

Especially there being no car, the woman had a difficult time relating to the trio's situation. Coincidently of no social it was about that time, a sudden downpour with sounds of boom cracks occurred. While waters were used as the main beverage treated with spots of syrup or sugar it was only one coffee was ordered with two extra cups, then divided into thirds it was added with the water. The rest of the orders each being different were split among each other. Soon, having heard what the waitress had told, the cook wanted to know about the situation. Then after going outside looking he admitted his disbelief. Overtaken with frustration, Stan noted how he was no longer interested in answering any more questions.

Smiling, Bill and Dave showed the licenses and sales slip while mentioning their partner's deep emotions where the cook responded how he understood. Shortly the waitress gave each a cup of coffee stating how the beverage was on her while the cook was going back and forth to the kitchen in between discussing the trip. Minutes later the waitress dropped off slices of hot apple pie and large glasses of milk with complements from the cook where the meal ended on a good note. Later as the storm passed, while outside feeling better, the three found it easier to cope with the cars not stopping. But the endless highway of walk, rest and walk took its mental toll.

Getting toward evening, while looking for a spot to sleep, a man pulled up asking where going. When Bill replied to Philadelphia but would settle for Pittsburgh, laughing, the driver blurted out how he wasn't going that far. Like others it was the usual questions until after some time, the man pointed out the road he was going to take. What a surprise, when instead of stopping, he kept on driving. Showing his good nature he later dropped the team off in front of a small motel where the man made a U turn going back west having gone out of his way simply to help.

As the three entered the office with a short discussion the manager noted the grubby appearance. Unable to help it was the man asserted adding he didn't think there were any rooms available. But as the trio pushed he was overheard making a telephone call to the diner that the trio had just come from. While he reviewed the identifications, the man mentioned the prices to which the trio showed him the empty wallets. Bill explained the lack of funds where smartly, Dave suggested being only necessary to get a shower, as not interested in any extras. Yeah, Stan added, just wanted to get cleaned up.

Clearly the man had a hard time believing what was told as repeatedly asked how going, where, and where the car was. Finally after speaking with some woman behind a curtain he advised of the two places on the end of the row being of lesser prices. But, not taking to the man's attitude, in disappointment the trio headed for the exit. However, just as Bill opened the door, the man hollered for us to hold up a minute. Noting of hearing of the boys really being that broke, the man stated that since there was nothing going on he could allow a reduction of about a third.

So, while Stan signed in with Bill paying the fee, Dave grabbed the key. Failing to look first the trio rushed out of the office where, almost instantly it was easy to see why he had cut the price. Not only was the room small in size but so was the bed. Totally upset at what they paid for but knowing each one's conditions, it was decided to stay. Shortly, along with extra blankets the man also provided a thick mattress cover that was used for underneath sleeping on the floor. Making the most of it everyone felt better being cleaned up especially able to wash the under garments. Times along with their circumstance, the trio was with no change of clothes, no beer, snacks, radio, watch, plus no card playing. Even limited to conversation the sad situation drastically affected the trio's minds.

First thing, next morning Bill asked whether such was the way they did things in the old days. But neither gave any response, only wondering if things could get worse. Before leaving the man bringing from under the counter offered wrapped saltine crackers, candy bars and other items. A little revitalized the trio was greeted by the radio forecast of scattered showers with heavy downpours, high winds and dangerous thunderstorms of lightening. Warnings for everyone to take cover were all being broadcasted but since the man didn't say anything about it the message was ignored.

Shortly the team made full use of the snacks while hoping for early rides, but as time passed, there were no rides yet, at least the three were feeling clean and refreshed. Often there was laughing at what was not even funny just to perk some good spirits. With people refusing to even slow down amid one moment feeling disgusted, the trio plopped on the ground. Later acting on Dave's prompting Bill pulled a pant leg up even doing a little wiggle but, the only thing that did was to bring on a couple of toots with finger displayed.

SEGMENT – 22.   Times of a short ride and walking it was when the trio came across a side road. A detour from the highway but necessary it was. A farmhouse was hoped where dry throats could be quenched. The dirt foundation of the skinny road was appreciated being not nearly as hot as the highway, then seeing the barn, Stan reflected on his childhood visiting his grand parents farm in south Jersey. Grandfather Nicholas Gurska would trade some of their corn, milk, berries and other crops with neighbors who had other items they didn't have.

After knocking on the door an older woman was seen inside peeking where the three asked if possible to get some water. However, hearing from out of state she quickly shut the door where shortly she was seen looking the three over through her side bowed window. Not to bother her, the trio started to walk away. Unexpectedly, wearing a smile the woman holding a pitcher of ice water and glasses yelled, hello boys, come on back.
Following an inquiry of the usual, the woman's personality blossomed as the talk developed into a nice discussion. Shortly the woman even brought out fresh coffee with toast and fixings.
     Enjoying a real friendly social on the porch with a roof over head it was really appreciated. Watching the rain Dave noted how nice it was not being caught in it. Time passed when thinking was to leave but the older woman came out carrying a tray of toast, cold cuts, lettuce, cheese and jelly for sandwiches.
While Stan attempted to say thanks he was also pressing for leaving but Bill put a stop to him noting how rude it would be to refuse her hospitality
     Concerned, Stan mentioned of the military time constraint but with all smiles Bill rebuffed how it didn't matter, since the reporting date had already been missed. So, while the woman described the destructive weather of the previous month, the three also noted their experience coping with the same. Such allowed common ground for conversation where each became comfortable allowing all to relax.

Without realizing it, time had passed into late afternoon, when the woman alerted to the forecasted unstable weather. For safety she suggested to stay the night but, her being alone there was only sleeping in the barn.

However, seeing the foreboding clouds quick nodding of heads was shown with replies of yes and many thanks. Later with the little dog at her feet she served some old fashion soup containing everything but the kitchen sink with rye bread. Afterward, although refusing to accept help, upon Stan's persistence the three washed the dishes while helping to clean up.

Later showing some gratitude it was shoveling the cow's droppings into the pasture while adding grain along with hay close to the cows. Apparent was that the old house and barn had been there years before the couple arrived. As the woman provided several blankets, towels and a bar of yellow soap she inquired if either knew about cows. While Stan took hold of the three-gallon bucket he asked the woman what was the name of the cow. Of course no one paid any attention to his question which was disregarded as simple talk. Meanwhile Stan found peace recalling his happy days spent on his grandparent's farm near Elmer, New Jersey. His parents visiting often would leave him there for a day or two where late recollections of making butter, ice cream and preserves along with eating fresh vegetables and meat, sleep came easy.

Dawn broke early as the team noticed the lady already in the coop feeding the chickens. As the other stood in disbelief at what they two watching, unbeknownst to them what was coming down, Stan picked up the bucket while talking to the cow. Then after grabbing a stool he put the bucket in place as he sat down. Blurting out their comical innuendos, the two could only watch as Stan stretched his arms while singing and patting the animal. Surprised the two were seeing Stan start with his hands on the udders.

Giving a few sounds, the animal gave a snarl. As the animal turned its head it seemed almost as if speaking. Immediately Stan patted the cow while he apologized, softly stating ok, ok, yeah, yeah, yeah, so it's been a few years. Soon it was visible how Stan was less than confident. Where a slower pace followed evidencing he was no longer sure of his self, resuming his singing while repeating the animal's name along with a few more pats, slowly the two seemed to jell. Then as the guy's hands moved in a steady rhythm with the cow not giving a sound, control was realized.

Stopping to rest his fingers and hands he badgered the two for them to get on using the tools where astounded by seeing the farm boy's ability they whispered an oky doky as the two manned the rakes and shovel.
Not an organized team for sure but, at least it wasn't three ding-a-lings fumbling around. Only about a third of the way full, as his hands just weren't up to the chore and not wanting to hurt the animal Stan stopped. Enjoying a quick shower outside the barn to the three it was next to heaven.

Then seeing the bucket causing the woman to smile the trio realizing some good was done they all felt a little of heaven. Pondering that Stan may have known a little bit farm work conversations often drifted with her curiosity.

At breakfast with the woman doing the cooking the eager eagles took over. Stan having helped his mom then grandmother, with Bill and Dave always assisting their mothers there was little the woman needed to do. Mealtime became an extravaganza with dialogue enjoyable as Stan's mind was swirling in bliss almost feeling at home. Then with the other three enjoying the time turned into a social. Finishing the coffee was the sad conclusion when a parting of the ways amid an emotional cloud was forced by the time element. Such highly sincere thank yous were expressed that a person would have actually needed to be there to appreciate the emotions especially understanding the woman didn't know either of the three. Back down the dirt road, the guys ignored the weather warnings as they walked.

Reaching the highway it was thumbs back to work when unexpectedly in a short time a very old small pickup truck pulled over. As an elderly man asked where heading, all excited, Bill hollered state of Pennsylvania. Scratching his ear, the man responded how it was ok, as knew we were fooling. Quietly, Dave asked why people keep saying the same thing thinking the man didn't hear then was surprised hearing him holler yeah, yeah so, two jump on the back. The very old model of box design with a bed made of wood gave off an odor where it was assumed the truck was used for fresh produce. While the two's pants had absorbed the odor a ride was a ride.

Eagerly the man spoke of his earlier years of hitchhiking even riding the rails where Dave inquired about a hobo camp in the area. He never thought the old man would have known of such a place but surprised he was when the man uttered, may be. Once Bill mentioned of the yardman along with the diner person having noted the place, the man smiled. While describing the spot the man even suggested where to cut across the highway for proceeding into the wooded area. Then as Dave opened the door for getting out of the truck the man suggested to look for unusual signs. Watching the man drive off once again the three were at another spot of no traffic light or intersection. Soon the trio was able to get a short ride then, it was walking until each step became a chore.

After some time and distance appearing as if sick, Dave stopped walking. Then while pointing he shouted out for the guys to look where, dumbfounded at seeing his seemingly pointing to nothing the two stood wondering. Unknowing what was happening, Stan inquired if he was ill while, Bill asked what they were supposed to look at. There it is guys, Dave screamed, while rumbling in how he saw it. Uncanny, but Dave easily saw the location of what had been described.

Hard at first, then after a few moments almost simultaneously Bill and Stan hollered their expression of, well I'll be darn. Feeling excited with optimism arms began waving with a burst of energy as the three ran in a frenzy. As fast as the legs would carry across the highway's wide span, not even stopping to look back the trio headed into the wooded area. Walking through a maze of big trees and fallen limbs each was shaking their heads wondering if they did right.

Dead wood and thick brush, the woods was also overcast as clouds created a dreary feeling like walking in a dense fog plus overhanging tree parts created large shadows. No idea of what signs to look for while in the unfamiliar area plus having no directions, the trio lost its bearings. Unable to hear automobile sounds or see any signs Stan asserted how the whole thing was just a bunch of bull. Then when Dave mentioned how those people told of what may have been years ago, Bill asked whats doos wees doos if there ain'ts no camp. Stan sarcastically replied trying something like walking yet, unknown was that they were not far from Ellis.

Not looking to go backwards the three spread out apart from each other to help prevent walking in circles then steadily moved forward. Forging through the dense trees and brush it was as if caught up in some mysterious challenge but after some distance, unexpectedly the three stumbled onto what could have been a theatre stage. No music or big lights, yet it was as if a huge curtain had lifted where there appeared an oval clearing. Instant happy moments but not a word was spoken where seen standing as if statues, were five men. Then hearing an invitation the team moved in where there was a pup tent, several sleeping bag rolls, laundry hanging on a string type clothes line plus a coffee pot over top a fire pit.

Politely the men introduced each other with joyous exuberance of welcoming new faces. Then with fresh coffee grinds added everybody gathered around in a reserved social where questions and answers flowed. Shortly metal cups along with passing the pot around each told some of their stories while hearing the trio's story. Extraordinarily thick able to be applied with a white wash brush Stan recalled how his grandmother Catherine made the same as didn't measure but simply filled the basket. After all she had six children that meant a lot of cups. As age and ethnic barriers fell away recalled were times of the Sunnybrook Ballroom and bands such as Woody

Herman's Herd. Gleefully, Bill overwhelmed by the moment without forethought uttered how he thought the social with the bums was great.

Red faces showed their displeasure where one of the men vehemently asserted for the young punk to hold it right there. Built like a linebacker the man displayed his anger while another held the angry man back. Upset with rage the man could have taken Bill's head off. In a quiet barking tone he aggressively advised for the trio to watch what the heck they say. While the trio backed up right away another explained how no one ever calls a hobo a bum where instantly Dave inquired about the problem.

Squashing the joy of the whole group, Bill caused embarrassment because the insulting reference of being bums hit the wrong nerves. Not knowing what affect his words nor their impact would have, Bill had blundered. Not intended but the guy had made a huge verbal association mistake. Alerted to a misunderstanding, one of the men suggested for everyone to take a deep breath while, another blurted out how bums are slouches where it was they were doers actually working for a living. Understanding the unintended offense Bill and Dave quickly apologized. Stan added a thank you for the education while explaining how they didn't know about train hopping manners.

Then as the men heard the three's ages noting they understood it was back to enjoying the social. Informed of having to move along, another mentioned of a train arriving as going east. Instantly hearing it could end up in Kansas City Stan questioned where the three could catch it. Seeing how serious the trio was, the men provided information on how to jump on the boxcars but hearing of the trio's experience with the caboose all went quiet.

Once agreed to follow the man's instructions the three tagged along. Without any flags or telling signs showing anywhere, some distance later the four reached the exact area the man had previously described. A secluded area, the spot was where he explained how signs were the natural growth of things. While advising when and where to run, time passed until heard was a loud whistle where a locomotive was seen in the distance. Hearing mumbling of conversation the man strongly blurted out to be quiet since there were spotters around.

Minutes later the four moved into a crouched position, anxiously with nerves stretched like rubber bands. The man mentioned the car's number noting it being the only one that could be used but neither of the three had any idea what he was talking about. But having played football, and track the trio understood the term of get ready. Loud duck like sounds were heard as the engine blew its horn. Overwhelmed, the four watched as the boiler blew out large gushes of steam with the metal monster releasing some anger.

Billowing out dark smoke from its stack the engine chugged, forcing the wheels to turn. Seeing the big horse move forward, overly excited Dave asked if we go now but, the man replied no, and wait for his signal. The trio's hurry up attitude conflicted with the man's displayed patience. Then as the car came into view the man jumped waving his arm while hollering how it was ok guys, now, let's do it. As hopping frogs, the four leaped up, running for the car. So precise, it was as if the four had even practiced. Following the man's example each ran, grabbed, jumped and climbed onto the car's floor.

Excited, as the trio had seen pictures of people riding with their legs out over the edge, they attempted to do the same. Immediately, the man grabbed the first two with his arms, yelling no. With the trio back against the other wall the man yelled out how such could never be done because of paid spotters with field glasses. Suddenly the three realized how much they didn't know.

Some distance later, as the train slowed down, Stan and Dave moved to the far corner of the car while the other two grabbed the other far corner while laid down. Felt were the repeated motions of the car going back and forth as the train moved cars around. Meanwhile the loud noises of the metal clanging and banging echoed inside as if inside a large drum where it was a new experience. Stan asked why so much hiding but, the man merely motioned for silence by putting his finger to his lips. Shortly at the door opening appeared two men waving their flashlight while looking around as if searching for something. Thinking the trainmen had moved away the three attempted to stand, but the hobo instantly motioned to stay put and be quiet.

Minutes later yelling by trainmen was heard followed by toots of their whistles. Then as the engine's horn sounded its toots the engine cranked out its power moving the train forward where the man waved his all clear signal. Shortly when Dave complained about there being no boxes or crates to sit on the man replied of actually riding in style since the car had been swept broom clean of animal matter. Enjoying a social, the miles went by where later the train came to another stop. That time, no instructions were needed as each moved quickly into position. Then as the train chugged forward the man advised how it was only a pick up and dropped off point.

SEGMENT – 23. Following a short nap over some long distance the train arrived at the final stop. As the train reduced its speed the hobo gave instructions of necessity to get off before the actual stop to avoid trouble with guards or the police. Time after advising the guys to follow him it was out of the car where the four stooped, jumped, rolled and ran until the man advised it was safe. Only close but, it was his usual spot for getting to his job destination. Being around the dinner hour Stan asked if he knew any reasonable eateries where smiling, the man pointed to the area north of the yard where places served good food at fair prices. With warm farewells bided shortly seen was him heading in the southwest direction where expressions were made of another friend being made yet, lost to time.

Topeka, where each felt good, aware of not being far from the next border. Seeing puddles of water neither paid much mind assuming they were due from showers and the humid weather., then being hungry, right away was to find one of the cafés the man suggested. Too much talk with little thinking, led the trio walking until unable to recall anything about crossing a highway yet, there they were. Spotting a man leaning against a light pole the trio approached as smartly Dave inquired about cafes. While the man inquired if price or quality was preferred thinking by the three was him being either a hobo or a company undercover person. Stan blurted out how neither of the guys were choosy where responding the man directed the trio back the way they had come.

Along the way, Dave mentioned of him finding it interesting how it was to have found the way to the coast yet couldn't find a café when given directions. Low foreboding clouds had approached with spritzing yet, neither one paid any attention. While reaching Topeka Avenue again, decided was each taking turns to find a decent place. Some fuss there was over a few places until the three agreed upon a café yet, not on quality or price but rather its name. Looking at the sign while laughing, Bill quizzed whether it was a car wash? "Ten Pennny", an elaborate beer place it served hot and cold sandwiches plus select platters.

With the main crowd gone, good seating choices remained where enjoyed was the simple pleasure of sitting on padded seats. Smiling, the waitress arrived with waters where doing a review of the two-sided dirty menus Dave uttered a grunt resembling that of a pig. Such noise generated several stares from other customers that caused comments from the other two. Minutes later as the woman in her late thirties returned with the usual service greeting, showing some spunk, Stan put on the charm. Noting her smile and being attractive Stan asked why such a pretty woman was not on the menu. Sternly the waitress cleared the air of her only wanting to hear what was being ordered.

Meanwhile weather reports on the café's radio gave warnings on storms of heavy downpours, lightening and wind but, not seeing people react, the three gave such no thought. When the cute Oriental American waitress returned, Bill ordered the roast beef special with extra gravy along with a large water for the beverage.

Quietly, Stan requested a large dish of mixed vegetables and extra water while Dave ordered a double order of toast with a large glass of milk and a large glass of water. As the waitress smiled she suggestively asked if the water was for dunking the veggies, Stan replied how it was actually to make them grow. As time passed, the woman was seen watching the food being divided up, where it must have appeared as some sort of food checkers.

Soon the guys requested water refills and extra toast with lots of jelly adding if there was no extra charge. Solemnly the woman responding asked if the guys were having some sort of hard luck time where Bill feeling embarrassed slouched with his head bent. Smartly, Dave showed his finesse while giving her a quick synopsis where Stan added to, for him not to forget the lack of funds. As before in other places, it seemed that most people assumed the three were yarn spinners where the woman persisted to know whether from Missouri or Illinois. Almost choking, the three replied how it had already been mentioned of being from outside Philadelphia. Upon hearing the reply she asserted having been to Pennsylvania being fully aware of how far the city was. Then following a pause, she added how no one ever told her such a bunch of malarkey.

Having taken her words as an insult, instantly Dave with temper jumped up bringing out his billfold. Angrily he handed her the driver's license while blurting out for the genius to look at it. What really hurt was overhearing another customer's expression how the three were just a bunch of liars. While she handed the document back Bill noted how he had enough of everyone's lousy arrogant attitude. Moments later, Stan seeing an ugly situation grow he attempted to alleviate it by asserting how she was attracted to him then added, please no more questions.

Surprise it was when later the waitress served cups of coffee for each, noting how it was her treat while also delivering a triple order of toast with extra jellies. When leaving Bill stated how the three appreciated her kindness where Stan all excited, blew her a kiss with a big smile. Customers were questioned regarding cities going east but received were only statements to buzz off or, to get lost. Mentally the daily drudgery thinking of saving pennies generated a deception of success leaving each with a false sense of confidence. Inside the new territory the three was not familiar with the area's weather history and with only hitch hiking and rails remaining, the three took the road leading to the train yard in optimism.

In the dimness of night each knew impossible was any hitch hiking where after much time it was close to midnight when the freight yard was reached. Looking for some help, forgotten were the previous warnings when in a hurry Bill rushed toward a watchman. Getting close, the uniformed man shined his bright flashlight on everyone in the face while hollering about being on private property. hen he added to get out of the yard or he calls the police. But quick thinking Dave, blurted out how Charlie suggested to speak to him.

 All the while standing in a breeze, the watchman raised questions similar to others as several gusts with drizzle caused the man to adjust his gear. asserting his having heard enough about Charlie, while scratching his chin he pointed to a specific train also noting the box car 's last digits of a box car's number. Then as the man yelled how the three were to disappear from his sight he added how the train would leave the yard early but only going to Kansas City. Boldly he added that if caught by police it was that he never spoke to us.

Not knowing whether another train would leave until two or three days later, it was decided not to wait. Unexpectedly a flash of a lightning lit up the area as if a huge camera light bulb had gone off when only seconds later the roar of thunder caught each by surprise. Hearing the thunder sound bounce between the empty cars built with metal bodies was a neat experience where the only concern was about being wet. Shortly noticed was the temperature dropping while walking as if at a vacation resort. But as it was turned into a speedy trot, needing to find the car Bill suggested splitting up. Thinking was that if it got worse it could have made it too difficult to find each other where the idea was shot down.

 Minutes later as another flash lit up the area Dave hollered how it was simply a cloud burst which the other two agreed. Thinking was it being only cloudbursts. It would be over soon, but things deteriorated as the drizzle gradually turned into drops of a steady hard rain. Rushing to find the car, felt was a whoosh followed by other whooshes as pushes of the wind increased in strength. Stumbling, as if chased by a mad dog replaced the running where such forced the trio into a slow trot. Electrifying cloudbursts opened up with roaring of rolling thunder as a thousand drums beating then while small things were blowing around large puddles of water, slippery stones and wood ties had become the challenge of the night.

As if on a schedule, multiple pow-pow strikes of lightening occurred where the three turned around only to observe a small strike hit the ground. Though some distance away the pow-pow with the quick as the thunder sounded, caused each a fright. Ducking large pieces of cardboard, sheet metal and boxes that were flying around was alarming forcing the guys to constantly turn around. If the bright flashes along with the big bang sounds didn't cause alarm, the sloppy wet under footing helped heighten the fears. Those matters along with things flying through the air the team became rattled.

Repeatedly one or the other kept asking what the hell was going on but, there were no answers. Meanwhile the situation had become a carnival act where Bill suggested getting out of the yard but the other two responded no, as only needing to find the car. Temperatures dropping along with fighting the wind took its toll then with the shoes full of the slimy yucky water each could feel losing his strength. Actually the three held up until the yard lights went out where from then it was a disaster waiting. Three yokes were moving as if one in a shell and man was the shell large.

Soon it was the team was also straddling downed hot power lines that were shooting off bolts of electricity. That along with the cracks of more flashes along with the banging noises sounded moment after moment had each scared out of their wits. No more simple struggling where it had become a matter of surviving as Dave let out a screeching shrill of cuss words noting of being terrified. Holding on to each other it was as if rag dolls as the strong gushes of wind pushed the bodies around without effort where moving about became treacherous. Normally, praying for help in any activities was not the norm, yet during certain moments praying to survive was heard.

With weather having demonstrated who was boss there were no choices as either an open door or the correct numbers had to be found. In sheer determination the three kept moving along, going passed all types of cars such as cattle, coal, refrigerator, box, oil and milk cars. Such madness by others may have been considered thrilling but, for sure it was not the kind of thrill the team was looking for. Nowhere to run for cover along with nowhere to go for safety, then afraid to go to the yard police office, the team was stuck in their muck. Moments of thinking the worst exploded when caught in heavy downpour of flushing as if out of huge bucket.

Emotions of fear sounded as Bill expressed how those weren't simple clouds of rain. With the wind driving sideways mixed with ice pellets Bill yelled that whatever happens, don't let go, no matter what! Totally frustrated unable to run or trot, Dave hollered out asking where the hell the damn boxcar is, as there's just too many. Mumbling while reeling and rocking, prayers turned into hard praying as true fear of being blown away overtook us often forced to reach for something to grab hold of. Seeing the rail cars rocking only increased the helpless distressed feeling of confusion. Drunk with fear each was on the border of panicking as the rail cars were passed. Yet, struggling, Dave in anticipation, yelled to jump into the car when found but all the other two could do was reply of what car, as no car with those numbers or a door ajar had been seen.

About then, a big calm occurred as if someone had slammed shut a huge door. Instant insanity, as Dave expressed his feeling of how glad the stuff was over. Yah man, was all the other two could add. Noting his being uncertain, Stan added how to him something was not right, as the wind just doesn't stop on a dime. Head for the police building or look for the car each asked, as anxiety muddled the thinking. While Bill hollered of having passed the car Dave argued that all three would not have been so blind as not to see it. In disgust, the three cut between the cars getting to the other side of the train.

Then starting to return to some normalcy, the three made jokes of the situation assuming to be just a terrible bunch of cloudbursts. Unexpectedly the temperatures steadily dropped again while the wind returned seemingly even stronger. The entire prior scene began to repeat as the lightning and thunder returned with the blowing boxes, lamppost parts, and even larger things such as wooden shack sections and corrugated metal pieces. As a terrific gust lifted each a little ways off the ground with arms clinging to each other it was the wind blowing in one direction, while the bodies seemingly wanted to go in another. Squeezing each other's hands as if attempting to inflict pain on each other, Dave yelled for Bill not to tear his arm off.

Frantically each grabbed a hold of whatever parts of a car just to keep from being blown away. Suddenly there were no macho men to be found, as scared out of our wits it was latching on to air hoses or ladder parts, while praying. Shivering while trembling like frightened chickens the trio pushed past one car at a time drained of strength yet with adrenalin pumping. Only thinking of death with nerves ready to break Dave screamed out, "oh God please, please help us".

Unexpectedly, ouch was heard from Bill having fallen to the ground. Instantly asked if he was hurt, Bill pulled his shoe off where it was seen that a sharp stone had penetrated the thin sole. Although the skin wasn't torn, the point had hit a nerve that caused pain bringing the man down. Untimely jovial comments were not what Bill wanted to hear but, being the nature of the two there was little they could do. Amid shouts of stupid, garbage, ridiculous, damn mess along with other cuss words, short prayers became the only constant. In a state of madness, while Bill fought to put his wet sock and shoe back on while sitting in the muddy puddle, Dave hollered out asking what the hell was going on as it's been too long for it to be simple cloud bursts.

While assisting Bill to stand a high gushing wind force struck violently pushing Stan against the car where he stubbed his thumb. Then as Dave tripped over Stan he slammed into the wooden car banging one hand while bruising the elbow on the other arm. Levels of fear had become beyond normal description. Hectically moving in sheer chaotic madness, "oh God help us, were the cries". Bam! Bang! Roaring crackling pow-pow thunder sounds erupted along with bright lightening flashes.

With Bill limping along, Dave showed his concern calling him the great hobble foot while emotionally adding his prayer of, please God, no more, please. Perhaps all of this struggling took place over a short period but, at the time it seemed like hours. Then, unexpectedly it happened! "Oh no", along with, "oh how stupid", were the expressions when seeing what was not anticipated.

There it was, the car with the door slightly open but, the numbers were a different matter. In the confusion a mix up had occurred plus the color was not white as thought but a light tan. While yelling out yeas and yippee, the door was moved wider as the trio jumped inside amid total darkness. Instantly, after closing the door most of the way, the three fell on their knees in a prayer of thanks for allowing the trio's survival. Not the Governor's mansion but it's better than being out there, Stan mentioned. Right away the other two hollered out their agreeing, "you betcha buddy and, you gots that aright".

Being totally soaked, shirts and pants were rung out then put on whatever nails could be found protruding from the walls. Carefully, most of the moving around was by feeling the way as too dark to see anything. Large and small, flattened cardboard boxes were found in walking around but, without real lighting it was moving almost in the blind. The thick cardboard was impossible to tear and since neither had a knife it was the strength of the three pulling against the pressed boxes.

Working by feel, the small nail type hooks caused each some pain when tugging as the hands would slip and slide. Using each one's strength to the maximum, the large containers were pulled apart. Not only did the physical struggle provide some release of tensions it also helped to take the minds off the situation. Something new was found as each coped with freezing. While each rolled up inside a large piece they moved tightly next to each other to maximize gathering of the body heat where slowly nerves calmed as sleep overtook the trio.

At the outset the three had made agreement of trust to stick together, relying on each other no matter what it took. But at the time no one had any idea of just how far reaching the statement was to be.

SEGMENT – 24.   Morning on the Twelfth day of July where Stan stated his being glad they hadn't taken the bus because he would have missed all the fun of the main event. Blowing locomotive whistle sounds along with the clanging and banging noises of the cars being joined resounded inside. Being tossed around assured everyone of staying awake. Joyfully feeling the warm weather, everyone put on their lightly damp under clothing but the pants had to stay hung as fully damp. Meanwhile decisions had to be made whether to leave for food or stay in the car hoping for the best.

Should the trio leave, then finding the train having departed it could be another day before the next one. Not having a schedule along with recalling what the watchman the night before had stated, it was decided to stay put. Precautionary actions were taken moving the large cardboard sections mixed with the small pieces creating a messed up appearance. And just in time it was when two guards stopped by doing with their flashlights as others had done. The incident caused the team to react as had been taught staying put under cover.

Then with the blowing of whistles complimented by horn blasts from the engine the locomotive moved the train forward. Finally a relaxed atmosphere had been allowed where breaths of relief were heard along with joyous expressions. Comments rambled from each where heard was, no more for me and, never wishing to ever go thru something like that again..A time of shock it was when a ways out of the yard the guys opened the door a short way more to see. And wow, did they see. Disaster from what nature had dealt the area stuck hard but, at least the trio was on its way.

Unable to take their eyes away, neither had ever seen the like of what had transpired the night before. Staring in disbelief, comments of holy smokes, and darn if we weren't lucky rang out. Emotionally moved, a silence of disbelief enveloped the car where mumbling of prayers were heard. Sadness had overcome the three thinking of what the people must have gone through. In one tree, seen dangling was a cow straddled over some large limbs while other animals were seen in many other places either dangling or lying torn apart. Also there was a car facing the ground upside down sitting in the lower portion of a tree trunk.

Other cars and trucks were overturned or leaning on things along with downed, split and uprooted trees scattered all over the area. Houses and farm dwellings showed roofs partially removed or twisted where other buildings were missing sides or stripped leaving large holes. Utter destruction, Stan belted out seeing the farm pieces, doors, window frames, fences, barn and even house wall sections scattered over the entire area. Such unexpected sights caused traumatic feelings where Dave and Bill mentioned how the whole area resembled some massive dumpsite. The bird's eyeful along with the three experiencing it firsthand was a weather education neither would forget. Aware of the fatal mishaps that had been seen, what or who prevented our loss or saved us became the big number one question.

Meanwhile with bladders needing release the three actually were concerned about not damaging the car but, where else was they supposed to go? Since no pail or jar was around Dave without any forethought let out his drain through the open door. Instantly the other two broke out in hysterics seeing the action. Having forgotten about the train's speed the guy suffered the consequences. Just as the water blew back inside onto his pant legs and shoes Dave could only show his unhappy face.

From then it was making use of the car's corners until eventually the time came when the train started slowing down. After a several toots of the horn, it was passing several very large cow and steer pens. Then there were the toots of the whistle when crossing of roads where either gates or persons holding railroad signs were seen. Oh what joy noticing the small signs indicating Kansas City. But delayed by too much seeing and talk, missed was the chance to jump off. As the train stopped inside the freight yard to get off or stay was pondered. Though hungry, while not knowing whether the train was to continue eastward had the three baffled.

Chancing it, decided was finding someone to get answers where after jumping out it was running alongside the line of cars keeping close for cover to speak to a yard worker. Assumed was that most of the guards were probably having lunch. But surprise it was, where out of nowhere came a voice shouting to hold it right there. Suddenly a guard appeared from in between two boxcars where an attempt was made to run. Hearing the man holler to stop and don't move the trio froze.

Approaching, the guard asserted how the three were trespassing on railroad property with him calling the police. Quickly, Stan hollered for him to wait up a minute where the guard reacted slinging his night stick. Angrily the big man asked how the three came to be in the yard where sadly, the other two stated being sorry but just taking a short cut. Sarcastically the guard questioned, of where going? Hearing Dave holler about getting to the exit the guard having gotten closer belted out how he saw the three were not older men.

Stunned, the man asserted how the trio looked like hell while asking if the boys were ok. Although Bill noted being from Chester Pennsylvania just trying to pass through, he demanded if from around the neighborhood. Failing to understand, the three in gruff tones responded how he had already been told. Upon seeing identification the guard's face lit up as if in shock knowing the three were telling true. Void of discussion but only short phrases, Dave all frustrated, blurted out how the three were looking for a train heading east causing Stan to move.

Angrily pointing his nightstick at Stan the guard hollered how he didn't want to hear any more bull. Then in response, Bill asked if he knew Charlie back at Topeka. Shaking his head, the guard stated no, while asserting his wanting to know who the heck Charlie was. All smiles Dave responded how he must have known Charlie from a ways back since he was the one who stated to use his name. Right away, the uniformed man asserted how the three had more guts than brains. Then he added how early the next morning the train would be leaving for St. Louis while pointing the location and blurting out how the three didn't hear that from him. Displaying anger he ordered the three out of the yard or it was the police where the three replied yes sir.

A mad dash for the exit was made non stop while sounding a bunch of whew, wows and thanks to be out of the place. Outside the yard without funds to rent a horse the three stood in wonderment. Bill found a day old newspaper lying against a fence where upon a brief look it was suggested of getting jobs but, noticed was mostly farm or factory work was listed. Aware of the time for filing out applications and background checking such thinking was put away. Corporation signs were seen such as Joseph Schlitz Brewing Company, Rutherford Food Corporation and other warehouse companies. While Pabst or Schlitz draught was Stan's favorite beers with

Snyder's Pretzels the other two enjoyed Ballentine and Miller. Thoughts were paying a visit maybe getting some free food but aware of the grubby appearance all visiting thoughts were squashed. Meanwhile it was taking turns checking out establishments, but due to prices of having no appeal, no place was found.

Seeing the D & S Café sign Bill started laughing until the two questioned what was so funny. Pointing to the sign he mentioned how it was Dave and Stan's place where joyfully Dave replied how it was a good idea except, that Stan was going in the service. Sophisticated, the local bar consisted of the usual kitchen, fancy booths, tables, counter, food and rest rooms plus, complimenting its small dance floor was a large floor standing juke box playing music paid for.

An attractive older, classy waitress appeared where right from the start she drew attention. Bending close she asked if everyone was feeling okay adding, how to her each looked a little peakish. While jovial, Bill uttered, "just what we need, a physician". As Stan stood up formally introducing his self along with the other two, smiling the waitress mentioned never seeing the three before. As the three responded about seeing the sign she asserted of never hearing of anyone fascinated by the initials. Shortly, it was back to business where she pressed whether it was the steak or pot roast special only hearing of the trio's planned orders. As the four broke out in a moment of laughter she split her sides laughing as she walked to the kitchen.

Serving the food the waitress questioned where from which led to others. Her noting it being all made up, it was the trio not knowing what to expect. Backing up the waitress responded seeing Dave standing up. Pulling out his wallet angrily he set the driver's license on the table. As if already knowing it was a fake she picked up the document while reading. As her face changed showing disbelief, the other two reached for theirs when the woman stated how it was ok, because she was a believer.

Over time the crowd dwindled where the waitress surprised the trio bringing out the man from the kitchen. Borrowing a chair the cook listened to the three then mentioned having friends in Johnstown. Also he told his story of being a cook in the service. With the two going into the military along with stopping in his place the man noted being on his good side where the cook had some cause to celebrate. Aware the three had portioned their meals while noting his understanding of the trio's situation the cook asserting his helping with the meals to help the guys celebration.

Frequently, the waitress mentioned how the place was where nothing exciting ever happens, when shortly the waitress served sides of bread with plates filled with slices of beef along with vegetables. All the three was able to do was thank her also noting of not having enough money. All smiles with enthusiasm, the woman responded how everything was with the cook's compliments while joining with the three enjoying a soda. Moments went by when at another table, in an excited voice the waitress hollered out how the trio was from southeast Pennsylvania!

Hearing the news, several customers clapped and others shouted cheery remarks. Meanwhile a few couples that had been dancing drifted close by offering word of encouragement. What a great time. But what to do as the three needed to sleep somewhere. The cook suggested directions to a wooded area but not much thought was given yet, it was all that remained. Thinking was the man had given the trio the beans yet followed his advice.

A long walk, proved was the man's directions ended with all being true where the small forest was reached located away from all traffic or pedestrians. Under open skies wasn't what the three had in mind however, since it was all that could be afforded the team applied its knowledge with the outdoors.

Using large trees to block the wind, good size limbs with branches were put making a few lean-tos. Meanwhile, branches, auto seat sections, beer case sides and parts of newspapers, beds were made.

Then while newspapers, book pages and leaves provided some covering inside the little dwellings, Bill and Stan mentioned being thankful for their Boy Scout training.

Chapter Twelve

SAWDUST, THRILLS, TERROR, AND A DRUG STORE

Sunday morning dawned with the trio in disgust of their deplorable situation. Getting back to the freight yard a stop was made at an automobile service station where permitted was to use the outhouse along with the man's bay area tubs to wash up. On the street while walking, a small store was stopped at where purchased was a large soda along with candy bars, chips and pretzels. Not breakfast food but it sufficed where half was saved looking forward to being inside a freight car. Meanwhile, reflecting on the hospitality enjoyed the night before it helped to perk up the spirits. All hope was in the magic of the thumbs but it was dissipated where only foot travel remained.

Arriving at the freight yard with doubts, the three stopped as if in a trance. Almost stunned, the three were seeing the train being in the very location the man had described. Along with a few main tracks there were many spurs inside the yard, Making sure of not being seen was the immediate trick, however too much yard activity hindered the team's movements. Original thinking was that the night would have been an advantage but as it was the daylight actually helped. Easy it was to distinguish the guards' pants from the yard workers, also looking underneath cars allowed us to see where guards may have been close by. Patience was tried where it seemed as if never getting to the right car in time.

With adrenaline pumping it was looking for that opportune moment of finding the one car that the man had mentioned. Around or in between cars it was whatever it took moving away from which direction it seemed guards were walking. Stress in worrying over getting caught controlled almost every sentence as each kept repeating to be careful. Hearts seemed pounding so hard that Dave uttered for Bill not to make so much noise. Oh geez, where the heck is that car, Bill whispered. Hop, look around, move, stop and look under. What a situation Dave belted out. Which side of the train to be on was the constant as move forward or backward, it was whichever doing it was nerve wracking. Only the word ouch was heard when scaring the daylights out of Stan, Dave poked him in the ribs.

Quietly, Dave pointed while the other two whispered of how they saw it. Cars in a straight line helped but, not being seen was another matter. All the dodging of the guards had each in a tizzy as the desire was to run for it, but couldn't. Nervously watching while waiting, the three were only able to move so slowly. Then for some reason a couple of the guards met for some conversation where seen was the coast being clear around the car. Feelings of Stan's hurt or small pains disappeared when in a dash the three ran as fast as the legs took them until the trio reached the car. Hopped inside each looked around only finding the car being empty from whatever it was carrying. Expressed was being lucky since they made it yet there was a big exception. Although there were large and small wooden crates, sawdust covered everything.

Just when starting to relax voices outside could be heard alerting to guards making inspections. Hide, Bill whispered, but where Dave asked? Things were different as the doors on both sides were open. Reaction was to close at least one yet, it was decided not to take the risk as closing either someone might hear the noise or even see. So, while leaving the large crates remaining in their spots, the smaller ones were arranged in a "v" shape. Such positioning allowed the three to lay and hide in between with sawdust scattered to cover the guys' foot tracks.

Several guards walked by with a couple of them stopping to look inside. Partially they closed the one door when minute's later guards on the other side closed the other door all the way. Soon hearing the men's voices drift away caused some optimism where neither one was complaining as the closing of the doors provided more seclusion from the spotters. It was a shame, that no one had a camera since looking at each other seen attached to the clothing and hair was the stuff. One big mess it was as the fine particles of stuff was everywhere. Although it made for a difficult time it would have been great for Halloween. Doing the best to brush each other off, the trio smiled as the locomotive giving off its toots got underway.

The train moving forward caused some feeling of relief with hope and although there was no way to find out its destination, at least known was it going east. Pushing the sawdust through the doorway was not possible because of someone seeing the action but the doorway opened a couple of feet allowed a good view. While enjoying a great view of the country unexpectedly, a strong wind blew in through the door opening where combined with the car rocking from side to side caused particles to fly around. Nowhere to hide and nowhere to run it was found even the corners didn't provide any protection.. No means of controlling the dust and without a broom along with no water there wasn't a whole lot of choices. But needing to do something the trio broke apart the crates removing the attached paper and cardboard. Torn to make brooms they were used to push the stuff into mounds where large pieces were laid over top of the mounds. Thoughts of how Larry and Tom were doing surfaced but with the mess the three were in, there was little conversation.

Finally, the pulled apart wood was scattered on top of the cardboard making a sort of lid. Though not perfect it did contain the mounds of dust. Viewing the scenery time passed as the engine's whistle sounded when it approached small towns causing the guys to take cover. Knowing they had missed mass on Sunday generated discussion that led to talk about other religions. Then other topics with the mounds holding, the three made use of the squashed chips, pretzels and hard candy where some a social atmosphere developed.

When a short stop somewhere near Warrensburg or Sedalia was made it secured the thinking of which direction the train was heading. Observing small villages, farms, horse and cow pens with the clear weather allowed improving of the three's minds stability. Well into the evening it was felt as having been in a steam bath but happy the trio was almost jumping with joy seeing signs noting the train was approaching the large city. Fully aware there was a long way to go but, heading into the large freight yard they knew they were close to the eastern border of Missouri. While Bill mentioned for the guys to look at the enormous size of the yard, Dave responded how there only being three more states to go. Both statements of good material caused the three to give a few hip hoorays, yippees and yahoos as their spirits improved.

Nighttime rolled around that presented a problem since neither knew where any of the eateries were located. Not having eaten a truly full meal in some time each couldn't help but know of their hunger. Yet each one respected each other aware that each was feeling the same lack of nourishment. Each refrained from complaining so as not to aggravate each other. Then rather than push our luck and get caught by roaming in the dark it was agreed to stay and sleep in the car. A well-lighted yard while no one was around the door was further closed all but about two feet for letting in the light. Falling asleep Stan all serious mentioned how lucky the guys were since everybody doesn't get an opportunity to sleep in the comfort of sawdust, paper and wood. Dave replied, not to forget the stuff also smelled good.

SEGMENT 25. Morning exploded in the West St. Louis freight yard where, seeing the light overcast blue skies with cloud puffs it was taken as a good omen. Noticing the immediate area to be free of any guards the three leaped out heading straight for the outside fence. No stopping, except for taking turns to look under cars for guards. With a steady breeze helping the trio to feel pretty good, assumed was that the coast was clear. Not far from the gate, while making a dash for the exit, stunned the three were.

Seemingly, out of nowhere a guard popped out from between the last group of cars. Blocking the way, while slinging his nightstick, the man hollered for the three to just hold up right there. Quickly, Stan asked where the heck he came from but rather than answer, the guard questioned what we were doing there. In response, Dave fed the bull as he mentioned about taking a short cut but, the man simply shook his head. Just the large size of the man along with swinging his nightstick caused each to use caution as the guard showing his temper blurted out how he better be told or we would be going to the police. Not looking for trouble, Bill and Dave mentioned a few comments on where going, but Stan was silent not knowing what to say. Right away the man demanded identification where the guard pointed his nightstick at Stan while hollering to bring them out slowly. Taking hold of Stan's driver's license the guard questioned about his address then also did the same with the other two.

As each tried to speak at the same time, the man waved his stick while shouting to shut up and speak one at a time. When Bill replied sarcastically how Dave had already told him, angrily the guard responded of having had enough and for each to face the car while keeping the hands where they could be seen as he was calling the police. Slowly, Stan pulled out the car receipt while explaining how the receipt was for the cash paid for the car. Seriously told about the guy's name, location and circumstance the guard listened where hearing of not having enough money for passenger train or bus fare he pressed about getting a job. Right away, Bill in frustration mentioned of the military situation when about then, another guard appeared. A short ways behind the man, the other guard asked if the man needed assistance.

For some unknown reason the man replied how the guard should be on his way being everything was under control.

While pointing, the guard advised of the main road leading across the river plus added of being extra careful, since the guards over there were tougher. Waving his nightstick as if to send a message the man hollered not to come that way again or it would be jail for trespassing. Following of yelling yes sir and thanks the trio ran thru the gate some distance until stopping in the brush. Shortly breezes helping, a strip was done for shaking out the clothes along with brushing each other off. Jesting, Bill blurted out how all weez gots to doozz was to gets to da udder sides of da bridge where Dave replied that with their luck it should only take one thumb five minutes.

Once the main road was reached it was quick stepping with thumbs out and all smiles hoping for a ride. A nice surprise it was, when only a short time had passed where an older couple provided a lift. Feeling on top of the world by the good luck of the ride the ego level of the three was really lifted when the couple dropped us off only a short distance from a diner.

Never had the three been so glad to use a sink. Thinking was getting back to feeling normal until each looked in the mirror. Only able to stare in disbelief when seeing what the others saw reality set in. Dirty, grubby, unshaven and worn it was a difficult time trying to comprehend. Taken aback, washing only provided what each was not prepared for. While his flat type crew cut allowed Stan only minimal washing the other two with bushy heads full of long hair found washing a problematic chore. Although the team saw each other daily as the days had passed none of what either had seen rang any bells as gradually the changes happened. It's amazing how cruel people were as looks by customers turned to ugly stares. So penetrating were some faces that it actually had an effect on the minds yet, attempting some humor while forcing a smile Stan noted being glad there was no dance to go to.

When the waitress showed up, Bill mentioned being hungry enough to eat a cow where sarcastically Dave responded how with the kitty eaten, there would be no cow. Then as the waitress attempted to provide her service Stan uttered for no more games where Dave followed asserting his needing to have all the cards on the table. Leaving the waters on the table the woman zoomed in on Stan and Bill as if some outlaws. No more bull, Dave asserted, as the two confronted Bill needing to know to the penny. Unlike the three it was distrust and disunity had taken over where with sullen looks, Bill responded noting of his disappointment with the guys' lack of trust. Sparks of ill feeling ignited as the three were unable to come to grips with their situation. Demonstrating a miserable attitude, Bill in a rage threw the plastic bag on the table hollering no more, as he had enough. Cussing, he asserted for the other two to decide things from then on.

Stunned from the outbreak the two sat staring in disbelief groping at what had just taken place. Seeing the remaining few dollars along with change it was as if some contamination had hit the table. Speechless like animals stuck in a cage the moment had developed into an ugly situation. Just in time the waitress returned. Showing signs of strain Bill belted out how he didn't want any frills but only the basic breakfast special with extra cream and water where the other two ordered the usual extra toast, waters and cups. Noticing things out of the norm, the waitress suggested how the three appeared to be having a time of it. Following a pause the woman displayed her candor mentioning that if the three was hurting not to be bashful, for she understood having also been in a few tough situations. Standing up, Stan muttered being beat and enough of the games telling the woman of being flat broke. Sarcastically, Bill suggested for Stan to tell the truth of having no money. In reply, the woman with apologetic words inquired when the parents where coming. Hearing Bill respond how they weren't, Stan asserted how if they didn't quit, he'd be moving to the counter. Again the woman pressed about adults or supervisor where Stan replied how there ain't no one else and enough is enough. Shaking her head the woman walked away as the trio assumed the last of her was seen.

Soon it was she brought out plates of large pastries noting that it was time to celebrate since us young guys were going into the service. Responding, the other two noted how the stuff was not ordered and couldn't be paid for adding how Stan's forwardness was a spectacle, but the waitress asserted that to her he was special, where it was her treat. Later, Stan stood up calling her over to his spot then as she moved close he whispered something causing her to show a raised eyebrow when a moment of intimate emotions could be felt. Upon departing, Stan blew her a kiss while the other two expressed their thanks. Slow it was, overcoming mental confusion and frustration although strong words were sounded the three emotionally patched up their differences.

The atmosphere upon arriving was so tense it could have been cut with scissors, but when leaving things had changed. Each wanted to remain close as a team, understanding the need for trusted unity, the value of comradely allowed the eventual softening of the spirits and shaking of hands. Back on the highway, all three holding cups of coffee took turns showing smiles with the thumb but Stan never revealed what was said to the waitress. While Stan attempted to do some sort of Indian dance, Dave tried to mimic Charlie Chaplin while Bill was clapping hard trying to draw attention. Nothing worked as the cars and trucks simply whiz by which left the trio feeling as if they weren't even there and though all three laughed from time to time, each understood the situation had badly deteriorated. If the team didn't get across the bridge for sure they would be stranded. Keeping up the spirits singing the tune of ninety-nine bottles of beer on the wall went on for a while followed by, I been working on de railroad.

As time passed with moods hurting, it's a long way to Penna. (Tippararee) was sung where even their walk looked as if in some death march. Seemingly hopeless, time was when a vehicle after going passed pulled over. Looking in wonderment the three thought they had a flat tire or mechanical problems. Shortly a door opened where an arm was extended showing a waving sign to come forward. Yelling at the top of his lungs Dave hollered for them to wait as the three ran. Upon reaching the car, Bill stood matting down his hair, where Dave sarcastically hollered for Mr. Hollywood to get his rear inside. Repeatedly, thank you rang out as the man pulled away.

Showing her smiles, the young woman mentioned of going to visit relatives in Illinois where after the trio noted where from and going to her husband responded. Recalling his past, the man noted how he also found it difficult hitchhiking after he got out of the service. Much conversation entailed when soon it was crossing the bridge. Each of the three strained to look for getting some bearings for when being dropped off where understanding the team's situation the man provided welcomed pointers on certain roads leading to the yard. Upon reaching the other side, the couple let the team out at what the man perceived it to be a good spot. Following hefty bunches of thanks along with expressions of feelings for best wishes the couple drove off. Such small effort by the couple was received as huge to the three hikers.

With the drizzle having stopped, along with good feelings the three started singing with anticipation "Five states over the ground we walked with four more to go". But as the trio walked, smiles made no difference since again were realized that people were not offering rides. Arriving at the East St. Louis, freight yard each of the team was in good spirits aware of being on the right side of the river. Hyped it was being aware that the place was where all freight trains were put together for heading east. Also it was recalled what had been told about a large freight train during the day which would leave the yard heading for the east region. Although discussed were the warnings regarding the toughness of the guards on the east side, enthusiasm was pushed by thinking of the east coast where along with large and small locomotives seen were many newer large type diesels. Only one side of the train was visible then with the yard surrounded by fence it all presented one big obstacle.

Yet, once inside it was sneaking around like cats on the prowl where several workers were located. However, when trying to speak all good intentions were quickly bashed. Disappointment time it was since the workmen refused to tell of any specific details other than mentioning certain types of boxcars to look for. When one of the men revealed the approximate time of the certain train's departure to be heading east, he angrily added for the three to quickly get away from him. Get out of the yard the man asserted where surely it was each was afraid of someone since they sternly advised to get lost being trespassers or they losing their jobs just for speaking to strangers.

Quick it was out of the yard as not looking to have any confrontation with anyone. Due to the fencing along with all of the guards there was no way of getting to the car before the train left the yard. Totally left in wonderment of what to do the tree looked on back on the nearby road. Finally it was decided not to hang around but move aware so as not to raise anyone's curiosity. More walking, when finally a young man pulled over offering a lift. Mentally suffering from the way they had been spoken to by the workmen, instant skepticism erupted with thoughts about the driver being an undercover guard. While the three climbed in, the man drove off while asserting to be careful since there were railroad detectives everywhere. Also he mentioned how from many years of making use of the trains he knew they were around.

Shortly it was on to a side street which was at the end of the yard where he dropped the three off.. Having no plan everything was guesswork Yet, things were as if plans had already been drawn when walking in the direction of the yard, a building came within view. Seeing windows the three moved into the cover of the bushes. Stoop while walking until reaching a good spot where it was to sit and watch. The yard's exit for the trains leaving the yard could be seen in the distance where each knew being so close, the train couldn't get up speed. Feeling of confidence were building as aware it was simply to wait and watch. Soon a small manually operated car approached with a couple of guards on it where the three instantly belly flopped, actually grabbing the weeds at the ground. no more was there any being scared of not knowing what to do as each had gained sufficient experience.

Confidence mixed with the young age and ego there was nothing they couldn't handle as the team was once again feeling its oats. Subsequent to a couple of steam locomotives pulling small trains, toots from the huge diesel engines could he heard warming the hearts. "Oh boy", Bill all excited whispered, "Chester here we come". Filled with anticipation the atmosphere was dense with glee as the three feeling their closeness shook hands along with tapping each other's shoulders. Shortly the big moment arrived when the engine's headlight could be seen approaching. All keyed up, Dave asked whether to grab the train or wait for another where quickly, the other two growled not waiting for other as if not this one which one.

Seeing the two new type of engines each knew it was going a long way. So many various types of cars heightened the expectations especially since the end was not visible. Then as cars went passed as if in a parade, noticed was that none of the boxcar doors were open. Yet eagerly, the three waited for that right car, aware that the end would soon be arriving. Anxiously, Stan hollered for the guys to do something. Boxcar after boxcar, cattle, log and tanker cars plus, more boxcars but with none with doors even ajar the guys lost all anticipation. Shortly Dave hollered requesting suggestions seeing the train wasn't to be ongoing forever. His blood pounding while in a dismal tone, Dave uttered of spotting the caboose where impulses took over the three. Quickly an agreement was made to grab onto any car that had space for the three. Unsure of his self, Stan shouted, "really then just grab on to the first having some room". Angrily, Dave responded hollering, "hell man, we're already frazzled, so stuff it". Acting on instinct, the struggle was on for anything that looked like something that could be handled. Time was running out as well did the number of cars where common sense turned into fear of not doing. Frantically all thinking about consequences had gone to the clouds as the three moved in absolute fright of losing the opportunity.

One after the other, the three jumped onto the only car that seemed right. And wow was it ever open. So thrilled were the three of what they found nothing else mattered other than jump aboard. With each one's burst of energy all thinking was squashed replaced by the intense desire to succeed in grabbing what was offered. Success it was finding their being located on the rear of a black colored tank car. Thankful for what they were able to find there was no squabbling.   They were moving east and not by their own feet where happy feelings abounded as rabbits in a lettuce patch.

Happy and happy and so happy the trio was where there was no thinking as   just being overly joyous at what they had done. Who cared of what, or how, after all, what mattered was that the three were on a train heading east. Standing on the metal platform while holding onto the railing it was as if going for a long joy ride. Shortly the three with ego all ablaze it was only confidence that remained as they sat down on the metal frame enjoying the ride.

While entertaining, the ride would also be taking them home, so the three assumed. With the nice breeze being steady and the weather just right while being on the right train heading home, who could ask for more, Stan uttered. But, slowly it was things started to change. Notions were made regarding rain or showers but the three were confident being able to handle whatever nature threw. After all it was summer time and with only seven plus hundred miles to the coast no one considered any consequences.

Attitudes were that even if matters went to the extreme the three would handle it. With air temperature up, the breeze felt good where smiles showed but then the train was only moving ten to fifteen miles an hour. Having so many cars it took time to get up speed and easily felt was it picking up speed. However for whatever reason, no one gave any thought as to what would be experienced when the train reached speeds of sixty miles an hour. Just a bunch of good ole young, care free, boys riding in a trance on their way home. Caught up in a false euphoria, totally ignored with closed minds was the danger each was exposed to. Even as speed increased the three only switched places to give whoever was sitting on the end a break from the wind. As if such was to solve everything the three ignored the danger they were in. Amusing fun of musical chairs while watching the scenery go by actually went on for some time.

Slowly the moods changed as the rear of the car's tank being round let itself be known. Similar to that of half a football caused the wind to end up as if being funneled where Bill noted of his being afraid. While his alarming remark got no attention, the speed of train was picking up. With the speed of the train increasing so was the speed of the wind blowing on the faces as if someone had turned up the controls on a fan. Also soon became aware was the effect on the rears of the hard metal when hitting a bump. Short concerns were shown but even then laughing it was as the silly three compared the wind and bumps to a roller coaster. Soon with speed over twenty miles per hour Stan getting alarmed asked, what would be done when it reaches over the forty mark. As if having seen a ghost, Dave and Bill realized their vulnerability. Indecisive suggestions began ranging from jumping off the train to climbing to another car but they knew no doors were open. Then looking down, seeing what was below caused hesitation. Added to the thinking were the obvious ends of the rail ties and stones, along with nail heads off to the sides which all combined denied any hasty decision making.

Demonstrating a shaking voice, Dave stated how the guys would probably break their necks trying to jump that sent the three reeling from doing anything. Stan suggested crawling back to the caboose where Bill responded not for him as from the weather there were the wet and slippery conditions of the wood. Short it was where thoughts of rolling off put a stop to all discussion. Moving tightly together for helping to block the wind while holding onto the railing with one hand, the other arm was used to partially cover the face breaking the wind's force. However no matter what was done, all intentions did little for the rest of the body. Gripping fear began taking its toll realizing the train's speed would soon be over fifty miles per hour. Often shaking with the situation beyond their control, Dave in fear yelled out asking God what to do.

Another moment in time of their lives it was where the ones always able to do while willing to try everything, had met there match. All of a sudden without mentioning anything to each other the three had become truly frightened being unable to do anything. Yet each knew each other where they each aware of the others' fears. Stuck in their helplessness, as rats caught in a cage the only thing each knew was that the train was continuously gaining speed and pulled by the engine that had no intention of letting up. Added to that were the thoughts of the miles to go, where mentioned it was easy to be days before the coast.

Persisted matters all combined had the minds enclosed in the box of the three considering the worst. Lacking all control along with having no solution while holding on to each other, praying was all that remained. Intensely full of gloom and doom the trio rode. In frustrating anger, Stan yelled out that no matter what, he ain't performing such a stupid trick again plus, the next time the train slows down he was jumping off. All smiles had gone to the wind as each had comprehended each ones haplessly dangerously death threatening position.

The train just kept picking up speed as if to make fun of the trio's desperation situation. Terror stuck hard as extreme levels of fear had risen disabling the minds where a discussion evolved regarding one to disrobe allowing the other two to use the clothing for added protection. With fear of dying heard it was not just the Lord's Prayer but actual pleadings for help. No short cuts and no bartering just simple pleadings of, "Oh God, help us".

No bashful strains and no such thing as bargaining where it was all heart and soul as the trio had become three different people holding on to each other for dear life. Geez, Bill hollered at least in the freight yard we had our feet on the ground but here we having nothing.

Time passed when finally, it happened. While being jolted around the three knew nothing of what was going on, yet the car was in the midst of mostly rocking forward and backward. Joyfully Bill expressed a yippee noting his feeling that the train was slowing down. Yet, in disbelief the other two failed to move or speak a word. The state of expecting the worst had peaked where the three paused trying to get some feel of any slowing motion. And then, there it was, the feeling of the train losing its forward momentum. Hearts exploded with joyful utterances of thank you God, thank you for hearing us, thank you and thank you, amen.

Right away, assumed was that the train was slowing down to pick up or drop off. Whatever it was doing neither really cared as suddenly all intentions shifted where it was focusing on getting off. Screeching sounds of brakes along with the wheels while jolts and couplers made their slamming noises caused all hearts to race. Immediately it was uttered not to wait for the train to stop but jump off. Realizing the trio was soon to be free from their trapped position nobody gave any thought to their locale. Then unexpected serious feelings of danger erupted. Each was aware that the train was not making the kind of normal stopping actions usually made where thoughts of fires or other catastrophe were expressed. Almost all at once, amid the noise and clamor, the train abruptly ground to a jolting stop. Sensing the unusual action kept the three in a trance of fear not knowing why. Extremely tense, yet each was feeling relieved, happy and shocked all at the same time. After all the train was stopping and that at the time was what mattered. With all that was recently experienced along with what was going on, it was the three's minds were stuck in a state of unknowing helplessness where the trio were frozen unable to move.

SEGMENT – 26. Instant alarm, when almost as if out of nowhere, several state police, the sheriff, along with no less than a half dozen railroad guards and local police appeared. Not only on both sides of the car but with pointed pistols, shotguns and rifles. All guns were seen at the ready position where absolutely speechless the three stood. Stunned at what was transpiring it was when loudly, someone yelled out for the three not to move. Then right away, another man yelled out for the three not to move but, just stay standing while keeping both hands on the railing where they could be seen. Quietly, Bill blurted out, "whatever you do guys, don't move".

Shaking he added, "am not interested in getting my head blown off guys so, don't move no matter what".

Smartly, the police moved closer repeating the same advice while advising to climb down while keeping one hand over our heads. Attempting to be funny, Dave stated how it was a different form of a welcoming committee but, the other two responded for him to stuff it and shut up. One by one it was down the steps till reaching the ground where each was forced to lean on the train car. Finding only empty wallets along with loose change after a through search amid the sawdust caused angry looks on the police apparently not finding what was expected.

The cop in charge ordered the men to put up their weapons while conducting a search of the car and grounds. Soon one of the state police spoke to the engineer while the regular cops handcuffed the three. Then as the officer in charge boisterously blurted out asserting the three were from Leavenworth he also inquired or from one of the local jails. Slowly all three simultaneously responded with a resounding no, from neither.

Totally frustrated while overwhelmed were all three by the sad turn of events where Dave attempted to explain. butt, instantly the officer yelled to shut up, asserting for the three to just answer his questions. Softly the policeman spoke as he pressed on wanting to know where the guns were tossed. Wearing the wrong expression of a smile, Bill blurted out asking what guns where such response caused the officer to show temper. Repeatedly in a boisterous voice he demanded to know where the guns were tossed when angry over the situation, Stan shaking his head yelled how neither one had any guns. In frustration Dave added that the trio was not running from any jail or prison.

Some talk between the different uniforms occurred as the officers put Dave and Bill in the back of one of the police cars while forcing Stan into the back of another car. Then it was off to jail when with guns drawn the three where put in separate cells while the police removed the handcuffs. Following the town's police, sheriff and state police conversation papers were signed and exchanged. Meanwhile, being finger printed along with our mug shots taken Stan asked the man if we would be getting a copy of the pictures. Bill being the only one having money they questioned him first as to where the bundle was stashed. But when he replied asking what bundle, the deputy replied to get smart and tell them where the stolen money was hidden. Round and round the group went regarding the stash and guns. Over and over the policemen persisted while Dave and Bill kept repeating there was no money, no stolen money plus never had any guns where Stan mentioned of simply making use of the train for a lift. With neither of the three having any idea of what the police were going to do, only short mumblings followed.

Although at some time each had been questioned by police, but at the present it was a new experience for the team, as neither had ever been cited, arrested or taken into custody. Only able to think in the negative, sarcasm seemed to relieve some pressure where off to a bad start. Dave sarcastically asked whether the police were having fun while Stan asked why the three hadn't been given the penthouse. Attempting to top the remarks Dave joked how the town probably received its name from Ming or the Joker as it was assumed being set free. But, instead the chief asked where who made the phony drivers licenses or where they had been bought. No matter how hard the three tried, it was always hearing something else as intensely the man showed his intent of refusing to listen. Noting of the three documents being of the same color, and state the man asserted they were done by the same forger while adding how he could see they had been mangled on purpose. Of course the dirty, raggedy appearance of the three meant very little but what could the three do, but stand, watch and listen. Then if that wasn't enough, the chief noted of Stan's birth date being Christmas, December twenty-fifth while Bill's being the last day of the year, December thirty-first during a leap year. It was simply too much where he asked Dave why his license didn't show Easter or the fourth of July.

Amid tempers the officer rambled on about supposedly being seventeen like he was twenty-one. Obvious it had become that the police were convinced that the three were jail birds. Back and forth, over and over went the questions asking how long the three had been on the run. Also thrown into the mad discussion was where the friends and rest of the gang was. Then while pointing to Dave the man asked how if only seventeen where the parents were. Shortly the mood changed when the officer questioned on having a bomb. Stunned by hearing the subject matter of the question, the three stood unable to even mumble. Ongoing it was about what doing on that car where again responded was how the three were just using it to get a ride. Suddenly, at the top of his lungs the chief yelled how he wasn't stupid, as nobody, but nobody rides an oil car unless they had bad intentions. By that time it was obvious the officer believed nothing told where minutes later he summed up everything. Belting out his story it was of being from Pennsylvania, then driving to California and staying with people they weren't related to or weren't close friends with then decided to walk back.

      Where are you really from the man demanded as he slammed his fist on the desk. Yet the three could only watch as the mood of the chief change to rage. Shaking his head the man continued noting of having left the stolen car in Kansas with somebody else the three didn't know, it was just happening to be on the freight train which was not even going to your own state. Angrily in a boisterous voice he yelled how really sick and tired of the games he was. Regardless of whether the licenses were forged or stolen, he asserted that the railroad was going to press charges of trespassing and vandalism, while he was charging the three with destroying private property and vagrancy. Showing a smirk, Dave asserted that since his group of idiots didn't believe the three why not just take them out shoot them and be done with it. Just what was needed another spark to heat up the ongoing madness. Right away responding to the statement the man commanded for each one at time to start at the beginning talking nothing but truth. Banging his hand on the desk he added, if found different from the truth to be found it would be our hides would be his before going to the pen. Then following a pause the man staring at each, blurted out how if found that the three lied, their necks would be worth nothing. Apparently the deplorable unshaven, dirty appearances only escalated the calamity. Not realizing it, the three had dug their selves into a hole where ongoing it went for hours. No change of pace, all the chief could do was shake his head, bang his fist on or kick the desk. Refusing to believe what he had been told, the officer responded how for sure they would be finding out soon enough.

Finally, after using our telephone numbers the chief appeared furiously wearing a grin that would have scared a grizzly bear. While letting the three out of the cells the chief stood them up in straight line. Displaying his anger in a boisterous lecture he yelled how the three weren't even eighteen and doing such bad things. Next it was on how close to death the three had come. Ensuring his message was getting across, the chief kept moving from one to the other standing toe to toe almost nose to nose with each one at a time.

 Not knowing what to expect, the three could actually feel the vibes from his rage where throwing his arms around he repeatedly pointed out the stupidity of the team's actions. Shouting out how the situation could have caused other persons to lose their jobs or even go to jail he belted out, how if someone hadn't spotted us and called the railroad, the train would not have stopped for hundreds of miles ending in three dead bodies. Demonstrating true concern, with a twisted face of emotion he asked what would the parents have done if either was found dead?

Then he quizzed, if not dead what if each lost a limb or two then what are your parents told? Following a pause while simmering down Stan attempted to say something but the chief belted out for him to just shut up.

Advising they had confirmed our ages the officer added how being minors without criminal charges he couldn't keep us in jail. But, he might just draw up some charges for all of the trouble the three caused the railroad, state police and his department.

Smiling he had the three detained where shortly the trio was taken to a local hotel. Locked in a large room, it was a very old wooden but sturdy building. The solid door had been rigged where it locked only from the outside. And although it prevented any leaving, it was heaven compared to the jail cell. Along with the very low ceiling, the room contained a few bunk beds, a table, chairs, a sink and toilet. While the trio was provided a late dinner perhaps to the officers it was just a meal but to the trio, the home style cooking with plates fully loaded was a feast. Slowly contention grew over the situation where sadly while also frustrated the three let their emotions get out of hand like cats and dogs in a cage.

Just in time there was a knock on the door. After it was unlocked an older man entered handing over wash rags, towels and soaps. Then surprising the trio, upon leaving he stated how such bickering wouldn't settle anything. Once the delivery person left a quiet settled in where discussions failed to materialize. Off and on thoughts were stated of being taken to a boarding school, a labor farm or some other place for runaways where under the circumstances neither could offer realistic suggestions.

Great, Stan mentioned, no television, no cards and no marbles, so much for kiddies' night out. As the three settled down, Bill uttered how the three gots to get their selves together as look what they were doing to each other.

All serious, Dave suggested for the guys to just shut up for awhile then start over with some realistic thinking. What the three had been through they still failed to comprehend where they were in life.

Was it the lack of using intelligence or, had ego so taken over that the minds were blurred with fantasy?

SECTION V -

DIRECTIONS AMONG

SCRAMBLED MINDS.

CHAPTER THIRTEEN

A CLASSROOM, MONEYGRAM, FOOD AND A BUS

July Sixteenth the three were treated to a greasy large breakfast then afterward it was back to the chief. Right away the three went reeling as the chief advised how they had contacted Dave's folks. All upset, Dave hollered out, "why me". His sudden outburst caused the other two to feel really low. Seeing the sad faces, the chief mentioned how they let the parent know that the three were healthy ok plus not in any legal trouble but only called to verify who they were.

Dave's mother stated that she would call the other parents and hearing that from the chief helped to relieve the teams' feelings. Following a pause, furiously the chief mentioned various ways how people had been killed hopping freights. Noting their losing their balance, or their grip then sucked under the wheels established his point of not good things. Settling down the man added how he had no interest in chasing after a few stupid young hoodlums but, since private property had been trespassed, if there was any damage whatsoever reported he would have the three picked and charged. Then sternly he mentioned some of the matters to be charged with that were damaging private property and stealing as matters of theft plus if any guards or workmen claimed they had been robbed or something stolen, the three would be charged with robbery.

Slowly as the deputy returned the wallets the chief mentioned how the word was put out across the state. Notices were sent to the affect that if ever caught on any railroad property the three would be jailed with the key tossed in the trash. After he asserted how he would be thankful if neither ever came back to his office again he yelled for the three to get out of his office. Stopped at the door, Dave mentioned needing some directions where the man replied. Almost screaming he asked, that with the three having been in the scouts, and knowing to be going into unknown areas how is it you all are without maps or a compass? Finally in conclusion he added for the three to remember, no and he meant no, freight riding of any kind.

By late morning that Wednesday, it was in the mid seventies with only a spotty drizzle while trying some humor, Stan admitted his being unable to recall the last four days being part of the original plans. However, Dave and Bill were so mad about the days that they responded how to them it was not funny and to stuff it. Ideal weather it was for trotting. But neither felt much like doing anything where being so preoccupied with getting out of the police station neither one thought to take notes on the name of the town, the hotel or the police officers. Plus over time for some reason the three totally forgot the town's name and location.

Yet able to be recalled was that the Ten Commandments was playing in the theaters while well known actors at the time were Bridgette Bardot and Charlton Heston. Drivers seemed to speed up while aiming for hitting the puddles. Then if it wasn't them, it was the occasional cloudbursts sending the three into detours of hiding under building overhangs of standing on porch steps.

Over time, the three arrived at route forty taking their place like mannequins where it appeared there was no life left in the three. Although some spurts of humor occurred it never lasted as what may have been jesting, innuendos or humorous before was no longer funny. Just past the edge of the corner, the trio stood as robots for it was the three had nothing to look forward to. Aware from experience that it was a good spot since the drivers couldn't help but take notice but, more important was that the three were aware that for all intense purposes the journey was over. Bodies were present but the spirit had gone by the wayside.

Watching the cars, and other vehicles go past being slow, it was noticed how some of the drivers smiled as they waved. Mentally such things took its toll where any other time such occurrences would have generated a response at least being made fun of. However at the time such only caused a response by the waving with finger salutes. As frustration grew, tempers heated where perhaps it was good that no one stopped to respond as the three were really hot, and it wasn't the weather. Soon considered was to start walking but, the three knew that once away from the intersection the traffic's speed would become a hindrance.

On edge there was no more happy as life seemed to have been drained where only existing was the doing.

Finally, when a car did pull over the usual comical remarks made in the past were absent where only you bet, and yes sir was heard. Wasting no time getting into the traffic the driver inquired how far going where right away Dave answered how it would be as far he was traveling east while Stan noted Pennsylvania. Moments later Bill mentioned going into the service where the driver advised of being an agriculture agent heading to some inspection. Then while Bill noted of which branch of service going into the man also mentioned of his army times along with hitchhiking after discharge.

Dropped off in Montrose, Illinois the trio felt a little better as the conversation with someone other police seemed to help. Another plus was that the driver let the trio out at an intersection that was inside a reduced speed zone. While Bill mentioned that the guys were back on the highway again, Dave noted how there only four states to go where Gene Autry couldn't have done it better in a song. Only a short wait for another ride, but from that time on, the only rides offered were short hops however, with each aware of their situation not a complaint was heard. What was in the short past a small time thing had become immensely significant as a ride was no longer simply just a ride but the only means of travel the three had available.

SEGMENT 27.   Getting thru the city of Terra Haute Bill hollered to hold up a minute. While the other two totally bored watched their partner he pointed while also generating a smile asked if it was a mirage. Totally disinterest the other two only responded with lame innuendos and him going bonkers. Right away, Bill yelled to look at the sign but the two being in their box of self, simply could not relate. Who would have believed it but, the large Howard Johnson sign was not just any sign but that belonging to the very place the foursome ate at the month before. Although not of the same joy as the original time, yet the occasion did give the three a lift.

Washing the faces helped settle the nerves as Bill blurted out, "thank God for restrooms and sinks as the three got cleaned up a bit. Flat out tired, the situation demanded some relaxing while grabbing at least some bits of food. Not really wanted due their predicament but necessary was the debate that ensued about how much to spend. Shaking his head Stan asserted of not giving a darn about the money, as he was hungry. With minds in chaos, tempers grew over assumptions there being more than five dollars left. When Dave asserted that Bill had been holding out, an argument followed. Just what the three did not need was more stress. Showing his being mad against the attitude of his buddies, Bill rebuked with dislike for the distrust by the two. Then with temper showing, he pulled his pockets inside out. Staring in disbelief the two then watched as Bill displayed his wallet of only a few single dollar bills.

Unity had vanished where it was just three separate bodies occupying the same booth mumbling words. Stan was emotionally breaking down when stunned by the outburst. Bill and Dave gathered close with their arms on his shoulder. Giving assurances of how they also felt the same way the two did their best to console the guy but he was down in the dumps. Their partner was really feeling bad mentioning of his being at fault by failing to prepare for taking care of Nashie that only caused the stress level among three to fall even further.

Bill and Dave sat refusing to say a word as the waitress asked if anything was going to be ordered. Requested the woman returned where an order was placed to fit the large budget. Shortly thereafter, the waitress seeing the three splitting the one coffee between them inquired whether things were really that bad. Quietly in response she was briefed by Bill who even told some of the team's particulars where she became speechless.

Emotions poured out as the other two understood what they had put their friend through. Yet, it was only days before when the same scenario happened when their friendship had been tested. Fires of disgust flowed from Bill, angry being so hurt. Tense as rubber bands stretched to the limit each was ready to pounce on each other where what prevented the fists from flying, nobody knows. How were they to act? Having being wrongly drawn against one another? Not knowing what to expect the trio flopped off the ground with each lost for words. Totally upset, unable to think straight the three sat like mummies. For each, it was a most strained moment of their life almost a disaster to the friendship.

Just in time some minutes later the waitress showing a huge smile set a double order of toast with extra butter and jellies while refilling the coffees for each. Quietly she mentioned how all was with her compliments and best wishes. Such good gesture actually caused the eyes of the three to water where the only responses were of multiple thanks and a thank you. What could either do as all three were stuck, sunk in the bottom of their muck. Perhaps it was the quiet, or the effort of the waitress or the combination. But, no one remembers as slowly the three realized the lousy situation they had created. Some communication started but, it was slow with bits of stuttering as each was afraid to say the wrong thing.

Whether it was the distraction of the Howard Johnson sign, who knew but, slowly, words expanded into explanations along with apologies. Slowly a regrouping emerged having come to grips with how stupid it was being over nothing without true cause as apologies and forgiving each other took place. Shortly it was agreed not to allow either one to repeat the same of what they had just experience along with no more negative talk. Following much coffee, toast and water afterward as Bill paid the check the three showered the woman with words of kindness.

Outside, it was helter-skelter thinking. With all money absolutely gone and riding the rails being out, walking or thumbing to get a lift was the only transportation that remained. Yet, rather than apply intelligence and use the phone, even then the three was hindered by what? Was it ego, pride or determination or a combination as they simply refused to quit. Even while getting no rides, the huge mental block remained. Beyond common sense, in their state of mind the three couldn't get over constantly thinking of only having three states to go. Along with that there were the hopes of a ride by someone going to the other border or even the east coast.

Meanwhile Bill and Stan aware of being already late for their military transport, neither one gave a damn. All the surviving three Chester Eagles Boys Club members knew was that they were in the state of Indiana without Nashie. Walk, a short ride, then walk some more where reflecting on some of the past occurrences led to small talks which helped take the minds off the situation at hand.

Just when things seemed to calm down one of Dave's shoes split with half the heel falling off. Then seeing him walk with a limp Bill, returned some of the favors recalling when he was felled by the stone. Later down the road Bill found a flat piece of metal that allowed Dave to pry off the remaining part. Then pinching a couple of stones together allowed the nails to be removed. Meanwhile, Bill and Stan's feet had suffered since their sneakers had worn to having holes in both soles. Inserting paper and green leaves helped cover the holes but after that all three were limping. Smile and walk became the rule of the day but as the miles and the time of day passed, reality drew closer. Mentally strained and physically beat with effort deleted and lacking funds, the day of reckoning had arrived.

Eventually, the three came to understand their hapless situation as they sat on the side of the road. With heads on their knees, it was really difficult for either of the three to even mention the thought ,yet the matter had reached its peak. So close yet, dividing the miles into days the three understood being forced to accept their not being able to go any further. A most difficult time it was being forced against their will to do what they didn't want to do. Unable to cope with the matter of being forced was the worst as didn't know how. It was beyond their nature to stop when not finished what they started where it was truly a devastating time of heartbreak. Even though the three had reached the final targeted destination realizing success, not getting home under their own means was devastating.

But there it was that fate had dealt the final blow as the team was dealt a hand void of choices. Into the depths of despair the three sank. With all options gone while so far down in the dumps there was little discussion as each knew it was useless. Too far from the last big city to turn around it was agreed that at the very next town a call to home would be made. In hindsight, many people may have thoughts of having answers yet not having ever experienced such situations hindsight remains what it is but fantasy. Thumbs were out, but with no one stopping, it was merely something to do while walking. Not having money was enough but the constant recalling of loosing Nashie really hit hard.

Surprise it was when someone actually honked their horn as they came to a stop. Like others, the passenger asked if looking for a lift but there was no reply when quick it was simply getting inside. After the driver introduced himself then his friend, he asked how far going. Still trying some humor, Stan replied about only going a short distance to Philadelphia where after the passenger asked if joking, a reasonable discussion took place. Naturally, the two middle aged men didn't believe. Responding to the passenger's suggestion of being on the run from the law Dave responded how the three were simply trying to get home. Subsequent responses also fell on deaf ears when all upset from the men's negativity Stan pulled out his driver's license, holding it up to the man's face. After Dave did the same, in a response of broken voice the man told the driver how he thought the three were telling the truth being down on their luck.

Soon they pulled into a small eatery. As the driver quizzed whether to wait or walk Dave asked about just sitting to rest where the driver offered to treat to some coffee. Totally skeptical, the three felt that the men were going to leave them at the place but being hungry his kind offer was taken.

When the time came for ordering over heard was the waitress told that all was to be put on his bill. However the three not wanting to be selfish did not take advantage where it was simply coffee with a Danish along with much water. Afterward heading east passing through tiny towns, finally the men arrived at the location where they had business in the town. For sure many thanks were given the men not only for the lift but their treat.

SEGMENT – 28. Into the city of Indianapolis the three limping along walked anticipating to find a place for a bus. But instead, after only a number of blocks the trio stumbled upon a police car. Parked a ways back from the corner of the intersection it was too late to change direction as he had seen us. Out of the car right away he was asked if he knew a place with a telephone booth where buses going east would stop. But, reviewing the identifications he inquired how the three happened to be at his location. Displaying apprehension the cop sat halfway on the front seat where he used the radio calling in our names and description while he inquired about our story. By then having told the story to so many people hearing only negative replies it became difficult. As Dave cut it short by telling from the police station, right away hearing about the trespassing on freight cars, the atmosphere changed.

Showing a stern look the patrolman asserted how he wasn't interested in any gibberish but just the truth from the California part. While Bill started explaining, Dave joined in but the cop was confused as noting the driver's licenses showing Pennsylvania having heard California. Swiftly, Stan asserted to tell the story from the beginning where even with radio interruptions the officer kept noting to keep going. Minutes later, taking off his hat while scratching his head, he asserted how you boys didn't really go through all that. Angrily in a gruff tone Stan belted out, how we knew he was going to say that where the cop responded asking how he could be expected to believe all of that stuff.

Shaking his head, Stan pulled out the receipt while belligerently Dave asked how he liked the guys' Sunday going to church clothes. Tempers of the three heated up where it was decided to walk away but the officer demanded to look at both sides of our hands along with the bottoms of our shoes. And that was all it took where the officer stated how he needed to think things out. Looking at the three as if expecting something to happen it was moments later he put his hat back on while expressing how through the years he had heard all kinds of stories but the guys' experience beat them all. Subsequently while hearing what the three wished to do he questioned about the east coast area.

Upon receiving an alerting call on the radio the patrolman reacted by ordering the three into the back seat while jumping behind the wheel. Then with overhead red lights flashing, while not stopping for traffic lights the officer advised of taking the three to a place he thought may help. With the doors secured where the three were locked in while hearing blasts of the siren it drove the minds into thinking it was on to the police station. Pushing the car's speed over several streets while around a few corners, it was as if in a race.

Then not even saying a word, he pulled to the curb while hollering, ok guys all out as this was your stop. In a blaze of continual motion the man jumped out while smiling as he advised of the store being a good place. Then while yelling good luck, he jumped back in and speed away.

In front of a small drug store the three stood watching as the shrill of the police siren faded. While Bill remarked how there went the Lone Ranger, all excited Dave yelled, "hi yo silver away". Boisterously Stan yelled out yeah, ok Keema Sobee and Tonto we ain't gots all night so letsa gets on with whats weez gots to dooz. The drug store was also a bus stop that provided service to the city's main bus depot. While the man operating the store behind the counter questioned where going he asserted how he didn't want either one touching anything as it was a drug store needing to be kept clean.

It took a couple of minutes for the three to gain some composure having felt the sting of the remark where each was embarrassed from what they heard. Maybe knock over some shelves Stan uttered as the man waited to hear. Struggling, for the words Stan asserted how the three's present appearance was not the trio's normal behavior but had a string of bad luck. Such statement only made it more difficult for the man to understand as with all of the man's confrontation it only made things more difficult. Slowly Bill and Dave struggled to explain but, it got frustrating. Only minutes before, the three had finally been in a cheerful mood but again as before it had been bashed. Enough of trying, the three in frustration asserted how they just wanted to use the phone.

Unlike the past days of uncertainty, at the time there was no more unknown, no need of decisions, no more calculated risks and no more hoping or chance taking. At the telephone booth located at the end of the store against the back corner, Dave called his mother reversing the charges. Meanwhile, the other two questioned on tickets cost along with the driving time where, seeing what was taking place the man explained being able to receive Western Union money telegrams and how the system worked. Overhearing his conversation was heart breaking as Dave's mom was very upset. Not hearing from him yet only the police, for sure the beginning of the call was a disaster. Not on the phone, but only close was enough as the two could hear him getting yelled at. His sobbing mom probably in tears, it wasn't long before Dave while leaning on the wall, broke down in tears. So upset the woman was explaining from not having heard from her young son, Dave was crushed.

Along with all that the three had gone through while also losing the car they had worked so hard for had already been mentally traumatic and then to hear her mother brow beat him was beyond difficult for his to take. Hollering of not knowing what may have befallen her son, uncontrolled had her voice become. Trembling from having realized what he had caused, his sad expressions and tears caused the other two to break down understanding how they had done the same. Struggling, Dave quietly settled his mother down, yet terribly distraught she kept repeating to Dave, wanting to know why either one had not been calling their families. But all efforts of general explanation fell on deaf ears.

Repeatedly noting of each being ok, Dave attempted to explain on the details being made but it was too much involved however, no matter how he tried the woman couldn't get passed the idea of a simple trip of celebration by car. Mentioning how much was needed for bus fares was easy but when he requested extra money for food it was terrible. Difficult in the least it was his telling of their not even having money for food. His mother being so upset and crying along with Dave mentally beat realizing his mother's anger caused the other two to emotionally break down.

So, heart wrenching was the terrible time that his speech became so slurred the poor guy wasn't even able to look at the other two. So depressed had Stan become that he couldn't even listen anymore where he walked outside. Shortly all upset, Bill joined him where the two attempted to console each other when later Dave met the other two outside where neither had any words to offer each other. Each was fully aware of what the others were thinking and feeling. Since Stan's mother had been taken when eleven and Bill had also lost his father, both had much understanding yet, feeling so low, words simply failed to help.

Several minutes later the trio went back to the clerk where showing some understanding, he brought out three big glasses of water. When the three returned to the booth hearing the phone ring all Dave could say was hello mom. Once his mother advised how she had contacted the other family members leaving word of our situation a short discussion of health and personal matters took place. Along with talk about the bus the two slowly engaged in some small talk.

Soon afterward Bill called his mother where thinking was that she was prepared having heard from Dave's mom. But her depressed words vibrated the emotional strain she was under. So affected by the call it took more toll leaving all three unable to converse.

Outside it seemed forever consoling each other as all spirits had been squashed where the mental condition had been bashed down into the dumps. Shortly dragging our selves back inside the three listened as the manager advised of what was to transpire and how. Meanwhile the clerk had provided information on an eatery called the Fountain Diner, recommending it of having good service along good food. At the moment it was the last thing each wanted to hear about but the name was remembered.

Wait and more waiting where it was to walk around, then stopping back only to walk and wait some more where not receiving any news drove the three bonkers as it had gotten early into the evening. Soon the man requested for the three not to be hanging around inside the store while also advised that if the parents called he would relay any message. Much later it was learned the money gram was soon to be sent where the clerk added how Dave's father wanted details on the bus expenses along with how much money each had for food.

Upon calling back it was all that his father needed to hear was of neither having any money. When his voice exploded over the phone Dave moved backward while holding the receiver far from his ear. Sounds from the man even outside the booth caused the other two to be affected. Then as close as Dave was to his dad he had another breakdown. No laughs and nothing funny as the three were trapped in what sadness they could never have imagined.

Understanding the miserable situation the clerk was kind enough to loan enough change for a couple of sodas and candy bars. Back outside the three passed the time walking or sitting on steps that helped the minds to settle and the three able to get a hold of their selves.

SEGMENT 29. Finally the money-gram arrived. While the funds were divided equally, Bill called his mother once more giving some assurance that all was well. Upon hearing of her to call Stan's house gave some comfort when afterward it off to the eatery. Hesitation was due to its being a part of a long row of other businesses.

Thoughts of the "Fountain Diner", were of it being an ice cream or sandwich place especially since from the outside it didn't have any appearance of being a restaurant, but, it was more than substantial. Serving of solid steak cooked to order, along with good desserts and beverages was just what the three needed. Customers without even enquiring were not hospitable where bad looks were shown. But not wishing to have trouble find us, each confined their looking to the menu and the immediate table.

As usual with others the waitress raised questions but, there just wasn't any interest. From time to time the guys smiled then once, Dave mentioned of having gone through some tough times appreciating some quiet. While nodding her head the socially able woman noted there being no problem with her fully understanding.
Expressing many thoughts the three raised their cups to each other, following with a prayer of thanking God for the good health enabling the three to return safely

Just what the doctor ordered as the meal allowed a refreshing of the minds where only statements of good feelings overtook the atmosphere. Each had lost several pounds where the three were not only of a weak strength but actually looked sickly. For sure, each had failed to give thought to what the lack of proper clothing, shelter, food and money will do to a person. So it was during desserts, the waitress while showing a big smile mentioned how she noticed a little change for the better in each one's disposition that added little positives. Soon there ensued a period of relaxation that the three hadn't been experienced in quite a while. Then upon leaving while appreciating her efforts, the three were compelled to praise the waitress for her unknowing mental help that she provided.

Then it was on to the bus terminal where tickets were purchased for the next morning. Subsequently the trio roamed around grabbing some delicacies ending with sleeping in the terminal. Early the next morning after the usual routine a place was found for breakfast where Stan borrowed a pen and scratch paper making keep sake notes of the night before. Then it was on to the bus when it didn't take long before other passengers showed their nasty looks with uppity attitudes. Feeling his oats Stan belted out, "Gee guys its segregation time at its finest" where   Dave in a raised voice responded for the two to ignore the bunch of no nothings as not being worth it. Not having any experience with long bus rides neither had given any thought to getting something to do. Time of riding was looking out the windows at the scenery where if there was ever an edgy time that could have led to a brawl, the three were in the midst of it.

Only a few wrong words by a passenger would have been all it would have taken to get Dave started while Stan kept trying to make conversation. Not able to discuss matters with the people along with their arrogant rudeness really magnified the situation. But as the big cruiser rolled on with a comfortable ride the miles passed by where also did the time as things settled down. After sitting like zombies a lift came when the bus made its next big stop.

Columbus Ohio where along with grabbing some food, there was the walking to stretch the legs when a newspaper was found. Providing something to read various articles generated some needed conversation where Stan held on to the front page as a souvenir. Afterward the time dragged on as if the turnpike had taken on extra miles when after stopping in Pittsburg it was another stop in Harrisburg.

Finally, the bus arrived at the terminal in Philadelphia on the Eighteenth of July where it was announced that the vehicle was not continuing on south. That meant there would be a transfer to another bus for reaching Chester. So, with the weather being comfortable it was decided to go for some refreshing snacks. With spirits up Bill noting of the limping, titled the three as the ballet-dancing club while Dave uttered the three as a bunch of hobos. Although some of the old spark had returned easily noted was how all three had changed. Personal were the matters but the three were just not the same boys that left only the month before.

Back at the depot it was just in time for boarding with each enjoying their selves aware of being less than an hour away from home. Stunned the three were when the driver blocked the doorway preventing the gaining entrance. Responding to the driver's action Dave and Bill asked the man what was going on, while Stan questioned if there was something wrong with the bus. Right away, the driver replied of nothing wrong with the bus but could not allow the three to board his bus in their condition.

Assertively, Stan hollered for him to explain himself as to what he meant as what condition. Boldly the man responded how he had to consider protecting the other passengers and their feelings. Showing his being insulted, Dave yelled out asking what about us passengers while angrily the three pressed the man showing having the proper tickets. Meanwhile the people had lined the windows watching the heated argument.

In temper, Dave stepped up close to the driver waving his ticket while blurting out how the man's action was crazy. Attempting to give assistance, Stan moved closer yelling, "the fare had already been paid, so let us pass". Immediately showing some fright while waving for assistance, the man hollered for the three to move backward as a guard arrived on the scene. Sternly with the three looking on, the driver belted out to the guard how he wasn't going to allow such grubby persons on his bus.

It was all that was needed where such words provoked Stan to step forward looking to get it on but, the guard stepped in between the three hollering for everyone to settle down and be quiet. Then as he turned to the driver it was mentioned how all the three had to get cleaned up or find some other means of transportation. Steaming, the three were beside their selves hearing the man's words where thinking was to make their point by crowding the entrance not allowing anyone else to pass. Frozen from seeing the passengers looking out the windows along with the guard making his stand, the three headed for the inside of the depot.

As the three washed up one thing led to another when, seeing each other's appearance it dawned on them where they comprehended the driver's position. Ridiculous, Stan screamed seeing it looking as if he had just rolled out of some dump heap. Such appearance noted by each was even magnified by the fact that each had lost some weight while not having shaved in many days, along with being void of any deodorant. Having lived with each other all twenty-four hours of each day together, the minds had absorbed the daily constant life's wearing. Constantly seeing the same clothes which daily deteriorated such objectionable appearance simply didn't take hold that others obviously easily recognized. Twas already departure time had been announced, when all through the room not a face was smiling. Once the gibberish had stopped the trio walked out optimistically, looking forward to the ride home. Surprise, it was, when back at the loading area seeing that the driver didn't wait. Feeling helpless, Bill yelled out asking what the hell does wees dooz now as angrily the three stood in the empty bus spot looking out.

Back inside the trio marched where another erroneous assumption had been realized finding there was no other bus. The last bus going south for the day had already gone leaving the next scheduled bus going to Chester not until early the next morning. Thoughts about hitch hiking were considered but getting dark such idea was deemed not safe plus walking to Chester was out of the question. Since ticket money for the bus had already been paid the guys simply wanted their ride.

Of course, there was the mind set as no way would they call home. Being so close to the home yet, it was so far. Decided was to take a walk for grabbing some deodorant and food where later a Bulletin and Inquirer newspaper was found. Noted were programs of Ed Sullivan, Jack Benny, Candid Camera plus the names of Ella Fitzgerald, Elvis Presley and Frank Sinatra stimulated some conversation. While the happy trio enjoyed use of a couple of park type benches for napping where being off the feet while getting some sleep all went well. Forced to move to other spots because of delivery vehicles or the police the night was what it was, another mess.

SEGMENT 30. It was the Nineteenth day of July, nineteen hundred and fifty-eight. Following a good wash and hot breakfast it was off to the bus depot. Right on time the three were where a small crowd was boarding. As the three made their attempt, again they were stunned when the bus driver got in the way. Though a different one, the man gave the impression of knowing we were coming as he started to make a scene similar to the night before.

Without any hesitation Dave asserted how the team was not hearing any more jibber jabber while Stan already livid added about having paid for tickets. Angrily as the man attempted to say something Bill and Dave interrupted him advising the man of the scene the night before where they were not going to be prevented from the ride already paid for. As the chaos peaked, letting out a yell, Bill hollered how if not allowed to use the tickets the three would lay down in front of the bus where it would be either on or under the bus.

Boldly Stan mentioned of him being friendly with the editor of the Bulletin and how they may be interested in how the bus company treats teenagers. Right away, Dave noted of him doing the same with the Inquirer through his printer friend. Reacting to seeing how upset the trio was, the driver locked the door and went inside the depot.

Minutes later the driver returned with a guard along with a supervisor. Meanwhile the driver had advised the supervisor of the threat that Bill made regarding physically blocking the bus from moving. Obviously displeased with the smirk he was getting from Stan, the supervisor approached him asking if he thought something was funny. Looking to respond but Stan held his peace for a moment as not wanting to be provoked. Shortly he replied how he thought their act was a mistreatment and not funny belonging on the television news.

Immediately the guard stepped in the middle stretching out his arms while telling everyone to be quiet while they discussed the matter. During the conversation of the three, a nice older woman sitting by the front door started loudly yelled for them to give the boys a brake letting them get on the bus. And right away when another man joined in quickly yelling basically the same thing others on the bus came to the doorway hollering the same.

Just what the trio needed, a fiasco of help by a live audience. Shortly the supervisor after responding to the two adults announced how the three could board. Then he added the conditions where the trio had to sit in the last seat all the way in the back. Of course had they made the three sit on the roof it would have been acceptable as what only mattered was for us to be on our way.

Once on the highway the three couldn't wait to engage in conversation about being glad when all the crap would end.Each one had enough of what was going on. Soon an older man seated in front moved to the rear quizzing whether the three were homeless or from out of state. Right away Stan stood up hollering," wow wee, guys, weez gots here a human person that's not arrogant".

Looks from other passengers were far from complementary to the situation yet, happy to engage in some conversation, the trio was fascinated hearing of the man's relative destitute situation when younger. When his gentleman friend joined in with his experiences it really made the ride enjoyable. Not of any extreme such as experienced by the boys, yet the man's episodes were worth listening to.

Arriving in the city of Chester, approaching the bus stop all went quiet. As the driver opened the door each paid a few kind words to the driver letting him know of no hard feelings. Stan asserted how each understood he was just doing his job but should have considered the trio's ages needing assistance.

Suddenly a moment of excitement erupted caused by the passengers clapping while offering cheers of well wishes. Bowing and waving was all the team could do as they walked down the steps out of the exit.

There weren't any greetings of a band, personal service or a limousine, nor was there any crowed waving but to the three they were just happy to have returned in one piece to where they had started from.

CHAPTER FOURTEEN

CONCLUSION

And so it was the Nineteenth day of July when the three had been dropped off in the center of Chester. The very place the four had passed through when setting out. It actually bothered the three being of a pitifully filthy and dirty condition smelling absolutely terrible. Yet, the repeated expressions of having survived and being alive established the priorities.

Not only did the three of the Chester Eagles Boys Club successfully visit every place originally planned but, triumphantly returned alive from surviving death threatening situations.

All Dave was able to way was that having walked across several states, a few more blocks of walking doesn't matter. Timely exuberant moments of close togetherness had taken over while strutting up Ninth Street.
With drizzle on the faces, the limping trio must have been a sight to behold as they walked a breast singing happy days are here again.
Along with thoughts of speaking to Tom and Larry sung was, hoora for CEBC, hoorah for CEBC, everyone in the crowd is hollering who ra for CEBC, one, two, three, four who you gonna yell for? Chester Eagles Boys Club that's who!

Finally arrived at Dave's house on Madison Street it was overhearing the ruckus Dave's mother came out screamingly chastising him for not telephoning. However over fresh coffee and pie his mother congratulated the three for overcoming the close calls. While tears showed weakness, it was the three knowing if Divine Providence had not intervened they may not have survived. Much close socializing there was over the moments, when upon leaving Bill all choked up, mentioned how the days of fun and learning were gone.

And so, that's the way it was in those days of yesteryear 1958, when the three of the Chester Eagles Boys Club successfully completed their high school celebration journey. Yahoo, yippee and amen!!!

Some unknown person had advised the Chester Times Newspaper about the trip but unfortunately, the paper never bothered to contact any of the five but printed the personal matter without any interview. Result was only a small article in the Monday's edition containing the guys' names noting of their trip void of any details. Yet, at least it gave credibility.

Days later the three found how people failed to comprehend where the only interest people showed was the trivial matters being of how long, and certain states or cities visited. No one believed the details of the story. And, the parents, they were so happy they threw the clothes in the trash not even considering their keepsake value to the three. Amazing how people made assumptions mentioning their being able to relate to our happy trip.

Easy it was for them to express their selves having gone on a trip in their new car or by train or plane staying at fine hotels. But with the three, any extreme situations mentioned were muted assumed as fabrication or overly exaggerated.

However, no one ever called any newspaper or historical societies to see if such weather existed at the time or the bus depot to see if there were any incidents. For sure though, the lives of the three had changed when some days later, the three even drove to the parish house offering personal thank yous for the priest's contacting the brothers at the monastery.

Little souvenirs, notations and pictures helped in restoring some memory but they didn't help Stan and Bill as the pair was AWOL from the Air Force. While Dave went in the army then on to work for a railroad, Tom had gone to work in a steel mill in Delaware also after serving in the Army. And Larry, well he didn't go to college but, ended up back on the east coast after also spending a hitch in the Air Force.

To be mentioned is that all five received honorable discharges. So it is was the Chester Eagles Boys Club Amazing Journey, the END. Whew! What a phenomenal journey of celebrations, then even alive to tell about it. Thank God for big favors, was all the author could say.   Hooray ,,, Yippee ,,, Yea ,,, Hurrah,, And ,,,,,,,,,, AMEN.

Author, Stanley E. Kornafel, 1137 Madison Ave., Prospect Park, Pa. 19076

First Date: 7 August, 2017   *NEW DATE: 26 April, 2023*

FAMOUS INTELLECTUAL EXPRESSIONS

Hard stuff at Pee Wees; Look at what a turtle; actually it's a boat; Oh man, Rolling wheels ; you guys ever had Greek food; Nature's way of helping to celebrate; quickly man, follow that car; a secret government project; oh crap, now what; It's Cinderella; and their off; string em up; sorry, but we're all sold out; hit the floor;

Sure glad we hadn't taken the bus because he would have missed the main event; never wishing to go thru something like that again; darn if we weren't lucky; hey, the fare had already been paid.

EPILOGUE

For sure anyone can dream adding if they only had the opportunity or if only there was enough money or relatives being rich. Yet people's dreams remain in space until carried into action. Watching television, warming seats in a tavern or in computer games initiates nothing.

Oh how great the prize for the person that acts as can truly say, at least they made the effort. The exciting feeling of joyous emotions realized by doing is awesome. It was a shame that neither of the guys' parents gave any thought for contacting any of the papers while at the time while the three were busy celebrating having survived.

CREDITS

Thanks must be extended to the other four for their hard attempts to remember when memory was lost to age and time. Chester Crozer Library and Historical Society along with the various newspapers and historical societies in the major cities across the country helped in allowing of correct places, areas and dates.

Also thanks for the assist received from Jessica and Nolan Green of Westville, N.J. who helped by discussion in clarifying and bring out relative forgotten information that helped to compile and format the notes into the story.

WRITING INFORMATION

Discussions, gathering facts, collecting material and making notes started in early 2004.

Compiled into a story format November, 2013 with the author suffering from two radiation treatments for cancer that completely wrecked his thought process while adversely affecting his mental stability.

Condensing while adding significant information ended when completed around November 2015.... Limited additions and corrections were made through 2016.... Under hardship, editing was completed in 2017.

www.ingramcontent.com/pod-product-compliance
Lightning Source LLC
Chambersburg PA
CBHW051510120626
46551CB00012B/862